ATLAS OF
WORLD HERITAGE

CHINA

National Commission of the People's Republic of China for UNESCO

LONG RIVER PRESS

The publication of this edition outside of China is authorized by SinoMaps Press.

This edition is edited and designed by the Editorial Committee of *Cultural China* series.
This book is compiled by National Commission of the People's Republic of China for UNESCO
and SinoMaps Press.

Managing Editors: Xu Naiqing, Wang Youbu, Wu Ying
Executive Editor: Wu Ying
Cover Design: Yuan Yinchang

ISBN 1-59265-060-0
Library of Congress Control Number: 2005934900

Published by
Long River Press
360 Swift Ave., Suite 48
South San Francisco, CA 94080
USA
and
Shanghai Press and Publishing Development Company
1110 Huaihai Middle Road, Donghu Villa F, Shanghai, China (200031)

Printed in China

1   2   3   4   5   6   7   8   9   10

The national boundaries of China in this Atlas are drawn after the 1:4 M Relief Map of the People's
Republic of China, published by SinoMaps Press in 1989.

PREFACE

China is a country with vast territory, beautiful landscape, long history and splendid culture. It has rich natural attractions and numerous historical sites: the Great Wall running 6,300 kilometers, the terracotta warriors and horses buried with the First Qin Emperor, the majestic Imperial Palaces of the Ming and Qing dynasties, the holy Taoist mountain of Wudang Shan, the sacred Buddhist mountain of Emei Shan, the great irrigation project of Dujiangyan, the picturesque nature reserve of Huanglong, and the perfect habitat of Suzhou Classical Gardens, etc. All these famous cultural treasures and natural attractions have become the precious heritage of the Chinese nation and the whole world.

At its 17th general conference in Paris in 1972, UNESCO adopted the Convention concerning the Protection of the World Cultural and Natural Heritage. Thanks to thirty-two years of persistent efforts, the noble cause of World Heritage protection has made tremendous progress worldwide. The international community has scored glorious achievements in protecting universal heritage of mankind and promoting the development of global economic, cultural and peace undertakings through joint actions. In 1985, China joined the Convention. By June 2004, a total of 177 countries (regions) in the world have become signatories to the Convention; 754 cultural and natural properties around the globe have been inscribed on the World Heritage List, of which 29 sites are in China.

Sustainable development is a common strategic goal of global social and economic development in the 21st century. It has a direct impact on the continuation of human civilizations. World Heritage protection is designed to coordinate the progress of material civilization with environmental protection and to seek sustainable development of humanity. This atlas attempts to give an environmental, aesthetic and comprehensive illustration of all China's 29 properties of World Heritage through maps, pictures and articles. It tries to brief the reader, in a brand-new angle, the geographic location, environmental characteristics, historical background and scientific and artistic value of each of the sites, so that he can broaden and deepen his understanding of the importance of World Heritage protection.

World Heritage properties are masterpieces created by man and nature. Their unique and common values crystallize the intertwining and integration of all civilizations in the world. They tell our future generations how to cherish the environment they live in and how to appreciate the evolution of human civilizations. They are the witnesses of human development, from benightedness to rationality and wisdom. They belong not only to an individual country, but also to the entire mankind. It is our historical duty to protect World Heritage properties and let them pass on from generation to generation, for the sustainable development of all mankind.

Zhang Xinsheng
Vice Minister of Education of P. R. China
Chairman of
28th UNESCO World Heritage Committee
Beijing
June 2004

CONTENTS

Provincial Map

▪	Capital		Seasonal river and lake
▪	Provincial capital		Dry river and lake
⊙	Prefecture-level administrative center		Waterfall
◎	County-level administrative center		Reservoir, dam
○	Town, village		Canal
	Railway		Swamp, salt swamp
	Railway under construction		Icecap
	High grade road	⊙	Cultural Heritage
	High grade road under construction	⊙	Natural Heritage
	National road	⊙	Cultural-Natural Heritage
	National boundary	✳	State-level scenic area
	Undefined national boundary		Great Wall
	Provincial boundary	✈	Airport
	Special Administrative Region boundary	▲	Peak
	Coastline	✕	Pass
	Perennial river		Desert
	Lake		Coral reef

Site Map/City Map

● Yanyu Tower	Key place of interest	– – – – – – –	Heritage protected area
● Qiwang Tower	Place of interest	·················	Heritage buffer zone
·	Building	—————————	High grade road
◎	Municipal government	– – – – – –	High grade road under construction
○	District government		Main street
Ⓗ	Hotel		Other street
⊠	Restaurant	—•—▢—•—	Railway, station
Ⓜ	Museum	—————————	Tourist route, path
⊕	Bank	⌐⌐⌐⌐⌐▢⌐⌐⌐⌐⌐	Great Wall, beacon tower
⊠	Post office	■ ■ ■ ■ ■ ■ ■ ■	City wall
🏫	School	—————————	Wall
✚	Hospital	▫——————▫	Cable car
●	Other building	⊓	Bridge
✈	Airport	▬	Block
⬯	Stadium, gym	▬▬	Built-up area
▭	Bus station	▨	Park, green belt
Dawangjing	Block name	**Mountain Resort**	Key scenic area
Lizhuang	Village	Huanglongdong Area	Other scenic area

Map of China

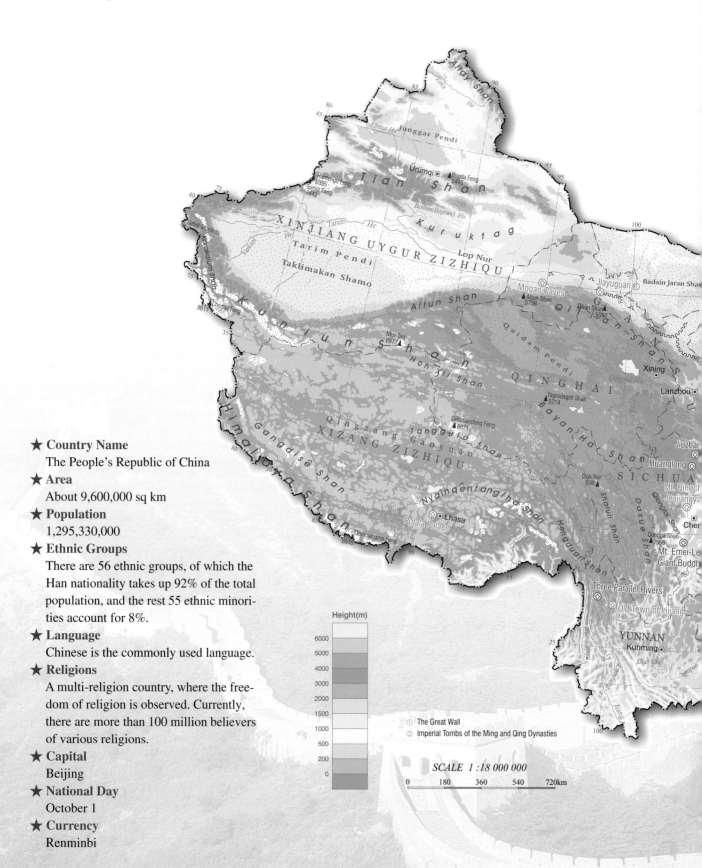

★ **Country Name**
  The People's Republic of China
★ **Area**
  About 9,600,000 sq km
★ **Population**
  1,295,330,000
★ **Ethnic Groups**
  There are 56 ethnic groups, of which the
  Han nationality takes up 92% of the total
  population, and the rest 55 ethnic minori-
  ties account for 8%.
★ **Language**
  Chinese is the commonly used language.
★ **Religions**
  A multi-religion country, where the free-
  dom of religion is observed. Currently,
  there are more than 100 million believers
  of various religions.
★ **Capital**
  Beijing
★ **National Day**
  October 1
★ **Currency**
  Renminbi

Height(m)

6000
5000
4000
3000
2000
1500
1000
500
200
0

① The Great Wall
② Imperial Tombs of the Ming and Qing Dynasties

SCALE 1 : 18 000 000

0   180   360   540   720km

125

120

Ergun He

Heilong

Xiao Hinggan Ling

Jiang

130

135

50

Hailar He

Da Hinggan Ling

Hulun Nur

HEILONGJIANG

Harbin

Songhua

115

Dongbei Pingyuan

Song hua

Changchun

Songhua Hu

Jiang

45

NEI MONGOL ZIZHIQU Gaoyuan

JILIN

Min

Xing

Jiang

Nei Mongol Gaoyuan

Yin shan

Shenyang

He

Yellow

Badaling ①

Chengde Mountain Resort

LIAONING

Hohhot

Imperial Palace

Summer Palace

Ming Tombs ②

Shanhaiguan ①

Yungang Grottoes

BEIJING

E. Qing Tombs ②

W. Qing Tombs ②

Beijing

TIANJIN

BO HAI

Peking Man Site

Tianjin

Yinchuan

Temple of Heaven

Taiyuan

HEBEI

120

QU

SHANXI

Shijiazhuang

SHAANXI

Taihang Shan

SHANDONG

Luliang Shan

Jinan

Ancient City of Pingyao

Mt. Taishan

Qin Emperor Mausoleum

Hua Shan 2160

Zhengzhou

Temple, Cemetery and Mansion of Confucius

YELLOW SEA

Qin Ling

Huang

Longmen Grottoes

He

Daba Shan

Xi'an

HENAN

JIANGSU

120

Rock ings

HUBEI

ANHUI

Xiaoling Tomb ②

Changjiang Kou

Chang Jiang

Ancient Buildings in Wudang Mts.

Xianling Tomb ②

Nanjing

Classical Gardens of Suzhou

SHANGHAI

Shu

Hefei

Shanghai

Yangtze

Hangzhou Wan

EAST CHINA SEA

Wulingyuan

Wuhan

Mt. Huangshan

Hangzhou

hongqing

Dongting Hu

Lushan National Park

Ancient Villages in Southern Anhui

CHONGQING

Chang Jiang

ZHEJIANG

IZHOU

HUNAN

JIANGXI

Poyang Hu

Nanchang

yang

Changsha

Mt. Wuyi

Tiaoyu Tao

Chihwei Yu

Fuzhou

20

25

FUJIAN

Taipei

JANGXI ZHUANGZU ZIZHIQU

GUANGDONG

TAIWAN

Nanning

Guangzhou

Yu Shan 3952

Taiwan Haixia

Tropic of Cancer

Taiwan Tao

Macau

HONG KONG SAR

Lan Yu

MACAU SAR

Hong Kong

BEIBU GULF

Dongsha Qundao

Qiongzhou Haixia

20

Haikou

20

SOUTH CHINA SEA

HAINAN

Wuzhi Shan 1867

Hainan Dao

10

Tropic of Cancer

GUANGDONG

FUJIAN TAIWAN

TAIWAN

GUANGXI ZHUANGZU ZIZHIQU

Macau

Hong Kong

Taiwan Tao

MACAU SAR

HONG KONG SAR

Lan Yu

20

Dongsha Qundao

20

Haikou

HAINAN

Hainan Dao

Xisha Qundao

Huangyan Dao

Zhongsha Qundao

SOUTH CHINA SEA

Liyue Tan

10

Nansha Qundao

10

Wan'an Tan

Zengmu Ansha

120

110

SOUTH CHINA SEA ISLANDS
1:36 000 000

BEIJING MUNICIPALITY

General Information

Beijing, also called in Jing in short, is the capital of the People's Republic of China. It is a municipality directly under the central government and a city opening to the outside world. With 16 districts and 2 counties under its administrative jurisdiction, Beijing has a total area of 16,800 sq km and a population of 11.43 million, with ethnic groups of Han, Man, Hui and Mongol.

Environment

Beijing is located at the northwest end of the North China Plain. It is surrounded by Hebei Province, except for eastern and southeastern corners, which are bordered with Tianjin Municipality. Its terrain is descending from northwest to southeast. It has a typical semi-humid warm continental monsoon climate, with an average temperature of -10 ~ -5°C in January and 22 ~ 26°C in July, and an average annual rainfall between 500 ~ 700 mm.

Places of Interest

Beijing is one of the seven major ancient cities in China, boasting a history of more than 3,000 years. The Peking Man, found in Zhoukoudian and dated back to 500,000 years ago, is the earliest origin of the ethnic groups of the Central Plains. Kublai Khan of the Yuan Dynasty constructed fortresses here and dug canals and then established the Grand Capital. The May 4 Movement and the founding of New China opened a new chapter in the history and culture of the city.

Beijing has the largest number of cultural sites in China. Among them are the towering Great Wall, the glittering and splendid Imperial Palace, the vast Ming Tombs, the magnificent Temple of Heaven, the Beihai Park, and the Summer Palace, as well as the Zhoukoudian site of Peking Man, the Lugou Bridge (Marco Polo Bridge) that is famous both at home and abroad, and the Ancient Observatory. Religious places of interest are the Biyun Temple, the Baiyun Taoist Temple, the Yonghe Lamasery and the Niujie Mosque that all have long enjoyed a good fame. The alleys and quadrangle courtyards in Beijing are permeated with a strong style of native Beijing.

The fame of the natural scenic spots of Beijing is carried far and wide. There are the Xiangshan Hill (Fragrant Hill) normally covered with the red leaves of maple trees in the fall season, the Zizhu (Purple Bamboo) Garden with exuberant bamboo woods, the Yuyuantan Park with an elegant and quiet environment, the Shidu Gorge in the suburbs of Beijing, the Miaofeng Mountain, the Longqing Gorge, and the Yougu Shentan (Secluded Dell and Immortal's Pond).

Local Specialties

Roast Peking duck, preserved fruits, crunchy candy, Fuling cake, cloisonne china (Jingtai Blue), Chinese carved lacquer ware, jade ware and carpets.

4

HEBEI

Shidongzi

Labagoumen

Songshutai

Changshaoying

Shan

Tanghekou

Baoshansi

Liulimiao

Xizhuangzi   Banchengzi Shuiku   Gubeikou   Xinchengzi

Banchengzi

Yunmeng Shan

Beishicheng   Miyun Shuiku   Songshuyu

Qiangzilu

Neilangkou

Sanduhe

Miyun   Jugezhuang

Huairou

Fumazhuang

Huairou Shuiku

Miaocheng

Jiangjunguan

Chawu

Mulin   Huangsongyu

Niushan

Jinbai Hu

angshan   Gaoliying

Zhaogezhuang   Xujiawu

Shunyi   Nancai   Pinggu

sanqi   Hualikan

Tianzhu   Beizhangdai

TIANJIN

Liqiao

Xuxinzhuang

HEBEI

ng

Imperial Palace   Tongzhou

Gaobeidian   Shuangqiao

emple of Heaven

ongmen

Dayangfang

Majuqiao   Matou

dahongmen

Weishanzhuang

TIANJIN

Fengheying

① The Great Wall
② Imperial Tombs of the Ming and Qing Dynasties

Height(m)

2000
1500
1000
500
200
100
0

SCALE 1 : 800 000

0   8   16   24   32km

Imperial Palace of the Ming and Qing Dynasties

☐ **Name:**
Imperial Palace of the Ming and Qing Dynasties

☐ **Geographical coordinates:**
39° 54' N, 116° 23' E

☐ **Date of inscription:**
December 11, 1987

☐ **Criteria for inclusion:**
III, IV of cultural properties

Triple terrace, Taihe Hall

⊙ Overview

The Forbidden City, located in the city center of Beijing, was the imperial palace of the Ming and Qing dynasties (1406-1911). It is the largest and best-preserved ancient palatial architectural complex in the world, representing the highest level of the palatial architecture in China since the Ming Dynasty. In the 500-odd years following its completion in the 18th year of Yongle in the Ming Dynasty (1420), 24 Ming and Qing emperors ruled the country from the Forbidden City. It boasts a grand art collection of more than 1 million relic and artistic pieces, all of which are now state-level artifacts. The palace is a key site of cultural relics under state protection.

Imperial seal

Blue-and-white flat bottle

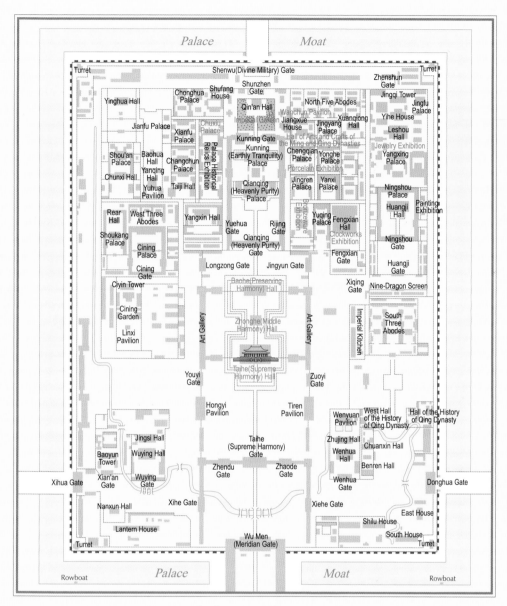

Palace Museum

⊙ Description

According to ancient Chinese astrological principles, the Purple Star (namely the North Star) was in the center of the universe and an abode of the Heavenly Emperor. Correspondingly, the earthly emperor dwelled in the "Imperial Palace", or the "Forbidden City". When Zhu Di, the third Emperor of the Ming Dynasty, took over the throne from his nephew, he decided to move the imperial capital from Nanjing to Beijing. Construction of the imperial palace got under way presently. The grand project was completed in 1420. The Imperial Palace had ever been the abode of the Ming and Qing emperors until 1911, when the Qing Dynasty was overthrown and Aisin-Gioro Puyi, its last emperor, was driven out of the Palace.

The Forbidden City is girdled by a 10-m-high city wall and a 52 m wide moat. It measures 961 m long from north to south and 753 m wide from east to west, covering an area of 780,000 sq m. There is a gate on each side of the rectangular city wall. The Wumen (Meridian) Gate in the south and Shenwu Gate in the north now serve as entrances for visitors. The layout of the architectural complex within the city wall centers on the north-south axis and sprawls eastward and westward. The architecture's red walls, golden glazed tiles, engraved beams, painted rafters rival in magnificence. The palace halls are arranged in majestic juxtaposition. All this looks like fairyland in the morning hues or in the shine of the setting

Interior of Qianqing Palace

million pieces in total according to the 28-volume *Report on Stock-taking of the Artistic Collections Left by the Qing Monarchy*, published in 1925. These include jade wares of the remote antiquity, calligraphy and paintings of the Tang, Song, Yuan and Ming dynasties, porcelain, ceramic, lacquer, gold and silver wares of the Song, Yuan and Ming dynasties. Besides, there are huge amount of extant classics, documents and archives. The Palace Museum was founded in 1925 to oversee the protection of such a huge trove of treasure. In the chaotic years, the museum frustrated the usurping efforts of the deposed Qing monarchy and its followers. After the September 18 Incident in 1931, the Palace Museum relocated thousands upon thousands of relics and art pieces to the south of the country in order to protect them from devastation inflicted by war and from plundering of the Japanese troops. The relics and art pieces were shipped to Nanjing in five batches and then moved to Sichuan in the southwest when the full-fledge War of Resistance Against Japan broke out in 1937. This relics protection activity lasted for a dozen or so years and its traveling route covered thousands of miles. In spite of the chaotic years of war, the huge amount of objects involved, and the tough journey covering thousands of miles, not a single art piece or relic got lost. It was really a wonder in terms of protecting the humankind's cultural heritage in the context of World War II. Since the founding of the People's Republic of China in 1949, in the recent decades in particular, the Palace Museum has made Herculean efforts in large-scale revamping of the palace, beefing up, management and protection of the relics, promoting academic research, improving exhibition and service, and in promoting digitalization.

sun. The frontal part in the south centers on Taihe (Supreme Harmony) Hall, Zhonghe (Middle Harmony) Hall and Baohe (Preserving Harmony) Hall, arranged along the north-south axis. On the east and west wings are Wenhua Hall and Wuying Hall. This part of the Forbidden City served as the venue where the emperor held morning court. In the north is the rear part of the Forbidden City centering on Qianqing Palace, Kunning Palace and Jiaotai Hall. The six eastern and western palaces are on the east and west and the Imperial Garden is situated behind Kunning Palace. Beyond this are Fengxian Hall and Huangji Hall in the east, Yangxin Hall and Cining Palace in the west-living quarters of the emperor and his queen and concubines. Sacrificial rites and religious ceremonies were also held in this part. The total floor space of the palatial architecture in these two parts is 163,000 sq m. The layout of the whole palace complex is meticulously designed to ensure the strictly stratified order of the feudal society and the supremacy of the emperor.

The existing relics and artifacts in the collections of the Forbidden City, left by the Qing monarchy, were 1.17

⊙ Highlights

Three Grand Halls in the Frontal Part With their overwhelming size, majesty, splendor and mystery, the three halls of Taihe, Zhonghe and Baohe form the climax in the spatial combination of the buildings in the Forbidden City. The three grand halls sit on three large-area elevated terraces, creating an impression of overlooking everything on earth. Of the three, Taihe Hall is the most majestic and largest in size. It represents the highest level of ancient wooden-structures in China in terms of size, standards and grade. Grand ceremonies were held here in the Ming and Qing dynasties.

Taihe Gate

Chuxiu (Gathering Elegance) Palace The palace is one of the six western palaces in the rear part of the Forbidden City. It was first built in the 18th year of Yongle (1420) in the Ming Dynasty for imperial concubines. The Empress Dowager Cixi once lived here when she was first selected as an imperial concubine. She gave birth to her son, who was later to become Emperor Tongzhi. In 1884 during the reign of Emperor Guangxu, the Empress Dowager moved back here on her grand 50th birthday. The courtyard here is planted with stately cypresses, presenting a tranquil beauty. On the wall of the winding corridor hangs the glazed ceramic plate inscribed with longevity odes composed by court officials for the Empress' birthday. Everything in the rooms is kept in the original state. The rooms are luxuriously furnished, reflecting the taste of the Empress Dowager Cixi.

Wanchun (Ten-thousand Spring) Pavilion This pavilion is located in the east of the Imperial Garden, coordinating from afar with Qianqiu (Thousand Autumn) Pavilion in the west. Built in the 15th year of Jiajing (1536) in the Ming Dynasty, it is formed by four verandas surrounding a square pavilion, with marble steps leading to the four verandas. The cone-shaped roof, covered with bamboo-joint golden glazed tiles, is round in the upper part and square in the lower, symbolizing the idea of "round sky and square earth". The pavilion is beautifully shaped and magnificently decorated and is therefore regarded as the best pavilion in the palace.

Theme Exhibition Rooms In addition to the three grand halls, the three rear palaces and the six western palaces which are displayed in their original appearances, there are specialized exhibition rooms for bronze wares, porcelain and pottery, crafts, calligraphy and painting, jewelry, and clockworks.

⊙ Information

■ **Transportation** *The Palace Museum is located in the center of Beijing, with Tian'anmen to the south and Jingshan Park to the north. Wangfujing, the major shopping mall in the city, is to the east, and Zhongnanhai lies in the west. Wumen Gate in the south of the Forbidden City and Shenwu Gate in the north are entrances for visitors. To enter the palace from Wumen Gate, one may take*

Wanchun Pavilion

buses No.1, 2, 4, 10, 20, 120, and 802 to Tian'anmen; to enter the palace from Shenwu Gate, one may take buses No. 101, 103, 109, 111, 810, 812, 814 and 846 or Kang'en special line to Jingshan Qianjie. Line 1 Subway has stop at Tian'anmen.

■ **Accomodation** *Beijing Hotel, Peninsula Palace Hotel in the east of the Forbidden City, Minzu Hotel in the west.*

■ **Others** *Tourist guide and audio guide in Chinese, English and Japanese, checkroom, shops selling brochures, souvenirs and food.*

Opening hours: 8:30 ~ 16:30 (Oct. 16 ~ Apr. 15), last entry at 15:30 (including the Clock Gallery and Treasure Gallery); 8:30 ~ 17:00 (Apr. 16 ~ Oct. 15), last entry at 16:00

Inquiry telephone: 010-65132255
Website: www.dpm.org.cn

Jade wine container

Bronze wine container

Life along Bianhe River at the Pure Brightness Festival (part)

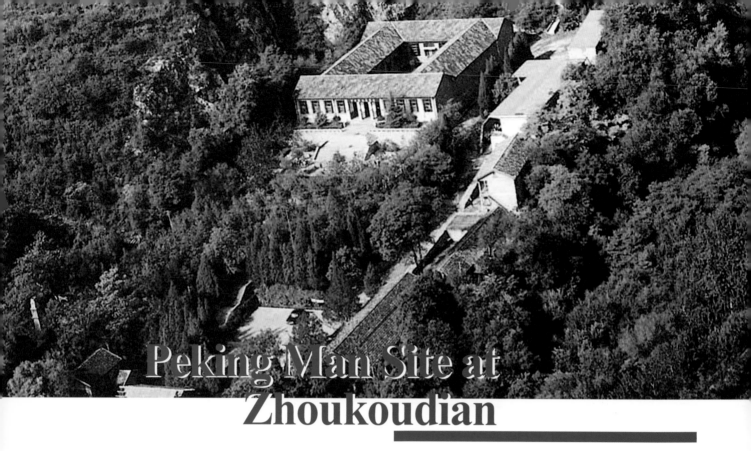

Peking Man Site at Zhoukoudian

☐ **Name:**

Peking Man Site at Zhoukoudian

☐ **Geographical coordinates:**

39° 41' N, 115° 51' E

☐ **Date of inscription:**

December 11, 1987

☐ **Criteria for inclusion:**

III, VI of cultural properties

Peking Man reconstructed

⊙ Overview

The Peking Man Site at Zhoukoudian is situated some 50 km southwest of Beijing city proper, at the juncture of Taihang Mountains and North China Plain. The site covers an area of 2.4 sq km, with 0.24 sq km of core area and 1.8 sq km of protected area.

The Peking Man Site at Zhoukoudian is the site with the richest and the most systematic palaeoanthropological information to date compared with any other site of the same age in the world, and occupies a critical position in palaeoanthropological and Quaternary geological research. The discovery of and research on Peking Man (*Sinanthropus pekinensis*), its cultural relics and artifacts has satisfactorily solved the half-a-century long dispute over whether the "*Homo erectus*" was ape or man in the scientific circles since the discovery of Java Man (*Pithecanthropus erectus*) in the 19th Century. As a pivotal breakthrough in the knowledge about human origin and evolution, it has established the evolutionary phase of *Homo erectus* and concluded the most important intermediate link in the full development chain from ape to man. On March 4, 1961, it was listed as a key site of cultural relics under state protection.

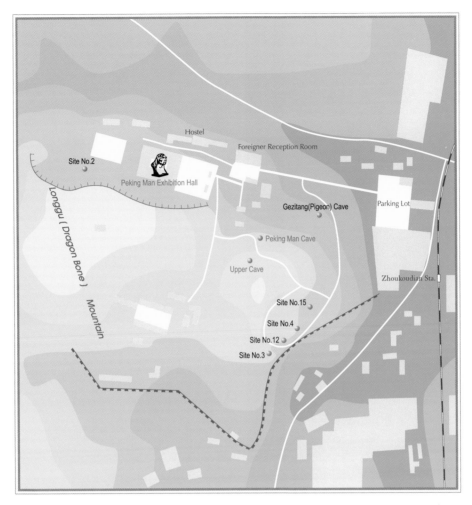

Site No.2

Hostel

Foreigner Reception Room

Peking Man Exhibition Hall

Longgu (Dragon Bone) Mountain

Gezitang(Pigeon) Cave

Parking Lot

Peking Man Cave

Upper Cave

Zhoukoudian Sta.

Site No.15

Site No.4

Site No.12

Site No.3

Peking Man Site at Zhoukoudian

⊙ Description

The Zhoukoudian area is important to geological study as it retains strata and sediments from Pliocene and Pleistocene. The geological formation of this region is limestone and bears many caves and fissures, with rich deposits of palaeoanthropological and palaeozoological remains.

For a long time, local residents in Zhoukoudian had lived by making lime and mining coal. During their limestone quarrying, small animal fossils were discovered, which attracted the attention of foreign scientists.

In 1921, Johann Gunnar Andersson, a famous Swedish geologist, and Otto Zdansky, an Austrian palaeontologist, conducted a small-scale excavation at Zhoukoudian. In 1923, they again carried out a short trial excavation and found two teeth that raised tremendous interest in Andersson. He believed that "the discovery at Zhoukoudian provides strong evidence for the hypothesis that mankind originated from Central Asia, adding an important link to the series of chains". In 1926, at the welcome ceremony for the Swedish Prince's visit to China, Andersson announced the discovery. At a time when there was hardly any discovery of ancient human fossil, the news shocked the scientific world. A new genus—*Sinanthropus pekinensis* was thereby confirmed. From 1927 to 1937, a 10-year extensive and systematic excavation was conducted at Zhoukou-

dian, resulting in the unearthing of numerous palaeoanthropological fossils, cultural artifacts and mammal fossils.

On December 2, 1929, Pei Wenzhong, a famous Chinese palaeoanthropologist, independently conducted the excavation and discovered at Site No.1 the first complete fossilized skullcap of Peking Man that dated back about 500,000 ~ 600,000 years, which surprised the academic circle worldwide. The event was famed as the first "gold medal" by Chinese scientists in the world's scientific arena. Subsequently, stone tools and evidence of fire use by Peking Man were discovered, which proved the existence of *Homo erectus*, thereby identifying the basic sequence of the human evolution and confirming the theory of human origin from ape to man. This has firmly established the position of Zhoukoudian in the palaeoanthropological research.

The excavation at Zhoukoudian started in 1927. In the 20-odd years that followed, over 200 pieces of ape-man and Upper Cave Peking Man fossils, ten thousands of stone tools, abundant residues of ashes and mammal fossils had been unearthed. In the long process of human evolution, there lived at Zhoukoudian, the Peking Man (*Homo erectus*) 700,000 ~ 200,000 years ago, the New Cave Man (early *Homo sapiens*) 100,000 years ago, and the Upper Cave Man (*Homo sapiens*) 18,000 years ago. The local

Peking Man Cave

same as modern man, and their lower limbs, though slightly curved, could support them to walk upright. The life span of Peking Man was quite short: most of them died before 14 years old, only a very few could live over 50 years.

Other discoveries include over 100,000 pieces of stone tools and stone flakes, fossils of 97 species of mammals, and "ash layers" with a depth of several meters, which are absolute proof that "Peking Man" was already capable of making tools and had learned to use fire.

Peking Man lived collectively in the cave and depended on gathering and hunting. Due to the harsh conditions, survival on individual basis was nearly impossible. Joint effort as groups and inseparable association through collective work were inevitable. This shows that Peking Man had acquired the earliest form of human social organization of their day.

In December of 1941, at the break of the Pacific War in the midst of World War II, the Peking Man fossils and large amount of animal fossils and stone tools all disappeared, and their whereabouts remain a mystery.

On August 16, 2002, for the purpose of better protecting Zhoukoudian, the Beijing Municipal Government and the Chinese Academy of Sciences signed an agreement on the joint protection and administration of Zhoukoudian. The discovery of Tianyuan Cave in June of 2003 provided new evidence for the study of human evolution. With its scientific value, Tianyuan Cave thereupon became the Site No. 27 among the series of cultural site group at Zhoukoudian.

geological history covers Eopleistocene and Epipleistocene, or 5,000,000 ~ 10,000 years ago.

To date, the discoveries of Peking Man Site at Zhoukoudian include such fossils as 6 skullcaps, 15 mandibles, 157 teeth, 7 pieces of femur, 1 tibia, 3 pieces of humerus, 1 clavicle and 1 lunate, as well as some fragments of frontal skull. All these belong to some 40 individuals. As a result of fossil restoration and study, there is understanding about the physical features of Peking Man that the head is evidently primitive, characterized by a robust skull, low and flat forehead, wide and flat nose, sharply elevated ridge bone, protruded mouth, the front of mandible reclines backwards, and a cranial capacity of 915 ~ 1,250 ml, all proofs of *Homo erectus*. According to archaeologists, Peking Man had hands almost the

Highlights

Site No. 1 (Peking Man Cave) The Peking Man Cave is a karst cave of natural formation. It is about 140 m in east-west direction and the widest place from north to south is about 40 m. The artifacts deposit has 13 layers of over 40 m in depth. Starting from about 500,000 ~ 600,000 years ago, Peking Man lived here intermittently till about 200,000 years ago. The remains, artifacts and traces of Peking Man, together with the collapse of roof rocks and the entry of sand-gravel flow from outside covered one layer upon another in the cave, forming a very deep deposit of strata. The site was first discovered in 1921 and its systematic excavation started

A panorama of Zhoukoudian Site

Upper Cave   Zhoukoudian Site Museum

in 1927. The work was suspended in 1937, due to the "July 7th Incident" (Japanese invasion of China). The excavation was resumed after the founding of the People's Republic in 1949.

Upper Cave It is a cave where the Upper Cave Man lived about 20,000 ~ 10,000 years ago. It was found in 1930 and excavated from 1933 to 1934. The discoveries included fossil fragments that belong to at least eight Upper Cave Men, including three sculls and a large amount of animal fossils. Artifacts of the Upper Cave Man included ashes from fire, stone tools, bone-wares and perforated pebbles, animal teeth and shells for ornaments. Hematite residues were found around the human fossils, an evidence that the Upper Cave Man applied burial to their dead. The cave has four parts: the entrance, upper and lower chambers, and a lower recess. The upper chamber was for living and the lower for burial. The lower recess, believed to be natural traps, produced animal fossil of entire skeletons.

Site No. 27 (Tianyuan Cave) The Tianyuan Cave is about 6,000 m southwest of the Peking Man Site at Zhoukoudian. Its geographical coordinates are 39° 39' 31" N, 115° 52' 19" E. Excavation at this site started in June 2003 and there has unearthed human fossils and large amount of animal fossils. The human fossils have been initially dated to be 25,000 years ago, the same age as the Upper Cave Man fossils. As such, these fossils have made up for the missing Upper Cave Man fossils and therefore are of significant scientific value. This fossil site has been named as "Site No. 27 (Tianyuan Cave) of the Peking Man Site at Zhoukoudian".

⊙ Information

■ **Transportation** *Take bus No. 917 from Tianqiao or bus No. 616 from Xidan Department Store to Liangxiang, change to Ring Line No. 2 to reach the Site.*

■ **Others** *The Peking Man Site at Zhoukoudian offers all kinds of souvenirs for sale, including hominid and Upper Cave Man head busts, individualized post cachet, post-marked envelope, post cards, CDs, individualized wrist-watch, folded cards, series books about the Peking Man Site, and other relevant publications.*

Opening hour: 8:30 ~ 17:30 (no closed day)
Inquiry telephones: 010-69301287, 69301278
Website: www.zhoukoudiansite.com

Skullcap fossil   Stone tools

Summer Palace, an Imperial Garden in Beijing

☐ **Name:**
   Summer Palace, an Imperial Garden in Beijing
☐ **Geographical coordinates:**
   39° 59' N, 116° 16' E
☐ **Date of inscription:**
   December 2, 1998
☐ **Criteria for inclusion:**
   I, II, III of cultural properties

Wanshou Hill and Kunming Lake

⊙ Overview

The Summer Palace is located in Haidian District in the northwest suburbs of Beijing City, on the northern border of North China Plain. First built in 1750 and occupying an area of 297 ha, it served as a provisional palace and summer residence of the Qing emperors (1616-1911). The Summer Palace is one of the most magnificent and best-preserved imperial gardens in the world. It is a masterpiece of Chinese landscape garden design, which combines natural landscape with artificial features to form a harmonious ensemble of outstanding aesthetic value. It is an outstanding product for Chinese picturesque imperial garden, fully reflecting the idea and practice of Chinese picturesque garden making. The palace plays an important role in the development of the oriental art and culture on garden making. The splendid palaces, majestic architectural complex, fine landscape and top-level technique are invaluable asset of the Chinese people. In 1961, it was listed as a key site of cultural relics under state protection.

Bronze Ox

Summer Palace

⊙ Description

In the construction of the Summer Palace, ideas of Chinese painting, poetry and literature were successfully integrated to create a harmony of magnificent construction, splendid colors and green environment. A large-scale artificial garden built on natural hill and lake, it has been commonly regarded as an outstanding example of imperial gardens in China. The design gives prominence to Wanshou (Longevity) Hill and the Kunming Lake. The palace, consisting of more than 100 scenic spots, can be divided into three areas: the administrative area, the residential area, and the scenic area.

The administrative area is located within the East Palace Gate and its central building is Renshou (Benevolence and Longevity) Hall, where the Empress Dowager Cixi and Emperor Guangxu handled domestic and foreign affairs.

The residential area lies between administrative area and scenic area. The three large courtyards of Leshou (Happiness in Longevity) Hall, Yulan Hall and Yiyun House, connected by dozens of corridors, were the residence of the Empress Dowager Cixi, Emperor Guangxu and his empresses and concubines. In the eastern part of the area, there is a 21m high three-storey Grand Theatre Stage, built exclusively for Empress Dowager Cixi. More than 40,000 pieces of cultural relics, which were used by emperors and empresses, are preserved in the halls.

Covering ninety percent of the total area of the palace, the scenic area consists of the front side of Wanshou Hill, Kunming Lake, the rear side of Wanshou Hill, and the Back River. The front side of the hill, facing the Kunming Lake, is gentle and wide, with a broad view; while the rear side of the hill, with winding paths at the hillside and a river at the foot, is very tranquil. Various palaces, temples and other buildings with a floor space of 70,000 sq m scatter nicely in the framework of hill and lake. Featuring both imperial majesty and natural beauty, the Summer Palace embodies the principle of Chinese garden making, "a garden should look like a natural landscape though it was made by men". In the middle of the front hill, the Temple of Buddhist Virtue forms the core of a group of splendid and magnificent building complex rising upward from the bottom. The Long Corridor connecting the building complex in the front hill is an example of huge gallery with color

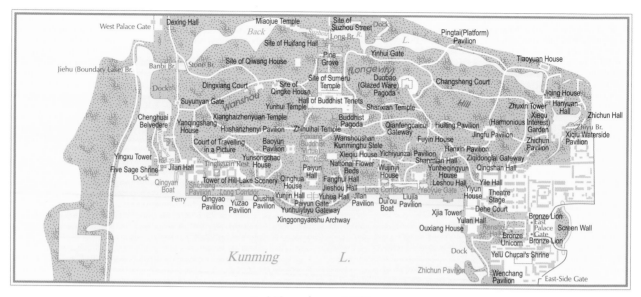

Wanshou Hill

paintings in Chinese gardens.

The beautiful Kunming Lake has the elegance of landscape south of the lower Yangtse, and three big islands in the lake are a perfect symbol of "fairyland in the sea", a goal pursued by Chinese garden designers. The 150-m-long Seventeen-Arch Bridge linking Nanhu Island with the east bank creates the most spectacular view of the lake. The West Causeway along the Kunming Lake is an imitation of the famous Song Dynasty Sudi Causeway at the West Lake in Hangzhou. The six bridges along the causeway and the West Mountain outside the park together form a wonderful landscape of mountains and waters. This method of borrowing the view of the West Mountain is the best example of its kind amongst the existing ancient gardens in China.

In the middle part of the rear side of Wanshou Hill, there is the Han-Tibetan style architectural complex, an imitation of the ancient Sangyuan Lamasery in Tibet. A business street in the style of South China waterside market place was laid out along the Back River. Located by the eastern slope of Wanshou Hill is Xiequ (Harmonious Interest) Garden, imitated after Jichang Garden, a private garden in Wuxi, Jiangsu Province. In the Summer Palace, landscapes from western plateaus of China to riverside towns south of the lower Yangtze are harmoniously condensed into one garden. The structures with styles of ethnic minorities reflect the excellent level of Chinese garden making. There were several exquisite small gardens in the rear side of the hill, which were destroyed by the allied forces of Britain and France in 1860, and by the invading troops of the eight nations in 1900, only some sites remain.

⊙ Highlights

Kunming Lake Occupying three-quarters of the area of the Summer Palace, it is one of the main components of the landscape. A reservoir for Beijing in the history, its water resources come from springs in the West Mountain. The lake was formed 3,500 years ago, and the water quality has always been pure until today. The Summer Palace was first named Garden of Clear Ripples for the water of the lake. Also known as immortal islands, the Nanhu Island, Zaojiantang Island and Zhijingge Island in the Kunming Lake reflect the Taoist belief in immortality. Along the lake there are many scenic spots, such as Zhichun Pavilion, Seventeen-Arch Bridge, Marble Boat, Bronze Ox and Six Bridges on West Causeway, Jingming Pavilion and Changguan Hall.

A distant view of Summer Palace

Foxiang (Buddhist Virtue) Temple It is the core and symbol of the Summer Palace, surrounded by all the scenic spots. The temple shows the emperors' wish for the blessing of Buddha. Built on a 20-m-high stone foundation in the middle of the front Wanshou Hill, the 41-m-high temple is an eight-faceted, quadruple-eaved three-storey wooden structure, supported by 8 atlas pillars of hard wood. The roof was laid by 184,172 glazed tiles of 35 kinds, showing the technical level of the ancient arts and crafts in China. The temple houses a 5-m-high gold-plated standing statue of One-Thousand Hand Bodhisattva, a treasure of arts and crafts made in the Ming Dynasty. From the temple one can get a bird's-eye view of the Summer Palace.

Long Corridor It is the most wonderful corridor among the ancient gardens in China. The 728-m-long corridor runs from Yaoyue Gate in the east to Shizhang Pavilion in the west, with 273 sections in total. The up-and-down base for Long Corridor circles around the southern side of Wanshou Hill like a colorful ribbon along the north bank of Kunming Lake, making the scenery of lake and mountain more beautiful. There are four double-eaved octagonal pavilions, namely Liujia, Jilan, Qiushui and Qingyao, representing four seasons. It links two waterside pavilions of Dui'ou

Long Corridor

Building complex of Foxiang Temple

Seventeen-Arch Bridge

and Yuzao, and connects the Tower of Lake-Hill Scenery in the northwest. Thanks to more than 14, 000 paintings of *Su* style on the roof beams, the corridor is also called Painting Gallery. In 1990, it was listed in the Guinness World Records for its unique length and rich paintings.

⊙ Information

■ **Transportation** *Visitors can take bus No.332, 333, 718, 726, 374, 904, 375, 384, 808 and 716 to get there. Taxi is also available. Pleasure-boats are available from Bayi Lake.*

■ **Accommodation** *Nearby the Summer Palace there are many hotels with different rates, such as Wofosi Hotel, Xiangshan Villa, Xiangshan Hotel, Shengtang Hotel, Shangri-La Hotel, Friendship Hotel, Yanshan Grand Hotel and Olympic Hotel.*

■ **Food** *To the north of the Long Corridor is Tingliguan Restaurant, a famous one in China featuring authentic court cuisine. There are restaurants providing fast food near Zhichun Pavilian, East Nine Houses and Marble Boat.*

■ **Others** *There are various small shops selling picture albums, books, arts and crafts and souvenir.*

Opening hours: Opens everyday 6:30 ~ 18:00 (Apr. 1 - Oct. 31); 7:00 ~ 17:00 (Nov. 1 - Apr. 1)

Inquiry telephone: 010-62881144

Website: www.summerpalace-china.com

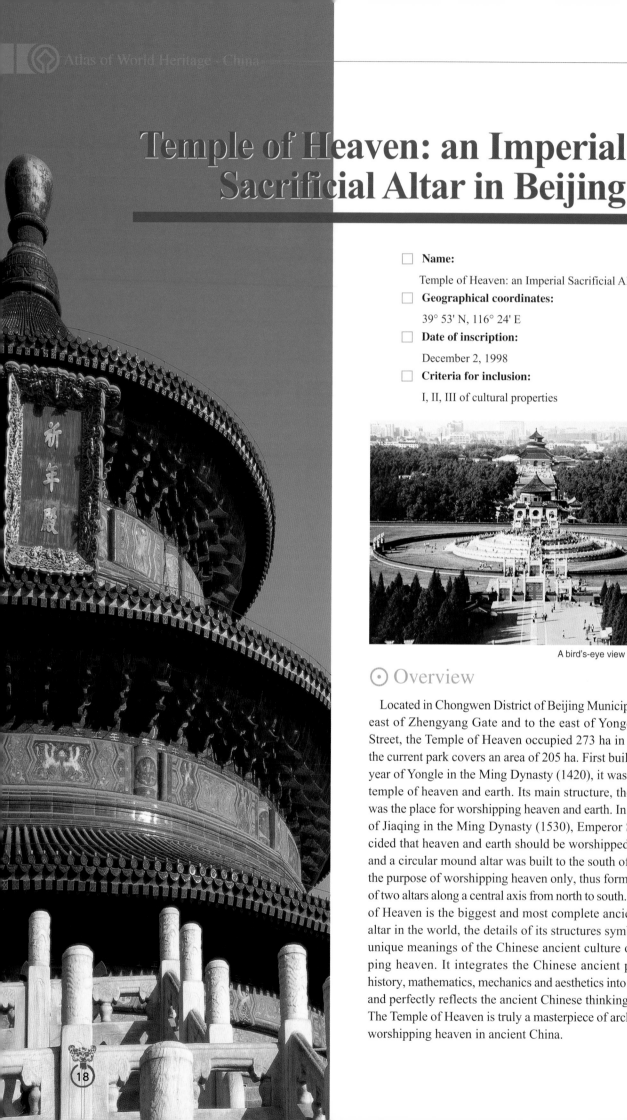

Temple of Heaven: an Imperial Sacrificial Altar in Beijing

☐ **Name:**

　Temple of Heaven: an Imperial Sacrificial Altar in Beijing

☐ **Geographical coordinates:**

　39° 53' N, 116° 24' E

☐ **Date of inscription:**

　December 2, 1998

☐ **Criteria for inclusion:**

　I, II, III of cultural properties

A bird's-eye view of the Temple

⊙ Overview

　Located in Chongwen District of Beijing Municipality, southeast of Zhengyang Gate and to the east of Yongdingmennei Street, the Temple of Heaven occupied 273 ha in history, and the current park covers an area of 205 ha. First built in the 18th year of Yongle in the Ming Dynasty (1420), it was originally a temple of heaven and earth. Its main structure, the Dasi Hall, was the place for worshipping heaven and earth. In the 9th year of Jiaqing in the Ming Dynasty (1530), Emperor Shizong decided that heaven and earth should be worshipped separately, and a circular mound altar was built to the south of the hall for the purpose of worshipping heaven only, thus forming a layout of two altars along a central axis from north to south. The Temple of Heaven is the biggest and most complete ancient imperial altar in the world, the details of its structures symbolizing the unique meanings of the Chinese ancient culture on worshipping heaven. It integrates the Chinese ancient philosophy, history, mathematics, mechanics and aesthetics into one entirety and perfectly reflects the ancient Chinese thinking on heaven. The Temple of Heaven is truly a masterpiece of architecture for worshipping heaven in ancient China.

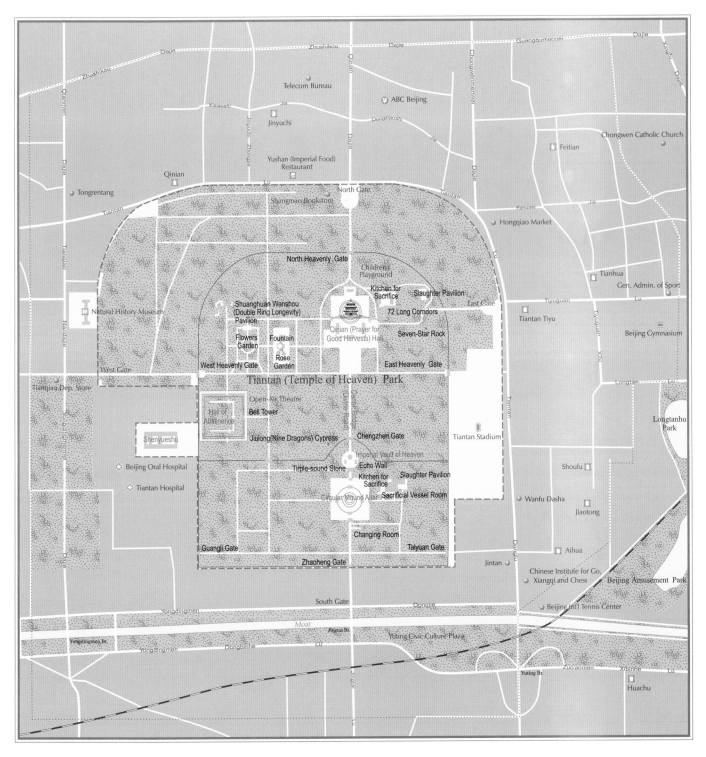

Temple of Heaven

Huangqian Hall

Circular Mound Altar

⊙ Description

The Temple of Heaven has two altars: the outer altar and the inner altar. The main structures are concentrated in the inner altar. At the southern end of the inner altar is the "Circular Mound Altar", and at the northern end is the Altar of Prayer for Good Harvests. A 360 m paved passage called Danbi Bridge (Divine Road) is built above the ground, which connects the two altars. Danbi Bridge is actually the central axis of the Temple of Heaven.

The Circular Mound Altar is a three-layer terrace made of blue glazed bricks in the Ming Dynasty. To the north of the altar is Taishen Hall (now Imperial Vault of Heaven), a round architecture with double eaves. The Circular Mound Altar and Dasi Hall are enclosed by a double wall, of which the southern half is square and the northern half semi-circular, representing the ancient belief

Iron burners

tectures in the Temple of Heaven. From the 7th year (1742) to the 9th year (1754) of Qianlong, the Hall of Abstinence was built, and the Circular Mound Altar was expanded and the Imperial Vault of Heaven renovated. The Daxiang Hall was renamed as the Hall of Prayer for Good Harvests and its tiles of three colors were replaced by blue ones. The earth walls of the Temple were changed into brick ones, and the gates of Circular Mound Altar were constructed. These projects of renovation made the Temple of Heaven loftier in architecture, more splendid in color and more meaningful in its symbolization. After such a large-scale reconstruction and expansion, the layout of the Temple of Heaven was finally formed in the 19th year of Qianlong (1754). Two altars exist together at the southern and northern ends, each with its own independent structure. The overall design was perfect with precise style. The layout and form have been kept for almost 200 years and remain the same until today.

In the Temple of Heaven, a vast area of cypress and other plantations creates an ecological environment of "harmony between nature and man" and makes up a beautiful garden. The Temple of Heaven is not only a masterpiece of architecture, but also a classic in Chinese art of ancient gardens.

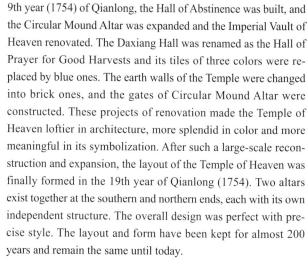

Qinian Hall

that the heaven was round and the earth square. It also made the two major structures, built at different times with a span of more than one hundred years, more harmonious, reflecting highly wisdom and originality of the designers. In the 21st year of Jiajing (1542) the emperor issued an order to demolish Dasi Hall. And in the 24th year of the Jiajing (1545), Daxiang Palace, a lofty cone-shaped structure with triple eaves based on a triple-tiered circular stone terrace, was built on the same site. This splendid and majestic building is the present Hall of Prayer for Good Harvests.

In the Qing Dynasty, Emperor Qianlong presided over a huge project on the expansion, renovation and refurbishing of the archi-

⊙ Highlights

Qinian (Prayer for Good Harvests) Hall It is the main building in the Temple of Heaven, and a rare example in ancient Chinese architecture. Located in Qigu Altar, the hall is a 32 m high structure with triple conical roof of deep blue glazed tiles, symbolizing the sky. Every part of the hall has its meaning. The four central pillars, called the Dragon-well Pillars, represent the four seasons of a year; there are two rings of 12 pillars each, the inner ring symbolizing the twelve months and the outer ring the twelve divisions of the day and night; together the 24 pillars represent 24 solar terms; and with the 4 central pillars, the 28 pillars for the 28 constellations in the sky; then plus the 8 small pillars at the top of big pillars, the number of 36 representing the 36 heavenly stems in Chinese era (corresponding to the 72 earthly branches of the Long Corridor). The caisson ceiling of the hall is painted with dragon and phoenix. At the center of the floor is a round marble slab, which has a natural pattern of dragon and phoenix, setting off the dragon and phoenix in the ceiling perfectly. The design of the hall reflects the idea of focusing on agriculture of the ancient people. Over the centuries, the ceremony of prayer for good harvests had become an important state protocol for feudal dynasties.

Huanqiu (Circular Mound Altar) Also known as Jitiantai, the altar is wholly built of white marble with fine craft and elegant style, a masterpiece of stone architecture in ancient times. Every year on Winter Solstice and in the 4th lunar month, the emperor would come here to pay homage to the heaven and pray for rains. Its structure totally reflects the ancient belief that heaven was round and the earth square. The Altar, consisting of three layers of circular marble terraces, has a round Tianxin (Heart of Heaven) Stone, placed and raised in the center of the upper terrace. When people stand on the Stone and speak in a low voice, the echo will be much louder, as if it were a dialogue between the human and the nature.

Imperial Vault of Heaven (Huangqiongyu) Located to the north of the Circular Mound Altar, it was used for placing the tablets of the Gods. The building is surrounded by the famous Echo Wall, which enable sound to travel for long distance, producing continuous echoes.

Hall of Abstinence Also called Little Imperial Palace, it is located to the southwest of the Hall of Prayer for Good Harvests. The hall is an east-facing palace for the emperor to fast before the sacrificial ceremony. The green tiles were used on the roof of every room in the hall, showing the emperors' subordination to Heaven. During the Ming and Qing dynasties, the emperors would stay and fast in the Hall of Abstinence before worshipping ceremony every time. To the north of the east gate of the hall is a bell tower. When the emperor left for the altar, the bell would start to ring, warning the officials to perform their duties. The main structure is a "beamless hall" built totally of bricks and tiles.

Shenyueshu Situated in the southwest of the Temple of Heaven, occupying a floor space of nearly 10,000 sq m, it is the drilling place for the ceremony. There are hundreds of rooms in the complex, used for practice and training of the dance with musical accompaniment for sacrificial ceremonies during the Ming and Qing dynasties. Main buildings include Ningxi Hall and Xianyou Hall. Shenyueshu is ranked among the five major architectures of the Temple of Heaven together with Qigu Altar, the Circular Mound Altar, Hall of Abstinence and the Sacrificial Place. All court officials who would participate in the ceremony should rehearse here for the protocol procedures.

⊙ Information

■ **Transportation** *Bus No. 6, 34, 35 and 106 stop at the north gate of the Temple of Heaven; Bus No.120 and 122 at the south gate; Bus No. 729 at west gate; and Bus No. 43 at the east gate.*

■ **Accommodation** *There are Tiantan Hotel and Chongwenmen Hotel nearby.*

■ **Others** *Opposite the east gate, Hongqiao Market is noted for its pearls, travel bags, and watches, etc.; Near the east gate, Yuanlong Silk Store is a must go for visitors.*

Opening hours: 6:00 ~ 21:00 (the park); 8:00 ~ 17:30 (major sightseeing spots)

Inquiry telephone: 010-67028866

Long Corridor   Imperial Vault of Heaven

Beijing

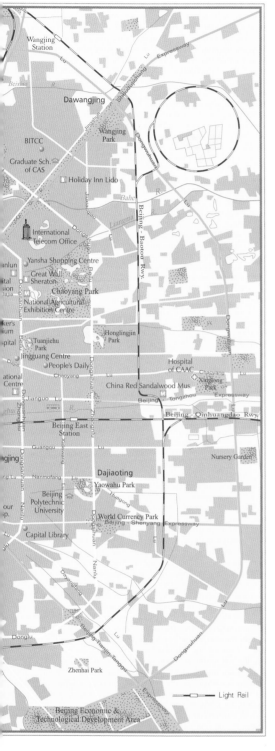

HEBEI PROVINCE

General Information

Hebei Province, also called Ji in short, has its capital in Shijiazhuang City. With an area of 190,000 sq km, it has under its administrative jurisdiction 11 prefecture-level cities, 22 county-level cities, 108 counties and 6 autonomous counties. The province has a population of 67.42 million and ethnic groups including Han, Man, Hui, Mongol and Zhuang.

Environment

Hebei is located in the northern part of North China Plain and the southeastern part of the Inner Mongolian Plateau, on the shore of Bohai Sea. Of the total area of the province, 60% are highlands and hilly areas, and 40% plains. The Haihe River is the largest river in the province. Most of Hebei Province has a warm temperate zone semi-humid monsoon climate. The average temperature is -16 ~ -3°C in January and 20 ~ 27°C in July, with an average annual rainfall between 400 ~ 800 mm.

Places of Interest

Hebei is a province of cultural relics, where historical sites can be found everywhere. Chengde Mountain Resort, the typical imperial classical garden of the Ming Dynasty, Eight Outer Monasteries, the imperial temple complex of the Qing Dynasty, and the Mulan Game Range of the imperial family of the Qing Dynasty pose a grand and magnificent view. The jade suit sewn with gold thread, unearthed from the Han Tomb in Lingshan Mountain in Mancheng, the world's oldest arch bridge, the Zhaozhou Bridge, and the Iron Lions of Cangzhou are well-known both at home and abroad. Shanhaiguan Pass of the Great Wall, the Eastern Qing Tombs, Western Qing Tombs and Chengde Mountain Resort are included in the World Heritage List. The site of Xibaipo, which once served as the headquarters of the Central Committee of the Communist Party of China, and the site of Ranzhuang Tunnel Warfare have become places for education on revolutionary traditions.

Time-honored fascinating natural landscapes of primitive simplicity are not uncommon in Hebei Province. There are the soul-soothing seashore beauty of Beidaihe, the vast and magnificent Bashang grassland, the Laishui Wild Slope full of wilderness funs, and the precipitous and beautiful Zhangshi Crag. Xin'ao Underwater World in Qinhuangdao and Qinhuangdao Wildlife Zoo have injected vitality and vigor to the vast land of Hebei Province.

Local Specialties

Angu medicinal material, Zhangbei edible mushrooms, Hebei juicy pears, Xuanhua grapes, Shenzhou sweet peaches, Cangzhou dates, Jingdong Chinese chestnuts, and Xinglong hawthorn.

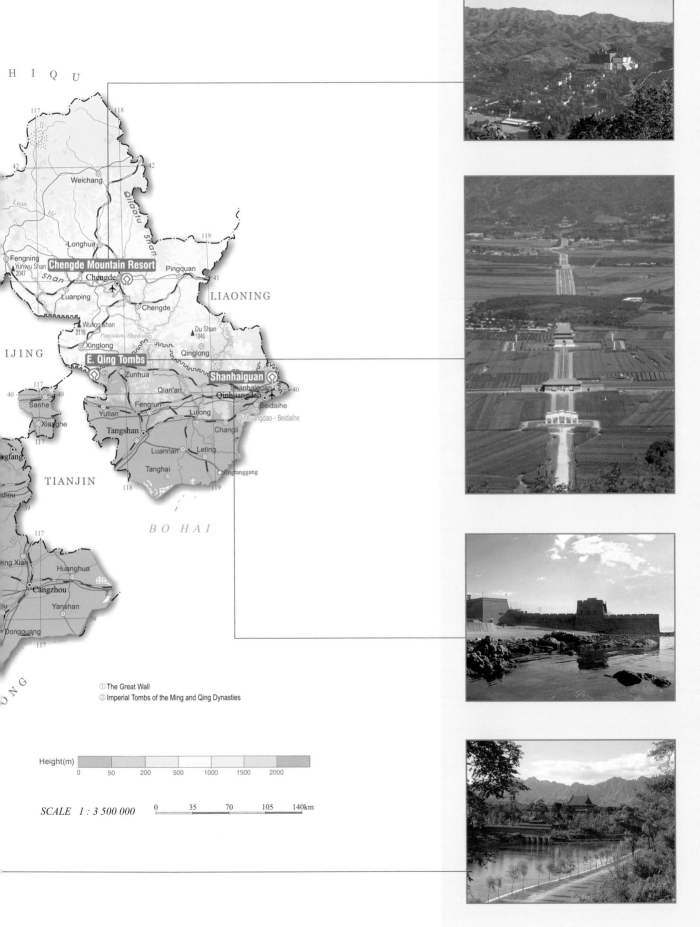

Map labels:
HIQU
117
118
42
Weichang
Luan
He
Qiaotu Shan
119
Longhua
Fengning
Yunwu Shan
2047
shan
Chengde Mountain Resort
Chengde
Pingquan
41
LIAONING
Luanping
Chengde
Wuling Shan
2116
Panjiakou Shuiku
Du Shan
1846
He
Xinglong
Qinglong
IJING
E. Qing Tombs
Zunhua
Shanhaiguan
Shanhaiguan
40
117
40
Qinhuangdao
40
Sanhe
Qian'an
Fengrun
Beidaihe
Yutian
Lulong
Qinhuangdao - Beidaihe
Xianghe
Changli
117
Tangshan
gfang
Luannan
Leting
Tanghai
Jingtanggang
TIANJIN
118
119
zhou
BO HAI
117
Huanghua
Cangzhou
Yanshan
Dongguang
117
ONG

① The Great Wall
② Imperial Tombs of the Ming and Qing Dynasties

Height(m)
0   50   200   500   1000   1500   2000

SCALE   1 : 3 500 000
0   35   70   105   140km

Chengde Mountain Resort and its Outlying Temples

☐ **Name:**

Chengde Mountain Resort and its Outlying Temples

☐ **Geographical coordinates:**

41° 00' N, 118° 00' E

☐ **Date of inscription:**

December 17, 1994

☐ **Criteria for inclusion:**

II, IV of cultural properties

A bird's-eye view of the mountain resort

⊙ Overview

Located in the city of Chengde, Hebei Province, and built in the 18th Century, the Mountain Resort was a summer retreat for the emperors of the Qing Dynasty (1616-1911). The resort consists of the emperors' palaces, the imperial gardens and the magnificent temple complex. During the reigns of Kangxi (1662-1723) and Qianlong (1736-1796), many important political, military, ethnic and foreign affairs were handled here, so the resort also witnessed the honor and disgrace, prosperity and decline of the Qing Empire. Two factors—the natural scenery and the classical Chinese culture, such as philosophy, aesthetics and literature—have been integrated into the resort, making it the epitome of Chinese traditional culture and an ideal homestead where man and nature coexist in harmony. It is a creative masterpiece embodying the great achievements of traditional Chinese garden making and architectural arts.

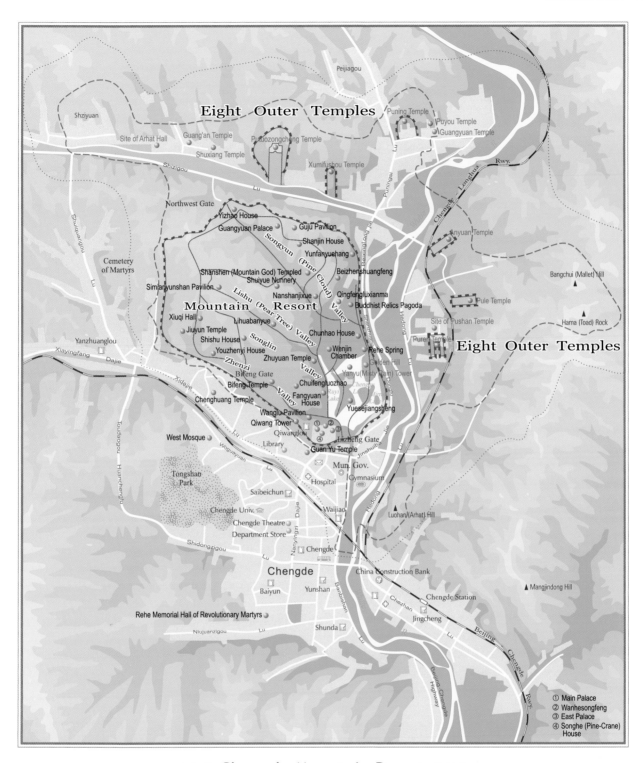

Chengde Mountain Resort

⊙ Description

The Mountain Resort and its outlying temples lie deep in the Yanshan Mountains in the north of Hebei Province. In its surroundings, there are undulating hills, odd-shaped peaks and grotesque-looking rocks. Wulie River runs from north to east and joins Luanhe River. This region was where the agricultural civilization of the Central Plains met with the nomadic civilization of the Northwest.

1. The Mountain Resort

Covering an area of 564 ha, the Mountain Resort (originally

called the Temporary Imperial Dwelling Palace in Rehe) is divided into two perfectly combined areas: the palace area and the scenic area. The natural environment is fully utilized and improved, which leads to a wonderful blending of the natural and human landscapes. The great scale, the large number of buildings and the huge consumption of labor and materials all display the grandeur of an imperial garden.

Situated at the south end of the Mountain Resort, the palace area consists of four groups of buildings: the Main Palace, Songhe

(Pine-crane) Palace, Wanhe Songfeng (Pine Soughing Valley) Palace and Eastern Palace. This area is where the Qing emperors lived, dealt with administrative affairs, and held grand ceremonies. The architectural style of the buildings is simple and elegant but not without the solemnity of all the imperial palaces. The place witnessed the death of two emperors, Jiaqing and Xianfeng, and the beginning of the "Xinyou Coup D'etat" that influenced the history of China.

The scenic area is further divided into the lake zone, plain zone and mountain zone.

The lake zone lies at the southeast of the Mountain Resort and consists of 8 lakes, which are the Chenghu Lake, Ruyi Lake, Silver Lake, Mirror Lake, Half-Moon Lake and others, collectively known as Saihu Lakes. The isles are surrounded by the water, and the water is enclosed by mountains. In its layout, traditional Chinese garden making techniques are adopted to compose a fairyland of Chinese myths and legends. Several groups of buildings were ingeniously constructed among islets, banks and lakes, presenting a scenic view of water town.

The plain zone is situated in the north of the Mountain Resort. This area is further divided into two sections: the grassland in the west and the woodland in the east. The grassland is centered on Shimadai where the emperors used to hold horse races. Named as "Ten-Thousand-Tree Garden", the woodland is one of the political centers within the Mountain Resort.

The mountain zone is located in the northwest of the resort and consists of four valleys, namely, from south to north, Zhenzi (Hazelnut) Valley, Songlin (Pinewood) Valley, Lishu (Pear) Valley and Songyun (Pine-cloud Gorge). On the undulating hills grow towering old pines and lush trees. Originally there were more than forty groups of buildings such as studios, pavilions, huts, Buddhist temples and Taoist temples, which are mostly ruins now.

2. The Outlying Temples

Covering a total area of 47.2 ha and consisting of 12 temples of different architectural styles, these are the imperial temples constructed by the Qing government to honor the minorities such as the Mongolians and Tibetans in Northwest China, to reinforce its power in the border areas. The high concentration of temples, the great scale of the complex, the exquisite construction and the superb workmanship in the numerous Buddhist figures and sacrificial utensils make this area one of the holy lands of Tibetan Buddhism.

Han style temples: They are temples with the architectural patterns of the traditional palace and mansions of the Han Nationality, including Puren Temple, Pushan Temple, Shuxiang Temple, Guangyuan Temple and the Arhat Hall.

Tibetan style temples: Most of the outlying temples are influenced to a certain degree by Tibetan lamaseries. Among them, Putuo Zongcheng Temple, Xumi Fushou Temple and Guang'an Temple mainly follow the Tibetan architectural style.

Han-Tibetan style temples: A combination of the architectural style of the Han temples and that of the Tibetan lamaseries is the most distinctive feature of the outlying temples, especially in Puning Temple, Puyou Temple, Anyuan Temple and Pule Temple. In these temples, generally, the architectural shape and structure of the Han style are adopted in the front, while that of the Tibetan style are adopted in the rear.

Shuixin (mid-lake) Pavilion

◉ Highlights

Jinshan (Golden Hill) It refers to a group of buildings in the lake zone of the resort modeled after Jinshan Temple in Zhenjiang, Jiangsu Province. It faces the lake on three sides and a stream on the remaining side. From the islet where the earth and rocks are piled into different heights, one can have a panoramic view of the natural beauty of the lakes and mountains. During his six visits to the regions south of the Yangtze, Emperor Kangxi ascended onto the Jinshan Jiangtian Temple in Zhenjiang several times to appreciate the magnificence of the Yangtze River. The beauty still lingered in the emperor's mind after his return, so he ordered his men to reproduce the temple and absorb its essence by constructing Jinshan Islet in the Mountain Resort. Compared with the original one in Zhenjiang, this Jinshan is smaller in scale but more refined aesthetically. Its main building, called "The Emperors' Pavilion", has six sides and three storeys. The eaves are hung with three tab-

Jinshan

lets inscribed with the handwriting of Emperor Kangxi. In the past, the Jade Emperor was enshrined and worshipped on the top floor, the Zhenwu Emperor on the middle floor, while the throne of the emperor on earth was on the ground floor. Ascending onto the pavilion, one can take in the lofty mountains and vast water at one glance.

Puning Temple In the 20th year of Qianlong (1755), the Qing government put down the rebellion of the Jungar Tribe in Mongolia. To commemorate this victory, unite the minorities in the northwest, consolidate the frontier defense in the north, and show respect to the religious beliefs of the Mongolian nationality, this large Tibetan Buddhist temple, modeled after the Samadhi Temple in Tibet, was constructed. It lies on the bank of Wulie River in the northeast of the Mountain Resort and occupies a central position among all the 12 temples. The temple, resplendent and magnificent, is divided into the southern and northern sections. In the southern section, the traditional temple layout of the Han style was adopted, while in the northern section, the Tibetan architectural layout was adopted. The biggest wood-carved Buddha in the world, the Thousand-Hand and Thousand-Eye Avalokitesvara, was enshrined and worshipped in the Mahayana Pavilion, the main building of the temple. The figure, 23.5 m in height and 110 tonnes in weight and made of five different types of wood, is a masterpiece of Chinese sculpture.

Yanyu (Misty Rain) Tower It is the main architecture on Qinglian (green lotus) Islet in the lake zone. Throughout his life, Emperor Qianlong paid six visits to the regions south of the Yangtze, and he appreciated very much the Mist and Rain Tower in Jiaxing of Zhejiang Province. In the 45th year of Qianlong (1780), a tower modeled after the one in Jiaxing was built in the Mountain Resort, and it became the venue from which the emperors and empresses viewed the beauty of the rain and the mist. Whenever it rained, viewed from the distance on the tower, in the drizzle, the water seems to have melted into the sky at the horizon, and the faraway mountains and nearby water are all wrapped in the mist, which turns this region into a fairyland. The Qingyang Study and the Duishan Studio around the tower were places where the emperors enjoyed reading. In front of the studio, there is an artificial hill on which stands a hexagonal pavilion named "Wing Pavilion", and on the stone wall beside the pavilion are inscribed three Chinese characters Qing Lian Dao, meaning "Green Lotus Islet".

⊙ Information

■ **Transportation** *Beijing Capital International Airport is 200 km from Chengde. The Beijing - Chengde and Jinzhou - Chengde railway lines link the city with the northeast and other regions of China. There are through trains between Chengde and Beijing, Tianjin, Shijiazhuang. The Beijing - Chengde Expressway and the Qinhuangdao - Chengde Highway lead directly to downtown Chengde. National roads 101, 111 and 112 run across the city. In addition, Beijing, Tianjin, Shijiazhuang and Qinhuangdao all have coaches heading for Chengde.*

■ **Accommodation** *Tourists can stay at Yunshan Hotel, Lulu Hotel, Shenghua Hotel, Qiwanglou Hotel, etc.*

■ **Food** *The restaurants serving special cuisines include the Imperial Palace Restaurant, the New Qianlong Restaurant, the Imperial Garden Restaurant and the Dongpo Restaurant.*

■ **Others** *Local special products include almonds, mushrooms, and bracken. The handicrafts are paper-cuts and Teng's cloth paste pictures.*

Opening hour: 8:00 ~ 18:00 in summer, 8:30 ~ 16:30 in winter (The Mountain Resort, Puning Temple, Putuo Zongcheng Temple, Xumi Fushou Temple, Pule Temple, Anyuan Temple, Puyou Temple)

Inquiry telephones: 0314-2037706, 2025918

Yanyu Tower

Puning Temple

SHANXI PROVINCE

General Information

Shanxi Province, also called Jin in short, has its capital in Taiyuan City. With an area of 150,000 sq km, it has under its administrative jurisdiction 11 prefecture-level cities, 11 county-level cities, and 85 counties. It has a population of 32.45 million and ethnic groups including Han, Hui, Man and Mongol.

Environment

Its terrain is mainly featured with highlands, plateaus and hills. Lakes are rare in the province. It is in the temperate and warm temperate zone with a semi-humid continental monsoon climate. The average temperature is -16 ~ 2°C in January and 19 ~ 28°C in July, with an average annual rainfall between 400 ~ 600 mm.

Places of Interest

Shanxi Province is one of the birthplaces of the ancient Chinese civilization. According to legends, emperors Yao, Shun and Yu all once established their capitals and started their careers in Shanxi, which was also home to the Xia Dynasty. Shanxi Province is truly a province with abundant cultural relics. Datong, Pingyao, Xinjiang, Daixian and Qixian are China's famous historical and cultural cities. There are 119 key historical monuments and cultural relics under state protection, such as the Hanging Monastery in Hunyuan County, the Sakyamuni Tower of the Buddhist Palace Temple in Yingxian County (the Yingxian Wooden Pagoda), the Jin Ancestral Temple in Taiyuan, and the Guangsheng Temple in Hongtong County. There are more than 4,000 historical monuments and cultural relics under province-level and county-level protection. Shanxi Province is famous for its numerous ancient architectures. There are more than 450 wooden architectural structures that dated back before the Yuan Dynasty. And architectural structures of the Ming and Qing dynasties can be seen all over the province.

Shanxi has abundant tourism resources. Yungang Grottoes in Datong and ancient city of Pingyao are included in the World Heritage List. Famous mountains such as the Buddhist Mount Wutai, Mount Hengshan, the Hukou Waterfall on the Yellow River, Wulao Peak in Yongji City, Beiwudang Mountain in Fangshan County are all key scenic spots and historical sites of the state. In addition, there are 18 national forest parks and four natural reserves under the state protection.

Local Specialties

Pingyao beef, Changzhi pilose asiabell root, Xinghuacun Fenjiu Spirits, Qingxu grapes and mature vinegar, Qinzhou millet, and Yuanping pears.

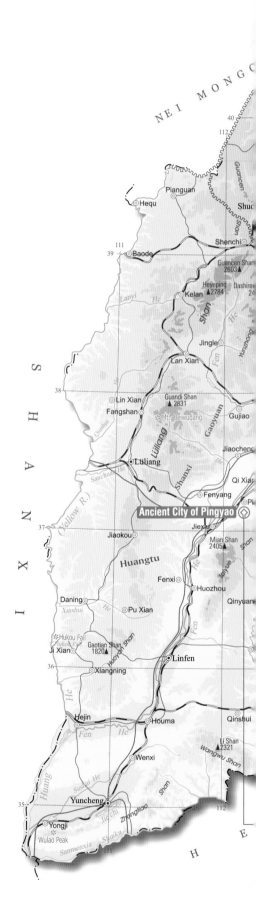

Height(m)

3000
2000
1500
1000
500
200
50

SCALE 1 : 3 000 000

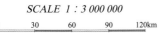

0   30   60   90   120km

Ancient City of Pingyao

Site of Rishengchang

Ming and Qing market tower

☐ **Name:**

Ancient City of Pingyao

☐ **Geographical coordinates:**

37° 14' N, 112° 11' E

☐ **Date of inscription:**

December 3, 1997

☐ **Criteria for inclusion:**

II, III, IV of cultural properties

⊙ Overview

The ancient town of Pingyao, located in the central part Shanxi Province, was built during the reign of King Xuanwang in the Western Zhou Dynasty (827-782 BC), having a history of over 2,700 years. With an area of 2.25 sq km, the ancient town comprises six large temple complexes, county government buildings, markets and more than 3,900 dwelling houses. The shops along the main streets still maintain the look of the 17th-19th Century. The existent layout reflects the scale of the town after the expansion in the 3rd year of Hongwu in the Ming Dynasty (1370). It is the best-preserved county town of the Ming and Qing Dynasties in China, where the complete city wall, streets, shops, temples and dwelling houses constitute a huge ancient architectural complex. The town is a famous historical and cultural city of China.

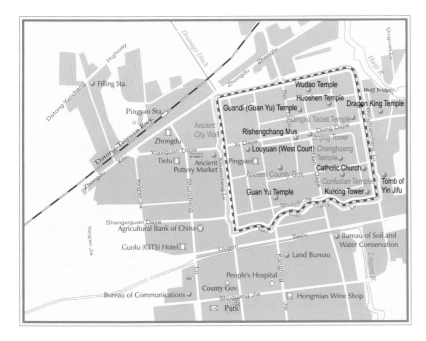

Kuixing Tower

✦✦✦ Ancient City of Pingyao ✦✦✦

⊙ Description

Situated at the southern end of Central Shanxi Plain, Pingyao neighbors Taihang Mountains in the east and adjoins Luliang Mountains in the west. Fenhe River, a tributary of the Yellow River, flows across the area.

Pingyao is a sample of ancient Chinese county towns. According to the county annals, the layout of the existent town has been unchanged in the past 600 years, and the ancient city wall is preserved completely. The town is of very important value to the research of the evolution of traditional Chinese cities, urban architectural pattern, mode of dwelling, and the development of traditional culture and art.

Pingyao is a carrier of history and culture of Han nationality, known as a museum above the ground. It has 5 key sites of cultural relics under state protection, 4 under province protection, 13 under city protection and 77 under county protection. The Wanfo (Ten Thousand Buddhas) Hall of Zhenguo Temple, built in the 7th year of Tianhui in the Northern Han Dynasty (963) and Shuanglin Temple built in the 2nd year of Wuping in the Northern Qi Dynasty (571), are treasuries of colored sculptures. The Qingxu Taoist Temple, first built in the 2nd year of Xianqing in the Tang Dynasty (657), is the valuable material evidence for the study of stage arts.

Pingyao is a milestone in the history of Chinese financial development that marked the beginning of remittance and cashing. In the Ming and Qing dynasties, merchants of Shanxi and Anhui held sway in China. Pingyao was one of the places where Shanxi merchants got started. With their expansion and prosperity, Shanxi merchants would often carry large amount of silver accompanied by heavy armed escort, which was unsafe and cost time and manpower. As a result, a new form of banking business—*piaohao* (money exchange)—appeared in Pingyao. In the 4th year of Daoguang in the Qing Dynasty (1824), Lei Lutai, manager of

Xiyucheng Dye Shop, founded the first draft bank on the West Street in Pingyao. That was China's first draft bank engaged in remittance and cashing business. The establishment of Rishengchang Piaohao was of epoch-making significance in the history of China's financial development, greatly strengthened the power of Shanxi merchants. As a result of 500-year dominance by Shanxi merchants in the business circle, Pingyao witnessed unprecedented prosperity of business and banking. It was regarded as the rural birthplace of China's banking industry. After Rishengchang, more than 50 *piaohao* emerged in the country, of which, over 20 based their head office in Pingyao. In the 100 years of rise and decline of *piaohao*, the banking industry had promoted not only the social, economic, cultural and artistic development in Pingyao, but also the commerce of the whole China.

Traditional dwelling houses reflect the unique local style. Still inhabited by local residents, the traditional courtyard houses in Pingyao are of great value for the study of folk custom and archi-

Thousand-hand Avalokitesvara in Shuanglin Temple

Wanfo Hall, Zhenguo Temple

Shuanglin Temple

tectural art. Some have been opened to tourists or used as hotels. They basically maintain the historical look of Shanxi-style residence during the Ming and Qing dynasties.

⊙ Highlights

City Wall of Pingyao A key site of cultural relics under state protection, it was first built during the reign of King Xuanwang of Western Zhou Dynasty. In the third year of Hongwu in the Ming Dynasty (1370), the wall was expanded to the present scale. It is the best-preserved ancient city wall in China. The wall is in the

shape of a square, with a total circumference of 6,163 m. Its body was piled with earth and covered with blue bricks. The base width is 10 m, the top width is 3 ~ 5 m, and the height ranges from 6 m to 10 m. The wall has six defensive towers, six city gates (three still exist) and four corner turrets (two still exist). On the city wall there are 72 watchtowers and 3,000 crenels.

Shuanglin Temple It is a key site of cultural relics under state protection, situated 6 km southwest of the old town. Originally named Zhongdu Temple, the temple got its name during the Northern Song Dynasty (960-1127). The temple was built in the 2nd year of Wuping in the Northern Qi Dynasty (571). The temple is full of colored sculptures with size ranging from several meters to

City wall of Pingyao

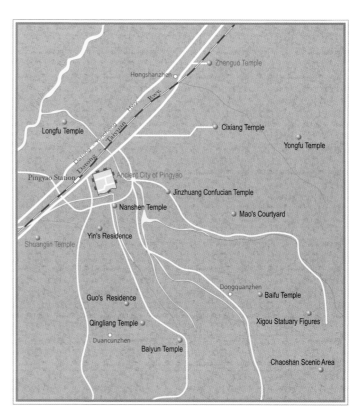

Qingxu Taoist Temple

Confucian Temple

Vicinity of Pingyao

Temple, it was built in the 2nd year of Xianqing in the Tang Dynasty (657). The Longhu (Dragon-Tiger) Hall in the temple has two 5-m high magnificent colored sculptures of a green dragon and a white tiger. There are also more than 30 stone steles of the Song, Yuan, Ming and Qing dynasties. The temple is a part of the Pingyao Museum.

⊙ Information

■ **Transportation** *Pingyao Railway Station is located northwest of the town. Datong-Fenglingdu Railway goes through the county from south to north, reaching Taiyuan and Shijiazhuang in the north and Linfen and Yuncheng in the south. Highway links Pingyao with Taiyuan, and the tip takes about two hours by bus.*

■ **Accommodation** *There are quite a few hotels in the town, including Yunfeng Hotel, Youzheng Hotel and Guifuxiang Hotel. Old dwelling houses are recommended to feel the atmosphere of the ancient town.*

■ **Food** *Noodles are the favorite food of local people, which include noodle with gravy (Dalu noodle), noodle with soybean paste, and Cuoyu'er (dough pieces). Visitors can taste Pingyao snacks on the Ming-Qing Street.*

■ **Others** *Native products include Guanyun beef, etc.*
  Opening hours: Summer 8:30 ~ 18:30, Winter 8:30 ~ 17:30
  Inquiry Telephones: 0354-5687805

a few inches. It is known as a museum of colored sculptures where more than 1,500 sculptures of the Song, Yuan, Ming and Qing dynasties (960-1911) are collected.

Confucian Temple A key site of cultural relics under state protection, it is located on Yunlu Street in the old town. The year of its construction is not clear, but the main building, Dacheng Hall, was rebuilt in the 3rd year of Dading in the Jin Dynasty (1163). The temple is composed of four courtyards. On the left of the central axis of the temple is Dongxue Hall, and on the right is Xixue Hall. In the rear part is Chaoshan Academy. Dacheng Hall is a precious example of ancient wood-structure buildings.

Qingxu Taoist Temple Located on Dongdajie Street in the old town and formerly called Taiping Xingguo

Yungang **Grottoes**

☐ **Name:**
Yungang Grottoes

☐ **Geographical coordinates:**
40° 06' 35" N, 113° 07' 20" E

☐ **Date of inscription:**
December 1, 2001

☐ **Criteria for inclusion:**
I, II, III, IV of cultural properties

Disciples, Cave No.8

⊙ Overview

Located at the southern foot of Wuzhou Mountain, to the west of Datong, a famous historical and cultural city of China, Yungang Grottoes started to be built in 460, flourished in the 60s and 90s of the 5th Century and lasted to the 20s of the 6th Century. They are the representative works of the early stage of grotto arts in China. There exist 252 caves with over 51,000 statues, extending 1,000 m from east to west. Yungang Grottoes display the grand-scale stone caves of imperial style of Northern Wei Dynasty (386-534). The exquisitely carved statues involve various themes and blend artistic styles of different areas in China and different countries in the world in its course of localization. They display, from various perspectives, the artistic style of China's grottoes and significant changes in the religious belief in northern China from the mid-5th Century to the 6th Century. Yungang Grottoes is a key site of cultural relics under state protection.

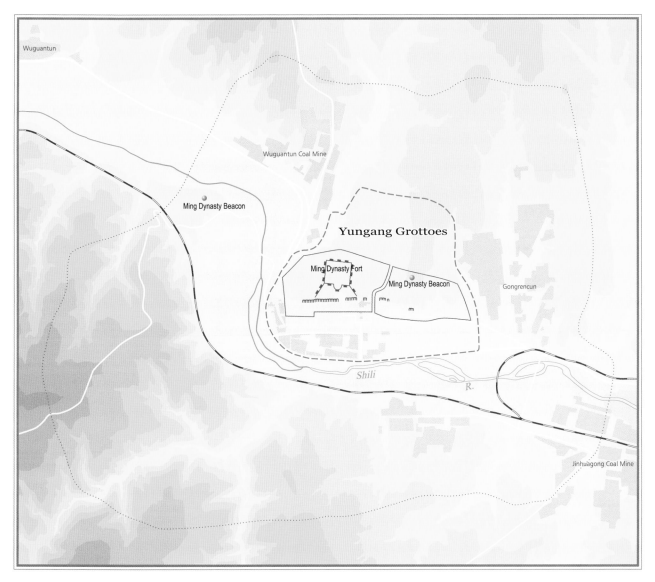

Yungang Grottoes

⊙ Description

Being actually a basin on the plateau, Datong is located in the transitional zone between Shanxi Plateau and Inner Mongolia Plateau. It was not only one of the largest metropolises in the world in the 5th Century, but also a hub that gathered culture and arts of India and Central Asia, as well as the ethnic culture and arts of the states in the Western Regions and the most developed regions in China, namely the six prefectures in Shandong, Shaanxi in Guanzhong, Liangzhou in Hexi, and Helong area in Northeast. The nearly 1 million people of the Han, Xianbei, Di, Qiang, Wuhuan and Dingling ethnic groups joined to forge the civilization of Northern Wei. The Chinese-style grottoes developed from the blending of diversified cultures reflect the achievements of Buddhist arts that were deeply rooted in the Central Plains area of China. Yungang Grottoes were the best works created during the second booming period of the world's Buddhist grotto arts.

Tan Yao Five Caves (Nos. 16-20) were excavated under the auspices of noted monk Tan Yao to symbolize Emperor Daowu, Emperor Mingyuan, Emperor Taiwu, Emperor Jingmu and Emperor Wencheng of the Northern Wei Dynasty. The statues, tall and solid, reflect the forever existence and circulation of Buddhism as well as the outstanding achievements in the caves' theme, exterior designs, artistic expression and religious connotation. "Loose clothes and wide belts" was a new form of dressing that resembled the Han style. Artistically, it was originated from the painting style of "thin and simple" of the Southern Dynasties. The new style brought great changes to the Yungang statues' garments and appearance and led to the creation of new form of Chinese grotto art. Yungang Grottoes is an outstanding example of Chinese localized stone grotto art.

Tan Yao Five Caves (Caves Nos. 16-20) were organized and designed in a unified form and of rigorous style. The five main statues, ranging from 13.5 m to 16.8 m, are the rare masterpieces of the grotto statues for its magnificent and imposing manner and beautiful decorations. The five caves, especially cave No. 20, started to evolve in terms of the appearance, manner and posture under the influence of the Chinese aesthetic feeling, but they also

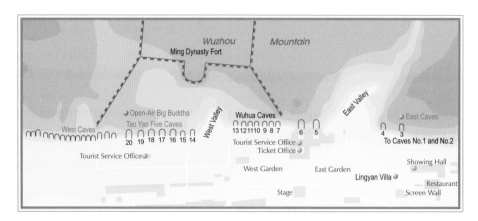

Wuzhou Mountain
Ming Dynasty Fort

Open-Air Big Buddha
Tao Yao Five Caves

West Caves
13 12 11 10 9 8 7
20 19 18 17 16 15 14

West Valley

Wuhua Caves
6 5

East Valley

East Caves

4 3
To Caves No.1 and No.2

Tourist Service Office
Ticket Office

Tourist Service Office

West Garden   East Garden

Lingyan Villa

Showing Hall

Restaurant
Screen Wall

Stage

Location of Caves

kept much artistic element of Gandharva and Mathura art in terms of garment and attire, thus maintaining the characteristics of "foreign look but Buddhist appearance" in statue carving. The caves No. 9 and No. 10 are known for its splendid design, fine carving of human figures and unique statue-making style. Caves No. 5 and No. 6 are the largest in scale. Cave No. 6 depicted the naturally connected 39 images from the birth of Sakyamuni under the tree to his first turning of the wheel of law. This is the earliest serial stone carving images of the Chinese grotto art that depicts the religious content. The Central Plains-style statues, represented by Cave No. 6, presented a new look in posture, attire and carving techniques. The attire of "loose clothes and wide belts" makes the figure dashing and vivid. The clean and elegant appearance impressed people with tranquility, kindness and mildness. This obviously reveals the change of artistic style from Buddhist to Chinese.

⊙ Highlights

Cave No. 6 This is a typical pagoda-temple cave with a door and a window. The central tower has two floors. On each of the four sides of the lower floor there is one niche, which houses separately

a sitting Buddha, a sitting-leaning Buddha, two sitting Buddhas, and a cross-ankled Bodhisattva. The four corners have four square thousand-Buddha columns. Two Buddhist legends are carved on each side of the niche. A standing Buddha is sculpted on each of the four sides on the top floor, with the height ranging between 4.5 ~ 4.75 m. On the two sides are assisting Bodhisattvas. A nine-floor pagoda standing on the back of an elephant was carved on each of the four corners. On the four walls of the cave there are niches arranged by layers. On the top part of the wall are 11 groups of niches. The figures are all one Buddha and two Bodhisattvas surrounded by dancing figures and Buddhist figures. The niches are separated by the disciple figures. In the middle are the niches with Buddhist legends such as "conquering the demons", "beating the fire dragons" and "preaching law at the deer garden". There are more than 30 such carved pictures in the cave.

Caves No. 9 and No. 10 This is a typical hall cave. Actually it is a group of double caves. The front wall has wood-like eaves supported by eight-edge thousand-Buddha column. The cave is a rectangle and divided into front and rear halls. Round niches with *goupian* rails were carved in the place where northern and southern walls met on the top roof. Inside the niches could be seen danc-

Statue of Vishnu, Cave No.8   Interior of Cave No.6

Open-air Buddha, Cave No.20

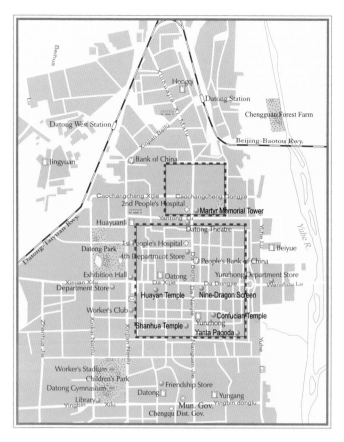

Datong

ers playing music. The main statue in the rear hall was 10 m tall. At the back of it was a religious service path. On the wall are carved the Buddhist stories.

Cave No. 20 This is a typical big statue cave. It belongs to Tan Yao Five Caves. It is one of the most representative caves of Yungang Grottoes. The front wall, top part and western wall have been ruined. The statue, 13.8 m tall, is a well-known open air Buddha statue.

Exterior of Caves Nos.5-13

⊙ Information

■ **Transportation** *There are trains to Beijing, Taiyuan, Xi'an, Yinchuan, Shijiazhuang, Baotou, Shenyang and Hangzhou (via Taiyuan, Pingyao, Luoyang and Nanjing) everyday. Beijing-Datong Expressway is available. Regular shuttle buses go directly to Yungang Grottoes and Mount Hengshan from Datong Bus Station.*

■ **Accommodation** *There are Hong'an International Hotel, Jingyuan Yingbin Hotel, Datong Hotel and Yungang International Hotel.*

■ **Food** *The well-known restaurants are Yonghe Restaurant, Yonghe Hongqi Food City and Laoyemaio Restaurant. Local snacks include Youmian noodle, yellow cake, simmered meat, Baihua Sumai, mutton chopsuey and fried dough pieces.*

■ **Others** *Local specialties are Datong Daily lily, Hengshan milk vetch, Datong buckthorn and Yanggao preserved apricot. Art craft include bronze hotpot and coal carving.*

Opening hour: summer 8:00 ~ 18:00; winter 8:30 ~ 17:00
Inquiry telephone: 0352-3026230
Website: www.yungang.org

JIANGSU PROVINCE

General Information

Jiangsu, also called Su in short, has its capital in Nanjing City. With an area of more than 100,000 sq km, it has under its administrative jurisdiction 13 prefecture-level cities, 27 county-level cities, and 26 counties. The province has a population of 71.27 million and ethnic groups including Han, Hui, Miao, Tujia and Mongol.

Environment

Located on the shore of the Yellow Sea, it is the mouth of the lower reaches of the Yangtze River on the sea. About 80 ~ 90% of the province's territory are plains, with the lowest and flattest land in China. Its southern part and northern part are influenced by northern subtropical humid monsoon climate and warm temperate semi-humid monsoon climate respectively. The average temperature is -1 ~ 3°C in January and 27 ~ 28°C in July, with an average annual rainfall between 800 ~ 1,200 mm.

Places of Interest

Jiangsu boasts green mountains and beautiful rivers, which give birth to many outstanding people. There are the Yangtze River that cuts straight through the province from east to west, the Grand Canal that flows from south to north, the vast Taihu Lake and the Hongze Lake with a mirage of flickering water, the simple and elegant Lean West Lake, Xuanwu Lake, Langshan Mountain and the Beigu Mountain that overlooking both banks of the river, and the Zijin Mountain sits defiantly like a crouching tiger. They have constituted a unique natural landscape dominated with rivers and lakes, which in combination with the mountains present a dazzling picture of natural beauty. Taihu Lake, Zhongshan Mountain, Yuntai Mountain, and the Yungang Lean West Lake are state-level scenic areas. The Suzhou Gardens and Xiaoling Tomb of the Ming Dynasty have been included in the World Heritage List. Zhouzhuang, Tongli and Luzhi have become favorite tourist attractions. Qixia Mountain, Huaguo Mountain, Shanjuan Cave, Yunlong Lake, Mochou Lake, Zhongleng Spring and Qinhuai River have enjoyed a good reputation far and wide. Nanjing, Suzhou, Yangzhou, Zhenjiang, Changshu, Xuzhou and Huai'an have become famous historical and cultural cities of China. Dr. Sun Yat-sen's Mausoleum, the site of the Heavenly King Hall, the site of Zhou Enlai's residence, and the site of the National Zijinshan Observatory are key sites of cultural relics under state protection. Jiangsu has centuries-old former residences of renowned figures and classical gardens, as well as thousand-year-old temples and mausoleums.

② Imperial Tombs of the Ming and Qing Dynasties

Local Specialties

Langshan chicken, Gaoyou duck, Taihu silver fish, Yangtze River hairtail, Yangcheng Lake crabs, Yanghe yeast-brewed liquor, Zhenjiang fragrant vinegar, Biluochun tea, Suzhou embroidery, Nanjing brocade, Changshu lace, Wuxi clay sculpture, Yangzhou lacquer ware, and Yixin chinaware.

SCALE 1 : 2 500 000

0   25   50   75   100km

Height(m)

0   100   200   500   1000

YELLOW

SEA

Lianyun
Dongxilian Dao
Lianyungang
Mt. Yuntai
anyungang

yun
Xinyi
Xiangshui
Guannan
Binhai
Lianshui
Funing
Sheyang
huaiyin
Jianhu
an
Yancheng
Baoying
Dafeng
hu
Gaoyou Hu
Xinghua
Gaoyou
Dongtai
Jiangyan
Hai'an
Shugang Lean West Lake
Taizhou
Rudong
Yangzhou
Jiangdu
Rugao
eng
Mt. Sanshan
Yangzhong
Tongzhou
Zhenjiang
Taixing
Nantong
ling Tomb
Jingjiang
Lang Shan
Haimen
Danyang
Jiangyin
Qidong
rong
Zhangjiagang
Jintan
Changzhou
Changshu
Wuxi
Taicang
Taihu Lake
Kunshan
Liyang
Suzhou
SHANGHAI
Yixing
Classical Gardens
of Suzhou
Tai Hu
Wujiang
Tongli
Zhouzhuang

ZHEJIANG

Classical Gardens of Suzhou

☐ **Name:**

Classical Gardens of Suzhou

☐ **Geographic coordinates:**

31° 19' N, 120° 37' E

☐ **Date of inscription:**

December 4, 1997 (Four Gardens including Zhuozheng Garden)

November 30, 2000 (Five Gardens including Canglang Pavilion)

☐ **Criteria for inclusion:**

I, II, III, IV, V of cultural propertiesa.

Wangshi Garden

⊙ Overview

The classical gardens are located in Suzhou City, Jiangsu Province and close to Taihu Lake on the Yangtze River Delta. The surrounding natural conditions of the city are excellent and the society, economy and culture are well developed. The origin of the classical gardens in Suzhou can be dated back to the garden of King Wu of the 6th Century BC, whereas the earliest privately-owned garden in record was the Pijiang Garden in the Eastern Jin Dynasty (4th Century). The 16th-18th Century saw the heyday of the garden making in Suzhou, when private gardens spread all over the ancient city and its environs. According to historical records, there were altogether more than 200 gardens at the time, and dozens of them are well preserved till today.

In the construction of the Suzhou classical gardens, the unique Chinese garden making techniques are adopted. Within limited space adjacent to urban dwellings, the gardens full of poetic and artistic conception of the traditional Chinese freehand brushwork paintings are made through the elaborate arrangement of rocks, water, vegetation and deliberate layout of the buildings.

These "Urban Landscapes" with natural charms create an amicable environment that brings man into harmony with nature, and they reflect the ancients' reverence for nature and their wish to return to nature. The classical gardens in Suzhou are the evidence of the Chinese garden history, the model of the Chinese

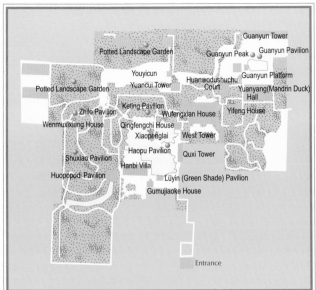

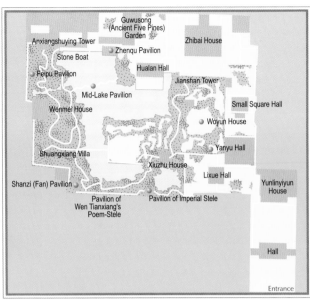

Liuyuan Garden

Shizilin Garden

garden making art and the important example for the theoretical research of the Chinese gardens. "China is the mother of the world garden making art, while the gardens in Suzhou are the outstanding representatives of the Chinese gardens".

⊙ Description

More than 2,000 years of continuous garden making history in Suzhou is a typical display of China's garden history in miniature. Suzhou classical gardens occupy an important position in the development history of the world gardens, and they are the chief representatives of the oriental gardens and one of the main origins from which the world's gardens have developed. Their architectural connotation covers many aspects of the natural and social sciences. Meanwhile, the existence value of Suzhou classical gardens must be reflected in their physical entities, and the research system of the gardens must be established on their collective form as a whole. The existing classical gardens are well preserved with complete structure, and they are able to reflect in an aspect the development process of the Chinese politics, economy and culture. These gardens are most important physical materials for people to research and understand the Chinese history and the traditional culture and their influence on the world culture. They are one of the major elements of Suzhou as a famous historical and cultural city in China.

Suzhou classical gardens fully exhibit the national feature and level of China's garden making art. Pavilions, platforms, storied buildings, springs, stones, flowers and plants are combined to simulate natural scenery and create an ideal space close to nature, through the application of various techniques and methods such as contrast, backdrop, measure, layer, opposite scenery and borrowed scenery. In enhancing the inhabited environment, integrat-

Ouyuan Garden

Xiangzhou Isle in Zhuozheng Garden

ing the architectural, natural and human beauties, the classical gardens of Suzhou have reached a historic high level, making them models of garden making art. Meanwhile, the gardens are also the carriers of the traditional Chinese ideology and culture. This is reflected in the naming, the inscribed horizontal tablets, the couplets hung on the columns, the block stones, the sculptures, and decorations of the hall structures in the gardens. In addition, a large amount of historical and cultural information has been stored with such techniques as implying morals and feelings through flowers, plants and stones, which endows these gardens with supreme artistic and historical values.

Suzhou classical gardens are the outstanding example of the freehand brushwork of gardens. The garden and the house are integrated into one structure that can be viewed and admired, visited and inhabited. The development of this kind of architectural form lies in man's attachment to nature, pursuit for a harmonious coexistence with nature, and aspiration for a better living environment in the densely populated city that lacks natural landscapes. The layout, structure, modeling, style, color and the fitment, furniture, furnishing of the buildings in the classical gardens of Suzhou are representatives of the local buildings south of the lower reaches of Yangtze River during the Ming and Qing dynasties (1368-1911). They have reflected the advanced inhabitation of this region at that time and influenced the architectural pattern of all the cities south of the lower Yangtze, setting examples to the design, layout, taste and building technique of the local folks. These gardens display the technological level and artistic achievement of the urban construction of the time and occupy an irreplaceable position in the history of garden science in China and the world.

Liuyuan Garden

⊙ Highlights

Zhuozheng (Humble Administrator) Garden Situated in the northeast of the ancient city of Suzhou, the garden, covering an area of 5.2 ha, is a typical example of the classical gardens in Suzhou and one of the four most famous gardens in China. It was first built in the 4th year of Zhengde in the Ming Dynasty (1509) by a dejected bureaucrat returning to his hometown after his relegation and therefore acquired its name. The garden is laid out to suit the physical conditions in which it was made. It is centered upon a broad expanse of water with a variety of buildings. Being simple and natural in pattern and rich in poetic meanings, the garden, with extensive water and exuberant vegetation, presents a typical image of the gardens south of the lower Yangtze in the Ming Dynasty.

Liuyuan (Lingering) Garden Located outside of the Changmen Gate and covering an area of 2.3 ha, it is one of the four famous gardens in China. The garden was first constructed by a retired bureaucrat during the reign of Wanli in the Ming Dynasty (1573-1620) and then renovated in the late period of the

Center of Zhuozheng Garden

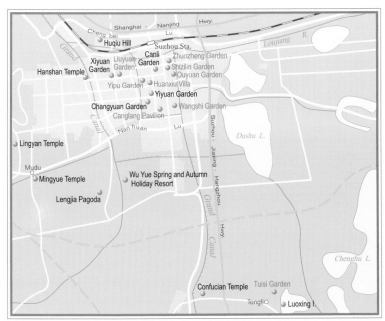

Huanxiu Villa

Suzhou Classical Gardens

Qing Dynasty. The garden is celebrated for its exquisite and artistic division of architectural space with halls, corridors, whitewashed walls and tunnel portals. The seemingly divided areas, combined with stones, water and vegetation, further form a variety of interlocking courts, which exhibits the artistic feature of the gardens south of the lower Yangtze.

Tuisi Garden

Wangshi (Master of the Fishing Nets) Garden Located in the southeast corner of the ancient city of Suzhou, it covers an area of 0.6 ha. Exquisite and ingenious in layout, the garden is a model of "the few surpassing the many" technique in China's garden making. It was originally constructed in the Southern Song Dynasty (1127-1279) and renovated during the reign of Qianlong in the Qing Dynasty (1736-1796). Being closely joined with the living quarters, it maintains the perfect feature of the classical gardens of the aristocratic families of Suzhou in old days. In the eastern side is the dwelling house, in the central area are some pavilions and platforms built around the pond, and in the western side is originally the study. The Astor Court in the Metropolitan Museum of Art, New York City, was modeled after this garden.

Minse House in Liuyuan Garden

Wangshi Garden

Canglang Pavilion

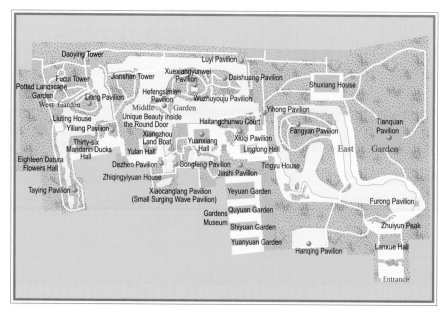

Map labels:
Daoying Tower, Luyi Pavilion, Fucui Tower, Xuexiangyunwei Pavilion, Jianshan Tower, Daishuang Pavilion, Potted Landscape Garden, Hefengsimian Pavilion, Shuxiang House, West Garden, Liting Pavilion, Wuzhuyouju Pavilion, Middle Garden, Yihong Pavilion, Liuting House, Unique Beauty inside the Round Door, Haitangchunwu Court, Tianquan Pavilion, Yiliang Pavilion, Xiangzhou Land Boat, Xiuqi Pavilion, Fangyan Pavilion, Thirty-six Mandarin Ducks Hall, Yulan Hall, Yuanxiang Hall, Linglong Hall, East Garden, Eighteen Datura Flowers Hall, Dezhen Pavilion, Songfeng Pavilion, Tingyu House, Zhiqingyiyuan House, Jiashi Pavilion, Taying Pavilion, Xiaocanglang Pavilion (Small Surging Wave Pavilion), Yeyuan Garden, Furong Pavilion, Gardens Museum, Quyuan Garden, Zhuiyun Peak, Shiyuan Garden, Yuanyuan Garden, Hanqing Pavilion, Lanxue Hall, Entrance

✥✥✥ Zhuozheng Garden ✥✥✥

Canglang (Surging Waters) Pavilion Located in the south of the ancient city of Suzhou, the pavilion covers an area of 1.1 ha. It was constructed between 1041-1048 by Su Shunqin, a prominent poet in the Northern Song Dynasty, and was named after the "Fisherman's Song" in *The Songs of Chu*. High hill and wide waterscape feature largely in the garden. Inside the garden, there are ancient sky-reaching trees and rugged blocks of stones. Outside the garden, there is a river running nearby in the open space. On the top of the hill stands the Canglang Pavilion rebuilt during the reign of Kangxi in the Qing Dynasty (1662-1723). The following couplets inscribed on the pillars are famous in China: "The refreshing breeze and the shining moon are priceless; the near water and the distant mountain strike a sentimental note."

Shizi (Lion Forest) Garden Lying adjacent to Zhuozheng Garden and covering an area of 1.1 ha, the garden was first constructed in the 2nd year of Zhizheng in the Yuan Dynasty (1342). Its name came from the Buddhist doctrine. Both Emperor Kangxi and Emperor Qianlong of the Qing Dynasty paid several visits to the garden and made a replica of it respectively in the Yuanmingyuan Garden of Beijing and the Mountain Resort of Chengde. The impressive and labyrinthine artificial limestone rockworks in the garden boast deep caverns and zigzagging paths. The whole garden is compactly laid out with corridors leading to all directions and small paths opening up on an enchanting view. It has also tall and graceful ancient trees.

Tuisi (Retreat and Reflection) Garden Located in Tongli, Wujiang City and covering an area of 0.65 ha, it is typical of the gardens in the ancient towns south of the lower Yangtze. Constructed during the reign of Guangxu in the Qing Dynasty, the garden acquires its name from one sentence in *Zuo Zhuan*, a Chinese classic, saying, "Advance to dedicate my loyalty to my country; retreat to reflect on mending my way." In layout, the garden consists of the reception area, housing complex area, courts area and garden area, all of which are aligned along the west-east axis. In the garden area in the east, all the various buildings, small but delicate, well arranged according to their heights, are constructed adjacent to a pool in the center, so this garden is known as Waterscape Garden.

Yipu Garden

Shizilin Garden

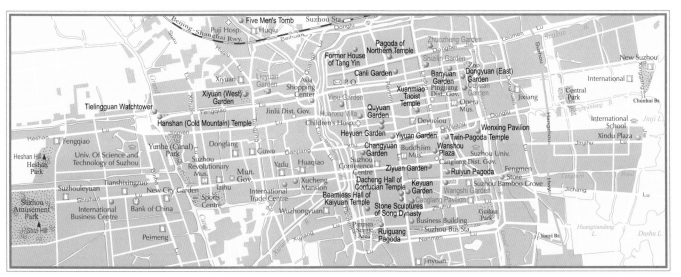

Suzhou

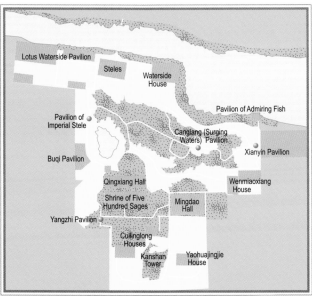

Lotus Waterside Pavilion
Steles
Waterside House
Pavilion of Imperial Stele
Pavilion of Admiring Fish
Buqi Pavilion
Canglang (Surging Waters) Pavilion
Xianyin Pavilion
Qingxiang Hall
Wenmiaoxiang House
Shrine of Five Hundred Sages
Mingdao Hall
Yangzhi Pavilion
Cuilinglong Houses
Kanshan Tower
Yaohuajingjie House

Canglang Pavilion

⊙ Information

■ **Transportation** *Railways: Suzhou Railway Station lies in the north end of the city, and trains link Suzhou with major cities of China. Roads: Shanghai-Nanjing Expressway linking Nanjing, Shanghai and Hangzhou facilitates the connection between Suzhou and other major cities. Three national roads, No. 312, 318 and 204, and seven provincial roads run across the city, so visitors from nearby cities are able to reach Suzhou directly by bus. Airlines: Visitors from abroad or China can first get to Shanghai Pudong International Airport, Shanghai Hongqiao Airport or Nanjing Airport by air, then take a coach or taxi to Suzhou via Shanghai-Nanjing Expressway.*

■ **Accommodation** *Five-star hotels include: Sheraton Suzhou, New Suzhou International Hotel; Four-star hotels include: Aster Hotel, Castle Hotel, Ramada Plaza Bamboo Grove, Lidu Hotel, Suzhou Gloria Plaza Hotel, Suzhou Conference Center; Three-star hotels include: Nanlin Hotel, Suzhou Hotel, Xincheng Garden Hotel, Lexiang Hotel and Gusu Hotel.*

■ **Food** *Suzhou boasts a rich variety of local cuisines, mainly including: Deep Fried Mandarin Fish with Sweet and Sour Sauce, Suzhou Braised Pork Seasoned with Soy Sauce, Coral Mandarin Fish, Quick-Fried Cuttlefish, Suzhou Lard Cake, Stir-Fried Meatball, Tofu Stewed in Clay-Pot, Gordon Euryale with Sweet Osmanthus, Stir-Fried Mustard Green with Chicken Fat, Spareribs Stewed with Dry Preserved Vegetable, Sweet and Sour Pork, First Dish under the Heaven, Tongli Min Cake, Aozao Noodles in Soup, Fengqiao Town Noodles in Soup.*

■ **Others** *Local and special products of Suzhou include Biluochun Tea, Dried Bean Curd with Soy Sauce, Suzhou Scented Tea, Yangcheng Lake Fresh Water Crab, Taihu Lake White Bait, Wujiang Perch, Taihu Lake Water Shield, Suzhou Sticky Rice, Souzhou-Style Candies, Baisha Loquat, Dongshan Red Bayberry, Lotus Roots and Gordon Euryale, Sweet Osmanthus Fried Chestnut, and Whelks.*

Inquiry telephone: 0512-65224929
Website: www.szgarden.com.cn

ANHUI PROVINCE

General Information

Anhui, also called Wan in short, has its capital in Hefei City. With an area of more than 130,000 sq km, it has under its administrative jurisdiction 17 prefecture-level cities, 5 county-level cities and 56 counties. The province has a population of 63.69 million and ethnic groups including Han, Hui, Mongol, Man and Miao.

Environment

It is located in the northwest of East China, straddling the Yangtze River and the Huaihe River. The province has a mixture of mountainous areas, hilly land and plains, with rivers and lakes crisscrossing the region. To the north of the Huaihe River is warm temperate zone semi-humid monsoon climate, while the south part is subtropical humid monsoon climate. The average temperature is -1 ~ 4°C in January (below 0°C north of Huaihe River) and 27 ~ 29°C in July, with an average annual rainfall between 750 ~ 1,700 mm.

Places of Interest

Anhui Province has many famous mountains and historical sites, as well as rich cultural relics. It has state-level scenic areas of Mount Huangshan, Jiuhua Mountain, Qiyun Mountain, Tianzhu Mountain, Langya Mountain, Caishi, Chaohu Lake, Huashan Mystic Caves and Taiji Cave. Mount Huangshan and ancient villages in southern Anhui are included in the World Heritage List. Shexian, Shouxian and Bozhou are famous historical and cultural cities of China. The dwelling houses of the Ming and Qing dynasties, ancestral temples and stone archway in Shexian and Yixian counties have survived centuries of ups and downs to remain as they were. They are the outstanding masterpieces of the folk architectural art. The ancient battlefield of Xiaoyaojin in Hefei during the Three Kingdom Period, the Ma'anshan Quarry, the Huatuo Temple of Bozhou, and the Tomb of Ming Dyansty Emperors in Fengyang are the top destinations for tours of adventures for ancient times. Among the 15 key sites of cultural relics under state protection, the ancient city of Emperor Zhongdu of the Ming Dynasty and the stone carving in the mausoleums, the Xuguo Stone Archway, the Xuejiagang site, and the site of the General Frontline Command of the PLA "River-crossing Campaign" in the Liberation War period.

Local Specialties

The Dangshan crispy pears, Xuanzhou sweet dates, Santan loquat, Huaiyuan Guava, Huizhou inkstick, She inkstone, Xuan brushes, Xuan paper, Gujinggong spirits, Huangshan Maofeng tea, and Lu'an melon slices.

SCALE 1 : 3 000 000

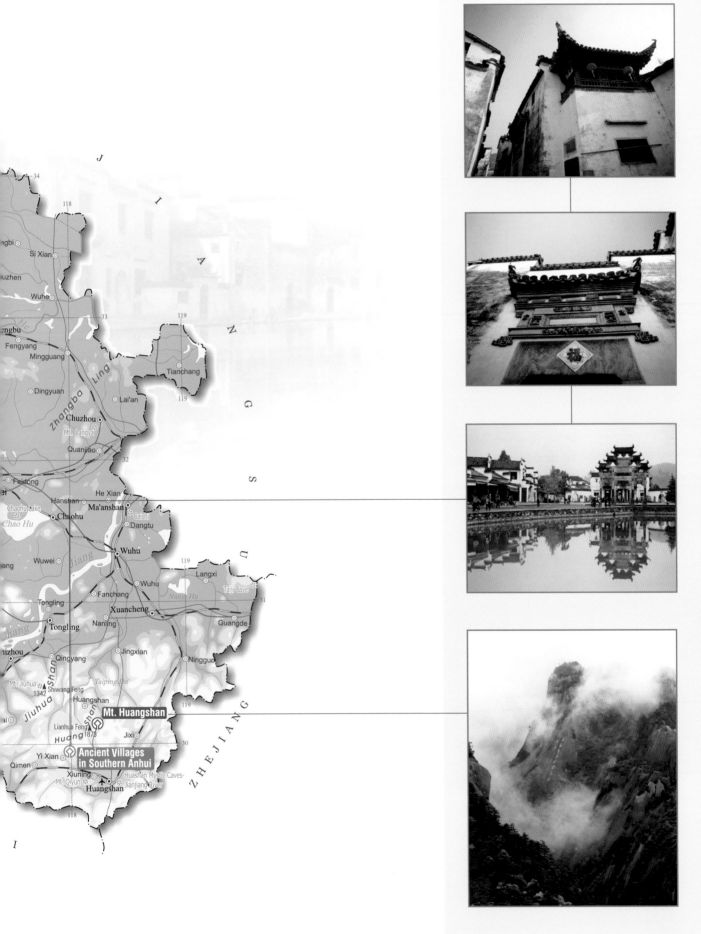

Mount Huangshan

☐ **Name:**

Mount Huangshan

☐ **Geographical coordinates:**

30° 01' N, 118° 01' E

☐ **Date of inscription:**

December 12, 1990

☐ **Criteria for inclusion:**

II of cultural properties

III, IV of natural properties

West Sea clouds

⊙ Overview

Mount Huangshan, 500 m to 1,864 m above sea level, is located in the city of Huangshan in the south of Anhui Province and covers an area of 154 sq km. It is a state-level scenic area in China.

As a site of natural heritage, Mount Huangshan boasts a seldom-seen forest of granite peaks and the remains of Quaternary glacier with significant research value. In addition, there are the unique scenery, rich biological resources, endangered plants species, rare wild animals, precious hot spring water and a wonderful sea of clouds.

As a site of cultural heritage, the mountain is the cradle of "Huangshan Culture". Well-preserved ancient buildings, ancient rocky mountain paths, cliff carvings and poetic names of scenic spots can be found everywhere. The number of literary and art works in praise of Mount Huangshan is beyond counting. These artistic works include both the inheritance and the innovation from the ancient Huizhou Culture and they have formed the mainstream of specific "Huangshan Culture". Their distinctive artistic features have greatly enriched the Chinese literary and art treasury.

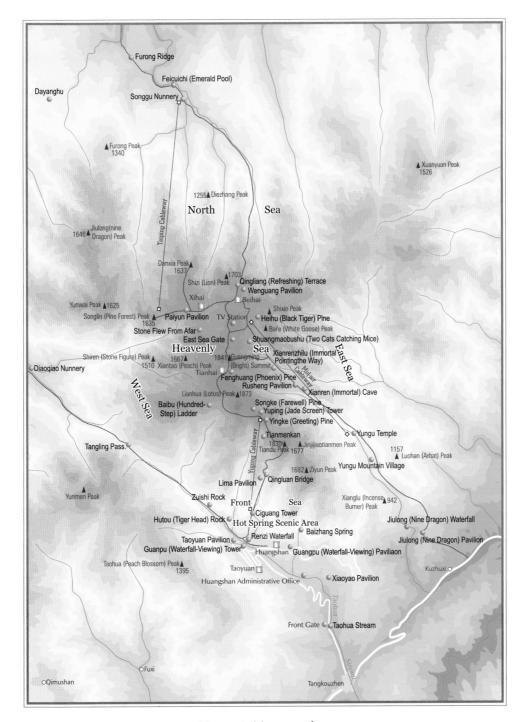

Mount Huangshan

⊙ Description

Mount Huangshan enjoys a high reputation both at home and abroad as a famous scenic area endowed with rich resources, a varied ecological system, and significant scientific and aesthetic value. As famous as the Yellow River, the Yangtze and the Great Wall, it has become another symbol of the Chinese Nation.

Mount Huangshan boasts an intoxicating beauty. Within the scenic area, there are many lofty peaks, grotesque-looking rocks, verdant and sturdy pines, dimly discernible mists and clouds, secluded valleys and deep springs, all of which have bought the mountain the name of "wonderland on earth" since ancient times. Mount Huangshan also has an enchanting uniqueness. No matter

if it is spring with all nature reviving, or summer with the waterfalls dropping through the verdant vegetation, or autumn with the red leaves covering the mountain, or winter with the ice and frost forming jade-like engravings here and there, all the spectacles are natural creations without any trace of man. In particular, the odd-shaped pines, grotesque-looking rocks, sea of clouds and hot springs are the "four ultimate wonders" of Mount Huangshan. The integration of sentiment into spectacles and the harmony between tranquility with movement make the mountain an eternal wonder.

Mount Huangshan is a wonderland on earth. It is divided into six scenic zones: hot spring, cloud valley, pine valley, north sea, jade screen and fishing bridge, with each presenting a unique sight. Throughout the ages, the famous people of different dynasties, attracted by its beauty, have repeatedly visited Mount Huangshan despite the arduous trials presented by the mountain, and left for later generations many poems, essays, cliff carvings and landscape paintings. There is one poem in praise of the mountain, which says "Words of description, will not convince you; the real wonder, come here to know."

Mount Huangshan is also a treasure house for rare plants and a natural botanical garden of South China. The vertical zonation is distinctive, with complete biological communities, including 1,450 species of native plants, an alpine swamp and an alpine meadow, and over 470 species of wild animals, among which 1 is listed among the animals under Grade I state protection, 5 under Grade II state protection and 10 under the Grade III state protection.

The human landscapes on Mount Huangshan include nearly 100 temples built and preserved through the ages, over 60,000 m of rocky mountain paths, 40-odd ancient bridges, 280 cliff carvings and stone carvings, thousands of literary and art works and ancient passes and pavilions. They provide invaluable physical and historical materials for the research of the religions, Huizhou culture and folk customs, the history of scenic spots construction, the history of the Chinese painting as well as the Chinese calligraphy and stone inscription. Different stone inscriptions can be found here and there on Mount Huangshan. They not only form a major landscape but also provide the evidence of the ancients' affection for the mountain. On the cliff of the Lima (Standing Horse) Peak, are inscribed ten huge Chinese characters, meaning "stopping the horse in front of the vast Eastern Sea and appreciating the peace and tranquility on the top of the mountain." The total height of the ten characters is equal to that of a 35-story building, which makes it the king all the stone inscriptions on Mount Huangshan.

⊙ Highlights

Odd-shaped Pines On Mount Huangshan, rocks can be found everywhere, and where there are rocks, there are odd-shaped pines. The pines grow out of the cracks of the rocks on the cliffs and in the valleys and the world marvels at the shapes created by nature over thousands of years. The pines are also full of the spirits of the

Monkey watching the sea

different objects that they are shaped into, like a powerful dragon, a twisted beard, a crane with its head raised, a person standing, an upturned umbrella or an extending guardrail.

Grotesque-looking Rocks According to legend, Mount Huangshan is the dwelling place of many immortals. The magnificent and varied peaks rise one after another with numerous natural fantastic rocks all over the summits and the valleys. Both the peaks and the rocks are graceful and vivid in shape and endowed with complicated and fascinating legends. These stories have been told

Cliff inscriptions

Baizhang Spring

with delight for ages and the ancients had projected their longings and pursuit of a beautiful life onto them.

Sea of Clouds There have been sea-like clouds on Mount Huangshan since ancient times. The mountain is wrapped in clouds and fog for two-thirds of the year, so it is also called Huanghai (Yellow Sea). The sea of clouds is divided into East Sea, South Sea (front sea), West Sea, North Sea (rear sea) and Heavenly Sea, and they together form one of the wonders of the earth. In addition, the "Buddhist halo" on Mount Huangshan is also marvelous.

Hot Springs It is recorded in ancient books that "at the foot of the Eastern Peak of Mount Huangshan, there are vermilion and spring water that can be put into the tea...or used as bath water and as a drink. By doing so, all diseases are cured." The water temperature of the hot spring stays at 42°C throughout the year, and it has never run dry during severe droughts nor over-flooded during excessive rains. Its flow rate always remains normal. The spring water is suitable both for drinking and bathing and is effective in curing diseases, so it has gained the reputation of a world-famous spring. The lofty mountain and dense clouds lead to plenty of rainfall and therefore many waterscapes. "After one night of rain in the mountain, the flowing springs can be found everywhere." No less than 60 springs, brooks and waterfalls have been named, including Jiulong (Nine-Dragon) Waterfall, Renzi (Inverted-V) Waterfall, Baizhang Spring and Feicui (Jade) Pool.

⊙ Information

■ **Transportation** *There are scheduled flights leading from Huangshan Airport to over 20 cities, including Beijing, Chengdu, Chongqing, Guangzhou, Guilin, Haikou, Hangzhou, Hongkong, Kunming, Qingdao, Shanghai, Shenzhen and Zhangjiajie. The Anhui-Jiangxi railway line runs across Huangshan City, and the passenger trains facilitate the direct link with 10 cities, including Beijing, Shanghai and Nanjing. The national roads connect Huangshan with Shanghai, Hangzhou, Nanjing, Wuhan, Hefei, Jingdezhen and Shenzhen. Within the scenic area, there are cableways up and down the mountain.*

■ **Accommodation** *In the Hot Spring scenic zone, there are the three-star Taoyuan Hotel, two-star Huangshan Hotel and Wenquan Hotel; in the Jade Screen scenic zone, there is the four-star Yupinglou Hotel; in the North Sea scenic zone, there are the four-star Shilin Hotel, three-star Beihai Hotel and Xihai Hotel, two-star Paiyunlou Hotel and Baiyun Hotel.*

■ **Food** *The unique dishes include Salted Mandarin Fish, Stewed Soft-shelled Turtle with Ham, Stewed Partridge with Lichen, Yipin Pot, etc.*

■ **Others** *Local special products include Huangshan Maofeng Tea, chrysanthemums, glossy ganoderma, bamboo shoot, Santan Loquat, dried snake, etc. The handicrafts include the four treasures of the study (ink stone and ink slab), bamboo carvings, bamboo weaving articles and porcelains.*

Inquiry telephones: Flights 0559-2934111, 2541222; Trains 0559-2116222, 2116262; Accommodation 0559-5561156; Cableway 0559-5586060, 5585728

Huangshan

Greeting Pine

Wolong (Crouching Dragon) Pine

Ancient Villages in Southern Anhui—Xidi and Hongcun

Huizhou style architecture

Gate of Lexu Hall

☐ **Name:**
Ancient Villages in Southern Anhui—Xidi and Hongcun

☐ **Geographical coordinates:**
30° 11' N, 117° 38' E

☐ **Date of inscription:**
November 30, 2000

☐ **Criteria for inclusion:**
III, IV, V of cultural properties

⊙ Overview

Located in Yixian County of Huangshan City, Anhui Province, the villages were first established in the 11th-12th Century. In selecting the site and construction of these ancient villages, traditional Chinese *fengshui* theory (geomancy) was followed, and the unity of man and nature, the respect for nature were emphasized to achieve harmony between the layout of villages and the terrain, the landform, and the scenery. In Xidi and Hongcun, the villages are precisely laid out and the architectural techniques of the dwelling houses are exquisite. Closely combined with the surrounding environment, the villages present a rural vista complementing the natural landscape. The people living here are simple and honest and maintain the traditional folk customs with rich cultural connotations. Known as a "retreat from the turmoil of the world", these are the best example of Chinese villages in the mountain areas along the middle and lower reaches of the Yangtze River.

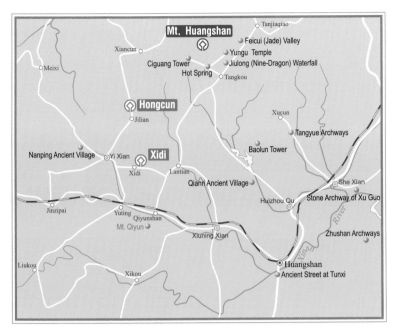

Balcony of Dafu House, Xidi

Ancient Villages in Southern Anhui

⊙ Description

The village of Xidi is situated at the foot of the hills with two brooks flowing across the north and east of the village and converging at Huiyuan Bridge at the southern end. The village is separated into different areas by three brooks named Qianbian, Houbian and Jin, and most of the dwellings are built by the water. The village covers a total area of 12.96 ha. Three roads, two of which run along the brooks, form the main transportation framework. The streets and alleys, all paved with the blue stones found only in Yixian County, generally run from east to west, with some extending southward or northward. Most of the ancient buildings are wood structures enclosed by brick walls. The carvings on the bricks, wood and stones combine into a colorful picture. Both the layout and the scale of the streets and lanes, the brooks and the buildings are appropriately arranged. 1,500 m to the west of Xidi in a valley between two mountains, there used to be a garden with several buildings constructed according to the *fengshui* theory. This beautiful place was used for teaching and learning in ancient times. Even now the Dongyuan Middle School is located there.

The village of Hongcun, covering an area of 19.11 ha, lies against Leigang Hill, an extension of Mt. Huangshan and faces Jicun Village across Yixi River and Yangzhan River in the west. To the east and west of Hongcun stand Dongshan Hill and Shigu Hill respectively, both are covered with verdant vegetation. In the south, there is a large expanse of water, the South Lake. The village basically faces south and is at the center of an area enclosed by mountains and rivers, which accords with *fengshu* theory of "Store the *Feng* and gather the *Qi*, Shoulder the *Yin* and embrace the *Yang*".

An irrigation canal over 400 years old flows across the village and reaches every household, forming two water areas in the center and the south of the village—the Moon Pond and the South Lake. The canal, the pond and the lake together have a prominent role in shaping the overall layout of the village, and create the unique artistic and scenic features of Hongcun. The streets and lanes within the village are mostly constructed close to the irrigation canal and paved with stone slabs. The ancient buildings found here include academies, ancestral halls and dwellings houses, which are characterized by their classic beauty.

Most of the ancient dwelling houses in Xidi and Hongcun reflect the characteristics of Anhui style of architecture. They generally have a basic unit of three rooms with an interior courtyard. The buildings are symmetrical in layout, with a hall in the middle and a wing-room on each side. The stairways are either at the front and back or on the left and right of the hall. An interior courtyard is set at the entrance of the hall for light and ventilation. On the above basis, the buildings can be extended vertically to two-row, three-row, four-side residential compounds. Some individual buildings extend horizontally to five rooms. The post and lintel or column and tie herringbone-fashioned ridge is often adopted in these dwelling houses, which are also enclosed by external walls and separated into different sections by gable walls. At the bottom, the bases are usually made of Yixian Blue Stones, and the tops are crenellated or convex-arc-shaped, with the black tile as the butterfly structure and horse-head-shaped fronts. To ensure security, the walls are tall with durable and graceful outward-opening windows

A panorama of Xidi

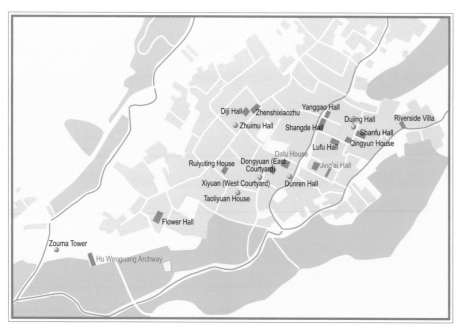

Nanhu Academy, Hongcun

Xidi

that are made of Yixian Blue Stones. Normally, the dwelling houses have long, narrow courtyards. After entering the door at the narrow end, one has to pass a long courtyard before reaching the halls. This makes the courtyards look larger within the limited space. Stone sculptures, miniature landscapes, raised ponds, waterside pavilions, platforms and towers are laid out in the courtyards, adding a special flavour to the houses.

Scholars and teachers are highly respected in Xidi and Hongcun villages. A large amount of ancient vocabularies and phonology are still in use today, so their dialect is quite different from standard Chinese, making it hard to understand on one hand but quite distinctive on the other. The well-known interpretation of their dialect by outsiders is: "ABCD", for "I don't know". There are many folk customs in the villages, the people living here are simple and honest, and the ancient charm is still well preserved.

Situated in the subtropical zone, Xidi and Hongcun have a humid monsoon climate, with an annual average temperature of 15.8°C, the highest temperature reaching 40°C and the lowest -12.2°C. The stunning mountain ranges, beautiful environment, mild climate, abundant rainfall and rich resources make these villages ideal dwelling places for human beings.

Highlights

Hu Wenguang Memorial Archway Standing at the entrance to the village of Xidi, the memorial archway was originally built in the 6th year of Wanli in the Ming Dynasty (1578). 12.3 m high and 9.95 m wide, it is a four-pillar, three-gate structure built of exquisitely carved marbles. Its pedestal consists of four rectangular columns. On the two pillars in the middle are carved four pairs of crawling lions. On the architrave of both sides are carved many auspicious images, such as kylins, red-crowned cranes, phoenixes and deers. On the facade are engraved four Chinese characters "Chancellor of Jingfan" and on the central tablet of the third level are engraved two Chinese characters "En Rong", meaning "favor and honor", with a relief of intertwining dragons on both sides. There are altogether 32 round hollowed out wings, exactly the same as the number of years of Hu Wenguang's political career.

Jing'ai Hall Lying at the center of the Xidi Village, the Jing'ai Hall covers a total floor space of over 1,800 sq m. Originally the residential house of Hu Shiheng, the fourteenth ancestor of the Hu Family of Xidi, it was rebuilt at the end of the 17th Century and expanded to be the ancestral hall of the Hu family where the Hu clan offer sacrifices and pay respects to their ancestors and carry out the traditions of the family. It is the largest existing ancestral hall in the village.

Dafu House This house lies in Xidi Village, at the junction of Zhengjie Street and Henglu Street. First built in the 13th year of Kangxi in the Qing Dynasty (1691), it was originally the dwelling house of Hu Wenzhao, a

Hu Wenguang Memorial Archway, Xidi

South Lake, Hongcun

Chengzhi Hall, Hongcun

senior government official. On the left side of the hall there is a tower facing the street where the young ladies of the family used to choose their husbands by tossing a silk ball. On the wooden board hanging on the tower are the engravings of six Chinese characters, meaning "the household in the peach garden".

Lexu Hall Lying in the middle of the north bank of the Moon Pond in Hongcun, this building is the ancestral hall of the Wang Family. It was first built at the beginning of the 15th Century, and its architectural style of the Ming Dynasty is well preserved till today.

Nanhu (South Lake) Academy Located on the north bank of the South Lake in Hongcun Village, the academy was first built during the reign of Emperor Jiajing in the Ming Dynasty and reconstructed in the 19th year of Jiaqing in the Qing Dynasty (1814), when six old-style private schools were established by the villagers of Hongcun on the north bank of the lake. The original name, "Six Schools by the Lake", was changed to Nanhu Academy in 1814.

Chengzhi Hall Located in the middle of Shangshuizhen Street of Hongcun and first built in the 5th year of Xianfeng in the Qing Dynasty (1855), it was the residence of Wang Dinggui, a major salt merchant at the end of the Qing Dynasty. It is a majestic wood and brick structure with rich interior carvings. Covering a total building area of around 1,600 sq m, the house has 9 atria, 60 rooms and several courtyards. It is a well-preserved large ancient dwelling house.

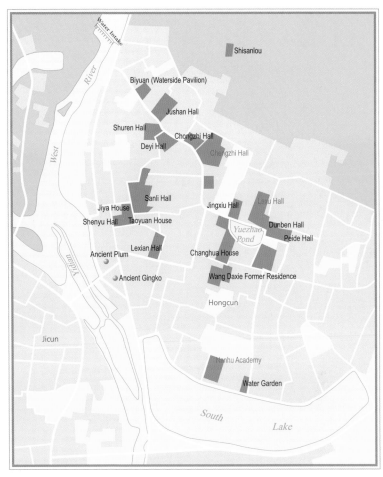

✂ Hongcun ✂

⊙ Information

■ **Transportation** *From Huangshan, there is a medium-sized coach bus heading for Xidi and Hongcun via Yixian County every 20 minutes. Visitors may also travel by taxi.*

■ **Accommodation** *In Huangshan City, there are the International Hotel and the Golf Hotel; in Yixian county seat, there are Shiwaitaoyuan Hotel, Xunyang Grand Hotel, Zhongcheng Villa, Daohuaxiang Hotel; in Xidi Town, there are Xidi Hotel and Wanchun Hotel; in Hongcun Village, there are Hongcun Hotel, Shisanlou Ancient Residential Villa.*

■ **Food** *Special cuisines are Salted Mandarin Fish, White-hair tofu, Laba tofu, Ham with Partridge, Shredded Meat with Bracken, Steamed Wild Soft-Shelled Turtle, Mingpu Fish with Bamboo Shoot, Ham and Bamboo Shoot, Hongtan Soy Cheese, Soybean Coat with Goose Neck and Mushroom, etc. The Xichuan Restaurant in Xidi Town mainly serves local dishes.*

■ **Others** *Local special products include torreya and bamboo shoot. Famous handicrafts are "OK" bamboo needle and different kinds of stone carvings and bamboo carvings.*

Inquiry telephones: 0559-5154030, 5523764

Website: www.yixian.gov.cn

Yuezhao (Moon) Pond

FUJIAN PROVINCE

General Information

Fujian Province, also called Min in short, has an area of more than 120,000 sq km. It has under its administrative jurisdiction 9 prefecture-level cities, 14 county-level cities and 45 counties. The province has a population of 33.32 million and ethnic groups including Han, She, Hui, Tujia and Miao.

Environment

Located in the southeast coast of China, Fujian faces Taiwan Province across the sea in the east. Hilly areas account for more than 80% of the province's total. The terrain descends from west to southeast, with zigzag coastlines and countless islands. It has a sub-tropical humid monsoon climate. The average temperature is 6 ~ 12°C in January and 28 ~ 29°C in July, with an average annual rainfall between 800 ~ 1,900 mm.

Places of Interest

Fujian Province has many beautiful mountains and rivers that are too stunning to be taken all at once. Cultural relics are found everywhere across the province. There are 13 state-level scenic areas that embrace all the natural beauty under the sky, including Wuyi Mountain, Gulang Island-Wanshi Mountain of Xiamen, Qingyuan Mountain in Quanzhou, Taimu Mountain in Fuding, Jinhu Lake in Taining, Taoyuan Cave in Yong'an-Linyin Stone Forest, Haitan of Pingtan, Guanzhi Mountain in Liancheng, Yuanyang Creek in Pingnan, the Gushan Mountain in Fuzhou and the Yuhua Cave in Jiangle. Among them, Wuyi Mountain is included in the World Heritage List.

Quanzhou, Fuzhou, Zhangzhou and Changting are famous historical and cultural cities of China. Other famous sites of human landscapes include Luoyang Bridge in Quanzhou, Mulanpo of Putian, the East-West Tower, Sitting Portrait of Laojun Rock, Stone Carving on Jiuri Mountain, Anping Bridge of Jinjiang, Tomb of Zheng chenggong in Nan'an, Chongwu ancient city in Hui'an, Tongshan ancient city in Dongshan, Zhao Family Castle in Zhangpu, Yongding Earth Tower and the Nanjing Earth Tower. Fujian has a developed religious culture, with 14 Buddhist temples under state protection including Xuefeng Temple in Minhou, the Welling Spring Temple in Fuzhou, the Guanghua Temple in Putian, the Kaiyuan Temple in Quanzhou and the South Putuo Temple in Xiamen. All of them are well-known ancient Buddhist temples both at home and abroad.

Local Specialties

Wuyiyan tea, Tieguanyin tea of Anxi, Xinhua Longan, Pingtan purple laver, Tong'an lancelet, Fuzhou bodiless lacquerware, Shoushan stone carving, and Dehua chinaware.

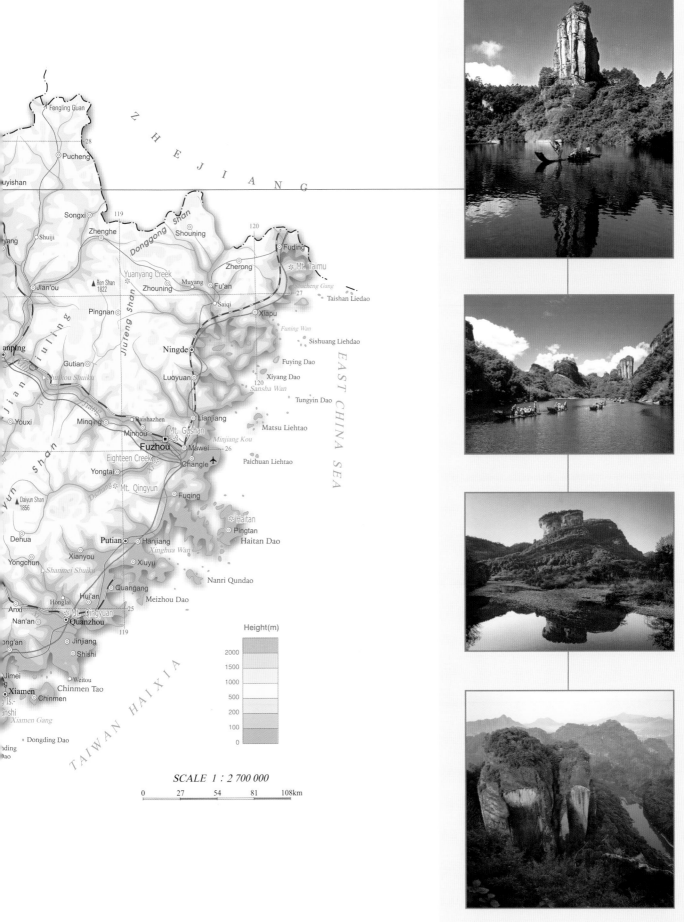

Fengling Guan

ZHEJIANG

Pucheng
28

Songxi
119

Zhenghe

Shuiji

Shouning

Donggong Shan

Jian'ou

Yuanyang Creek

Ren Shan
1822

Muyang

Zhouning

Zherong

Fu'an

Mt. Taimu

Fuding

120

Pingnan

Saiqi
27

Shacheng Gang

Xiapu

Jiufeng Shan

Funing Wan

Sishuang Liehdao

Ningde

Fuying Dao

Gutian

Luoyuan

Xiyang Dao
120

Sansha Wan

Shuikou Shuiku

Tungyin Dao

Youxi

Minqing

Baishazhen

Lianjiang

Matsu Liehtao

EAST CHINA SEA

Minhou

Mt. Gushan

Minjiang Kou

Fuzhou

Mawei
26

Eighteen Creek

Changle

Paichuan Liehtao

Yongtai

Dazhang

Mt. Qingyun

Fuqing

Daiyun Shan
1856

Haitan

Pingtan

Dehua

Putian

Hanjiang

Haitan Dao

Xianyou

Xinghua Wan

Yongchun

Xiuyu

Shanmei Shuiku

Nanri Qundao

Quangang

Meizhou Dao

Anxi

Honglai

Hui'an

Mt. Qingyuan

Nan'an

Quanzhou
25

119

Jinjiang

Shishi

Jimei

Weitou

Chinmen Tao

Xiamen

Chinmen

Xiamen Gang

Dongding Dao

TAIWAN HAIXIA

Height(m)

2000
1500
1000
500
200
100
0

SCALE 1 : 2 700 000

0   27   54   81   108km

59

Mount Wuyi

- ☐ **Name:**
  Mount Wuyi
- ☐ **Geographical coordinates:**
  27° 32' 36" ~ 27° 55' 15" N,
  117° 24' 12" ~ 118° 02' 50" E
- ☐ **Date of inscription:**
  December 1, 1999
- ☐ **Criteria for inclusion:**
  III, IV of natural properties
  III, VI of cultural properties

Dawang Peak, Jiuqu River

⊙ Overview

Located in the northwest of Fujian Province and covering an area of 999.75 sq km, Mount Wuyi boasts, in its western part, the key area of global biodiversity conservation. Lying here is the best conserved, most typical and largest ecological system of meso-subtropical virgin forests of the same latitude in the world. In its eastern part, the mountain and the waters integrate in a perfect entirety, and the humane and natural landscapes form an organic mix, with the beautiful waters, wonderful peaks, deep and secluded valleys, precipitous gullies, centuries-old history and culture, and numerous sites of relics claiming a wide reputation. The middle section of the mountain, which serves as the link between east and west, harbors the source of Jiuqu River and maintains an excellent ecological environment.

Mount Wuyi is rich in cultural relics. Located here are the site of ancient city of the Han Dynasty (1st Century BC), the study centers where Zhu Xi, philosopher of the Song Dynasty (1130-1200), carried out his academic activities, and the world's oldest boat coffins in the cliff caves. Viewed from a historical and scientific perspective, the mountain is of outstanding and universal value because it not only provides a witness to an ancient civilization and cultural tradition that had disappeared, but also a direct link to the civilization of Neo-Confucianism.

Mount Wuyi

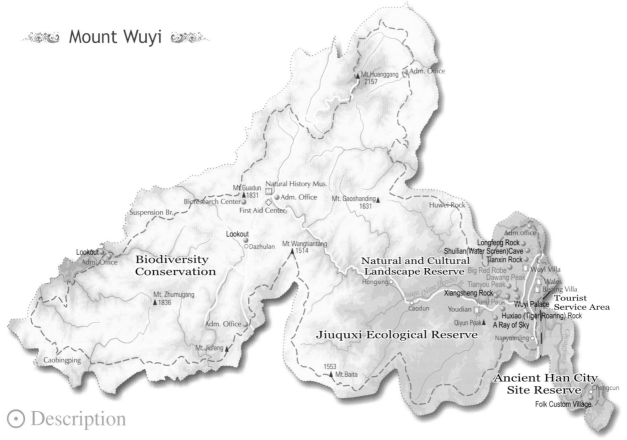

⊙ Description

1. Natural heritage Mount Wuyi is a typical example of the process of biological evolution and the interaction between man and nature. Conserved here is the ecological system of a meso-subtropical virgin forest most complete, most typical and biggest at the same latitude in the world.

Mount Wuyi is a key area of global biodiversity conservation and the habitat of endangered rare species. Rich in the resource of species of plants, it is a gene bank of rare wild life and a world-famous origin of modular specimens.

Featuring unique and rare landscapes, Mount Wuyi is a place of great beauty that has been protected for more than twelve centuries. The incomparable natural scenery of Jiuqu River, in particular, is a typical example of harmonious combination of mountains and waters, and perfect integration between man and nature.

2. Historical heritage The cultural relics of the ancient Minyue State and the ancient Minyue Nationality in Mount Wuyi provide a historical witness to an ancient civilization that is gone. As early as 4,000 years ago, ancients worked and lived in this region, who gradually developed a culture known as the ancient Min Nationality Culture and later the ancient Minyue Nationality Culture, which was unique to this area of China. Lasting for more than 2,000 years, this nationality left behind it mountains of cultural relics, most notably the boat coffins in the cliff caves, the *hongqiaoban* (Rainbow Bridge Plank), and the site of the capital town of the king of the Minyue State in the Han Dynasty.

The boat coffins in the cliff caves and *hongqiaoban* in the eastern part of Mount Wuyi are the relics of burials of the ancient Yue people who lived some 3,000 years ago. The remnant cotton cloth pieces were the earliest cotton and textile articles ever found in China. The boat coffins in Mount Wuyi are the oldest of their kind

ever discovered in China.

The ancient town of the Han Dynasty, covering an area of 48 ha, is of unprecedented high historical and cultural value. It is the best-preserved site of ancient Han city found south of the Yangtze River. Unearthed from this town are large amount of cultural relics, including potteries for daily use, building materials of porcelain, eaves tiles carrying writings, ironware and bronze ware. Representing the well-developed productive forces at that time and embodying the highest level of Chinese civilization, these articles provide important material evidences for the study of the rise and fall of the Minyue Nationality and the history of economic and cultural development south of the Yangtze during the Han Dynasty.

Mount Wuyi has been inseparably linked with the Neo-Confucianism developed by Zhu Xi, the greatest thinker, philosopher and educator in China's history after Confucius. Synthesizing the academic thinking developed after Confucius, Zhu developed Neo-Confucianism. His doctrine of Confucianism, established by the imperial court as the official and orthodox ideology of philosophy, structured the dominating ideology and theory in China for more than 700 years from the Song Dynasty to the Qing Dynasty (13th-20th century). As a symbol of traditional national spirit with universal significance, it left its influences on countries in East Asia, Europe and America, and stood as an embodiment of the civilization in East Asia. Even today, Neo-Confucianism of a Japanese type and that of a Korean type are still being studied in foreign countries, bringing together experts and scholars from dozens of countries for its study. The activities of Zhu Xi and his disciples and successors in Mount Wuyi had left cultural relics of extremely high value, such as the ancient site of Wuyi Jingshe Academy, the philosophical inscriptions by Zhu Xi and other Neo-Confucianists,

Ancient Han Dynasty city

such as "Time Flies", "Self-cultivation Comes First", and "Humanity Develops from Wise Thinking"; the stone tablet inscription on Liu Ziyu's tomb, and the society founded by Zhu Xi. All these cultural relics are precious for the study of the rise and fall of Neo-Confucianism, Confucianism, and China's history of philosophy and thinking. They are treasures of traditional Chinese culture.

ecological reserve in the middle section of the mountain and snakes across the *danxia* landform in the eastern section. The stream features deep valleys and sharp curves conditioned by rocks, gullies and rifts, and meanders along peaks and gullies for 9.5 km, of which the direct distance is merely 5 km, with a curving ratio of 1.9 km. The landscape on the banks of Jiuqu River is of typical monoclinal *danxia* landform where stand 36 peaks and 99 rocks. All the peaks and rocks are characterized by inclined top, steep

⊙ Highlights

Tianyou (Heavenly Tour) Peak Rising 408 m above sea level with a relative height of 215 m, this is a rock ridge extending from the north to south. Adjacent to Xianyou Rock in the east and Xianzhang Peak in the west, it has a steep precipice rising above all other peaks into the sky. Standing on the peak and looking at the ever-changing sea of clouds, makes one feel like as if he were in a fairyland or celestial palace, hence the name Tianyou. The Stand of Panoramic View, located in the center of the scenic area, is the best place for viewing the scenery of Mount Wuyi, including the five spectacles of sunrise, sunset, clouds and mists, Buddhist halo, and moonlight. Numerous ancient trees grow on the peak. On the stone cliffs by the Huma Stream at the top of the peak are scattered nearly 100 sites of rock carvings of different dynasties.

Jiuqu (Nine Bends) River Originating from the densely forested western part of Mount Wuyi, the river runs 62.8 km through the

Tianyou Peak

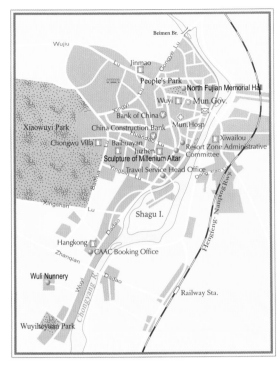

✤ Wuyishan ✤

cliff, and flat slope. Facing the east, they look like thousands of galloping horses. Imposing in look and varied in posture, the river forms a natural landscape of mountains and waters and claims to be the essence of the natural beauty of Mount Wuyi.

Big Red Robe Located in the central part of Mount Wuyi scenic area, inside the a famous scenic spot of Jiulongke (Nine Dragon Den), this is a deep and long valley developed under the control of the faulted structure running east-west. Sinking deep, the valley is flanked by long single-sided mountains and nine precipitous peaks facing each other from south and north. Due to unique joint development, the peak ridges rise and fall like nine dragons restraining themselves from attempts to fly off. Standing at the mouth

of the valley is a round rock looking like a ball for play by the dragons. In the valley and on the red precipice are growing verdant pines and slender bamboos. The Big Red Robe Tea, known far and wide, grows at the deepest part of the valley. The six ancient tea trees, about 340 years old, grows luxuriantly on the precipice north of the base of the Jiulongke. The tea from these trees compares favorably to all oolong tea in color, fragrance and taste, hence the title "the King of Tea".

⊙ Information

■ **Transportation** *There are over 20 flights to Beijing, Shanghai, Guangzhou, Shenzhen, Wuhan, Hong Kong, Wenzhou, Zhoushan, Fuzhou and Xiamen; Nanping-Hengfeng Railway runs across Mount Wuyi, linking it to Fuzhou, Xiamen, Quanzhou, Hefei, Nanjing, and Shanghai; daily long-distance bus service is available to most part of the country.*

■ **Accommodation** *There are many guesthouses and hotels available, such as Wuyi Villa, International Trade Hotel, Youdian Hotel, Qingzhu Villa, Changcheng Villa, Meihai Hotel, Huacai Hotel, Dianli Hotel, Baodao Hotel, Beijing Villa, Yun'an Hotel, Jade Maid Hotel, Wales Hotel, and Jiaotong Hotel.*

■ **Food** *Local dishes include Wengong vegetables, pressed salted duck, rabbit meat hotpot, Manting banquet, Bagua banquet, Wuyi medicinal food, and Dragon-Phoenix Soup. Other snacks of local flavor include litchi jelly, Kuzhu cake, Wuyi Fragrant Wine, potherb mustard, Shuqu fruit and Maci fruit.*

■ **Others** *Local special products are Wuyi Rock Tea, Xianggu mushroom, red mushroom, Cat's Claw, white lotus, Wuyi orchid, Wuyi orange, Wuyi walnut, Wuyi snaked wine, and Wuyi dried bamboo shoots.*

Inquiry telephone: 0599-5252579 (government); 0599-5113053, 5252884, 5105848 (scenic spots)

Website: www.whwy.org

Liuqu (6th bend) scenery

Meadow of Huanggang Mountain

JIANGXI PROVINCE

General Information

Jiangxi, also called Gan in short, has its capital in Nanchang City. With an area of more than 160,000 sq km, it has under its administrative jurisdiction 11 prefecture-level cities, 10 county-level cities and 70 counties. The province has a population of 42.63 million and ethnic groups including Han, She, Hui, Mongol, Miao and Man.

Environment

It is located on the southern bank of the middle and lower reaches of the Yangtze River, and by both banks of the Ganjiang River. The province is surrounded by mountains in the east, south and west. The central parts are hilly areas and in the north are plains. There are numerous lakes in the province. It has a sub-tropical humid monsoon climate. Plum rain is frequent in spring and rainstorms are more common in summer. It is dry in autumn. The average temperature is 4 ~ 9°C in January and 28 ~ 30°C in July, with an average annul rainfall between 1,300 ~ 1,900 mm.

Places of Interest

Jiangxi is bestowed with rich natural resources and treasures, as well as resources of human culture. Six state-level scenic areas are the summer resort of Lushan Mountain, the revolutionary cradle of Jinggang Mountain, the place of origin of Taoism—Longhu Mountain, the greatest fairy summit south of the Yangtze River—Sanqing Mountain, as well as Xiannu Lake, Sanbai Mountain, Meiling and Guifeng Peak. Of them, Lushan Mountain is included in the World Heritage List. Tengwang Tower, Shizhong Mountain, Hongyan Cave and Shazhouba of Ruijin are famous tourist attractions. Nanchang, Jingde-zhen and Ganzhou are famous historical and cultural cities of China. There are 24 key sites of cultural relics under state protection, including the Memorial Hall of the August 1 Nanchang Uprising. The Donglin Temple of Lushan Mountain, Nengren Temple of Jiujiang, Zhenru Temple on Yunju Mountain, Jingju Temple on Qingyuan Mountain and Tianshifu on Longhu Mountain are the key temples under state protection.

There are also four nature reserves under state protection, such as the Poyang Migratory Bird Nature Reserve, in addition to 20 national forest parks like Jing'an Sanzhualun Forest Park. Just as a saying goes: A sightseeing tour to visit the waterfall on Lushan Mountain and the fresh green bamboos on Jinggang Mountain and to remember the good old days at the city of chinaware is more than worthwhile.

Local Specialties

Three fresh delicious fish of the Poyang Lake—the white bait, the mandarin fish, and the long tail anchovy; sweet oranges of Nanfeng, Wuyan green tea, "Ninghong Tea" of Xiushui and Wuning, chinaware of Jingdezheng, and agate carving of Jinxi.

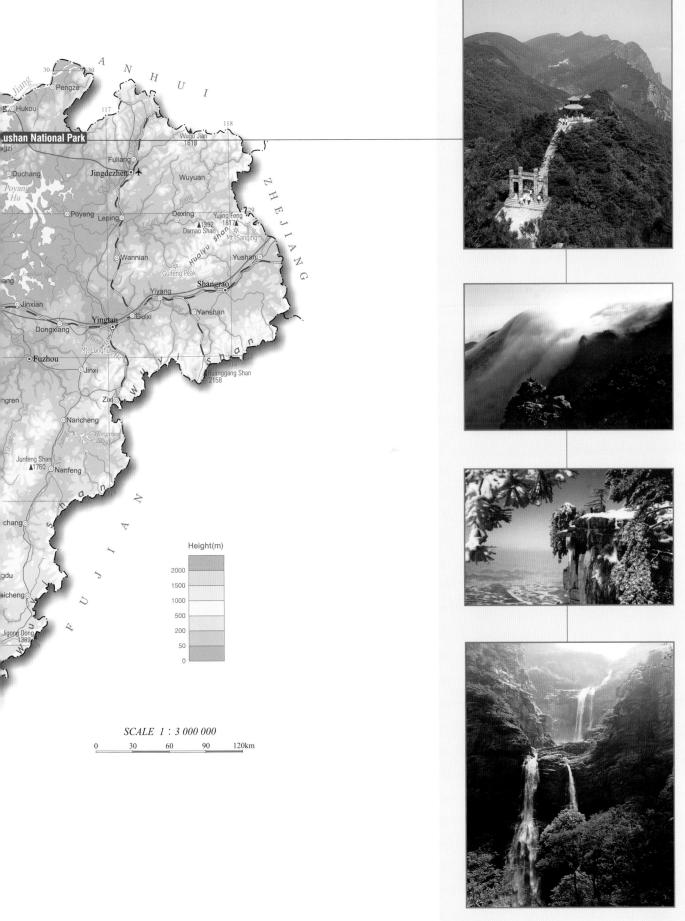

Map Labels

A N H U I

Jiang
Pengze
Hukou

ZHEJIANG

117
118

ushan National Park
Wugu Jian
1618

Fuliang
Jingdezhen ✈
Wuyuan

Duchang

Poyang
Hu

Poyang
Leping
Dexing
Yujing Feng
729
▲1392 1817▲
Damao Shan
Mt. Sanqing

Wannian
Yushan

Guifeng Peak
Yiyang
Shangrao

Jinxian
Yingtan
Guixi
Yanshan

Dongxiang

Mt. Longhu
Huanggang Shan
2158

Fuzhou
Jinxi

Zixi

ngren
Nancheng

Hongmen
Shuiku

Junfeng Shan
▲1760
Nanfeng

chang

gdu

Jigong Dong
1389

icheng

F U J I A N

Wuyi Shan

Height(m)

2000
1500
1000
500
200
50
0

SCALE 1 : 3 000 000

0   30   60   90   120km

Lushan National Park

☐ **Name:**

Lushan National Park

☐ **Geographic coordinates:**

29° 26' ~ 29° 41' N, 115° 57' ~ 116° 08' E

☐ **Date of inscription:**

December 6, 1996

☐ **Criteria for inclusion:**

II, III, IV, VI of cultural properties

Surging clouds at Hanpokou

⊙ Overview

Mount Lushan is located in the north of Jiangxi Province, on the southern bank of the middle reaches of the Yangtze. The mountain borders on Jiujiang, a famous historical and cultural city, and Poyang, China's largest freshwater lake. It covers an area of 302 sq km, with an outer protection zone of 500 sq km. Human activities on Mount Lushan can be traced back to 6,000 years ago, forming a rich and unique Lushan culture. Geotectonically, the mountain belongs to Yangtze Block of South China and is a unique a horst, or "fault-block mountain". This region boasts the geological remains of Quaternary glaciers, abundant biological resources, a complete ecosystem and more than 2, 200 species of alpine plants, including over 40 endangered species. Its forest coverage rate reaches as high as 80%. There are 12 scenic zones and 474 scenic spots on the mountain, which can be divided into waterfalls and springs, mountains and stones, meteorological phenomena, plants, geological landforms, rivers and lakes, human landscapes, and architectural villas. Since ancient times the mountain has achieved its reputation as "the finest mountain under heaven". In 1996, Mount Lushan was inscribed on the World Heritage List as Cultural Landscape.

⊙ Description

Facing the river and adjacent to the lake, with high peaks and deep valleys, Mount Lushan has a distinct mountain climate that features plenty of rain. The average annual precipitation is 1,917 mm, the average annual number of fog days is 191, and the average temperature between July and September is 16.9°C. Inside the precipitous Mt. Lushan, there are many beautiful landscapes. Its highest peak, Hanyang Peak, is 1,474 m above sea level, and 171 peaks have acquired their names since ancient times. Among the peaks are scattered 26 ridges, 20 vales, 16 caves and 22 grotesque-shaped rocks. The high mountain and flowing water work together to form numerous waterscapes, including 22 waterfalls, 18 streams and 14 lakes and ponds. The famed Three Tier Waterfall has a drop height of 155 m.

Mt. Lushan boasts a rich diversity of biological resources and a complete ecological system. Its forest coverage rate is 80%, with over 3,000 species of plants and 2,000 species of animals living there. The Poyang Lake Migratory Bird Protection Zone is located in the piedmont of Mt. Lushan, where the world's largest white crane flock of present time has been found.

Human activities on Mt. Lushan date from the later stage of the Neolithic Age, and Lushan Culture with rich connotation and far-reaching impact has taken shape here since ancient times. In 126 BC, Sima Qian visited Mount Lushan and recorded it in *Shi Ji* (Historical Records). In the Eastern Jin Dynasty (317-420 AD), a number of cultural celebrities such as Tao Yuanming and Xie Lingyun made Mount Lushan the source of the traditional Chinese pastoral poetry, scenic poems and landscape painting. Since then, more than 1,500 famous literati, statesmen and artists including Li Bai, Bai Juyi, Su Shi and Wang Anshi had lived in or visited Mount Lushan successively, and composed over 4,000 verses, ditties, odes and songs in eulogy of the mountain, most of which are masterpieces.

In the 4th Century AD, Monk Huiyuan first established the "Pure Land Method" in the Donglin Temple on Mount Lushan, which representing the trend of localization of Buddhism in China. Religions thrived on the mountain between 4th-13th Century, while the number of Buddhist and Taoist temples reached as high as 500. In 1924, World Buddhism Convention was held here. At the beginning of the 20th Century, Christian churches from over 20 countries gathered on Mount Lushan. Today, many structures of different religions and sects, such as Buddhism, Taoism, Muslim, Christianity and Catholicism, can still be found here.

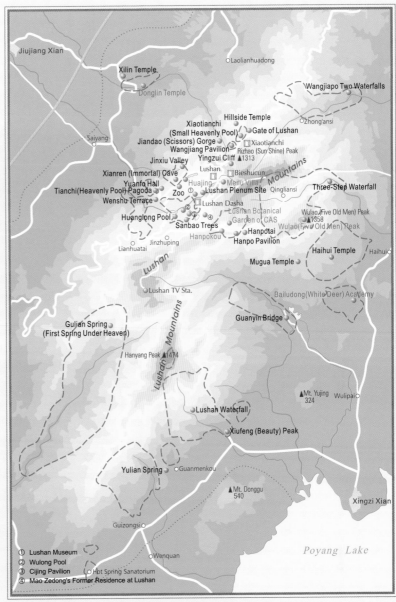

① Lushan Museum
② Wulong Pool
③ Cijing Pavilion
④ Mao Zedong's Former Residence at Lushan

Mount Lushan

Bailudong (White Deer Cave) Academy, the first among the four ancient Chinese academies of classical learning, was established on Mount Lushan in 940 and revived in 1179 by Zhu Xi, a famous Neo-Confucian philosopher and educationist of the Southern Song Dynasty (1127-1279). This academy embodies the major trends of the Neo-Confucianism in the past 700 years in China.

In the 1930s, Li Siguang, a geologist, first found the remains of

Ruqin Lake in autumn

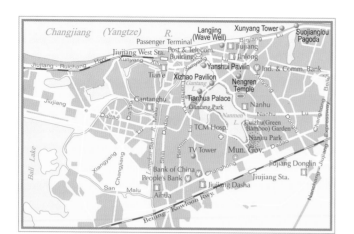

ꞏ✺ Jiujiang ✺ꞏ

Quaternary glaciers of China on Mount Lushan and thus established the Theory of China's Quaternary Glaciers. Hu Xiansu, a botanist, set up China's first formal alpine garden—Lushan Botanical Garden—after conducting thorough investigations into the flora on the mountain.

Since the 19th Century, people from over 20 countries including the United States, Britain, Russia, France and Japan started to build villas on Mount Lushan. In the 1930s, the mountain became the "summer capital" of the national government. After the founding of the People's Republic, Mao Zedong paid three visits to the mountain and presided over three significant meetings that had drawn world's attention.

⊙ Highlights

Wulao (Five-Old-Man) Peaks Situated 9 km from Guling Town, the center of Mount Lushan, the peaks rises 1,358 m above sea level, presenting an unrivalled beauty on the southeast side of the mountain. They border on Poyang Lake in the south, adjoin Hanpo Ridge in the west and lean against Dayue Mountain in the north. Being the highest of all the peaks of Moung Lushan, they acquire the name because of the five adjoining peaks that look like five meager-faced old men. Among the five peaks, the third is the steepest while the fourth is the highest. In front of the Wulao Peaks stand five lower peaks: Shizi (Lion) Peak, Jinyin (Gold Seal) Peak, Shichuan (Stone Boat) Peak, Lingyun (Cloud-Reaching) Peak and Qigan (Mast) Peak. The peaks present different shapes when viewed in different seasons or from different places, and they often impress visitors with the charm of obscurity.

Meilu Villa The villa is located by Changchong River in the eastern valley of Guling Town, about 1,000 m from the main street. It was first built in 1903 by Britain's Lord Lannoze and then transferred to Mrs. Bali in 1922, who later presented it as a gift to Song Meiling in 1933, because of their deep personal friendship. In 1934, Song Meiling and Chiang Kaishek moved to this villa and lived there for some time in the following years till their departure in 1948. Chiang Kai-shek named this villa as "Meilu" to express the meaning of "beautiful mountain, beautiful building and beautiful wife" and had his own handwriting inscribed on the stone. After the founding of the People's Republic, Mao Zedong used to stay here for several times. This villa is the only one in China where the highest leaders of both the Communist Party and the Kuomintang had resided, and it is now a key site of cultural relics under state protection.

Huajing (Flower Path) The path is 2,000 m from Guling Street. Its name comes from the poem composed by Bai Juyi, the famous poet of the Tang Dynasty, "Dedication to the Peach Blossom of the Dalin Temple". At the entrance stands a stone archway, in the middle of its horizontal tablet were inscribed the two Chinese characters "Hua Jing", while on the sides of which are two couplets, meaning: "The flowers bloom in the temple, while the poet stays here with his ode". Behind the Jingbai Pavilion, a stone tablet was erected, on

Meilu Villa   Stone archway of Bailudong

Wulao Peaks

Longshou (Dragon Head) Cliff

which there is the inscription of the *Record of the Jingbai Pavilion*, narrating the construction of the pavilion.

Hanpokou Located 6,000 m from the main street, the Hanpo Ridge in the southeast of Mount Lushan appears like a fleeing horse or a swimming dragon, running horizontally between Jiuqi Peak and Wulao Peaks. The ridge seems to be ready to swallow down the Poyang Lake, hence the name which means "Mouth Containing Poyang". Litoujian (one of the remains of Quaternary glaciers) is the best position to view the sunrise. From here, the second highest peak of Mount Lushan—Wulao Peaks—looks like an upturned face of an old man in the distance. It is also a good place to enjoy the sea of clouds.

⊙ Information

■ **Transportation** *Beijing-Kowloon and Wuhan-Shantou railway lines stop at Jiujiang. Scheduled flights connect Nanchang with major cities such as Beijing, Shanghai, Shenzhen, Chengdu, Kunming, Qingdao, Xiamen, Haikou, Shantou, Wenzhou, Zhuhai,* *Fuzhou, Jinan, Wuhan and Xi'an. Along the Yangtze River, there are some 20 regular ships berthing at Jiujiang everyday. Three highways link Wuhan, Hefei, Nanchang, Jingdezhen and other cities to the piedmont of Mount Lushan. Two roads on the north and south slopes of the mountain lead directly to Jiujiang and Nanchang. Within the mountain, there are highways to major scenic spots, and trails for tourist preferring walking.*

■ **Accommodation** *There are more than 150 hotels with a total of over 20,000 beds on Mount Lushan, including the four-star Xihu Hotel, three-star Jingwei Hotel, Lianglu Hotel, Lushan Hotel, Xinshiji Hotel; two-star Lushan Mansion, Yunzhong Hotel, Guling Hotel, Jiaxiu Hotel, as well as Lushan Villa Hotel, Lushan Yingbin Hotel and Guomai Hotel.*

■ **Others** *Special local products are abundant, the most famous ones are Three Stones (Stone Fish, Stone Chicken, Stone Gyrophora) and One Tea (Lushan Cloud and Fog Tea). There is a shopping street in the downtown area of Guling, where one can find various tourist souvenirs.*

Website: www.china-lushan.com

Waterfall of clouds

SHANDONG PROVINCE

General Information

Shandong Province, also called Lu in short, has its capital in Jinan City. With an area of more than 150,000 sq km, it has under its administrative jurisdiction 17 prefecture-level cities, 31 county-level cities and 60 counties. The province has a population of 90.69 million and ethnic groups including Han, Hui, Man, Chosen and Mongol.

Environment

Shandong Province is located in the coastal areas of East China at the lower reaches of the Yellow River. Its eastern part is a peninsula, its middle part is Mount Taishan, Mount Yimeng hilly areas, and its northwestern part is plain. It is in the warm temperate zone with a semi-humid continental monsoon climate. The average temperature is below 0°C in January and about 26°C in July, with an average annual rainfall between 500 ~ 1000 mm.

Places of Interest

Shandong Province is the birthplace of Confucius and Mencius who were exemplary masters for generations after generations. There are Mount Taishan that dwarfs other peaks, Zibo that was once the capital of Qi during the Warring States Period, Jinan the city of springs, Yantai the fairyland, and Weifang the hometown of kites. The land of stunning beauty of Shandong fosters a unique lifestyle of local people, and provides sources of nourishment for honest and unpretentious Shandong people. Jinan, Qufu, Qingdao, Liaocheng, Zoucheng and Zibo are famous historical and cultural cities of China. Mount Taishan and the Temple, Cemetery and Mansion of Confucius are included in the World Heritage List.

Shandong Province is famed for its great mountains and beautiful rivers, with fascinating landscapes. Mount Taishan, Laoshan Mountain in Qingdao, the seashore of Jiaodong peninsula, Mount Boshan and Qingzhou are state-level scenic areas. Qianfo (Thousand Buddhas) Mountain, Daming Lake, Baotu Spring and Penglai Pagoda are tourists' favorite choices, and Qingdao, Yantai and Weihai are ideal summer resorts.

Local Specialties

Qingdao beer, Yantai apples, Laiyang pears, Feicheng peaches, Longkou bean vermicelli, Dezhou braised chicken, Dong'e donkeyhide glue, Weifang kites and Zibo glassware.

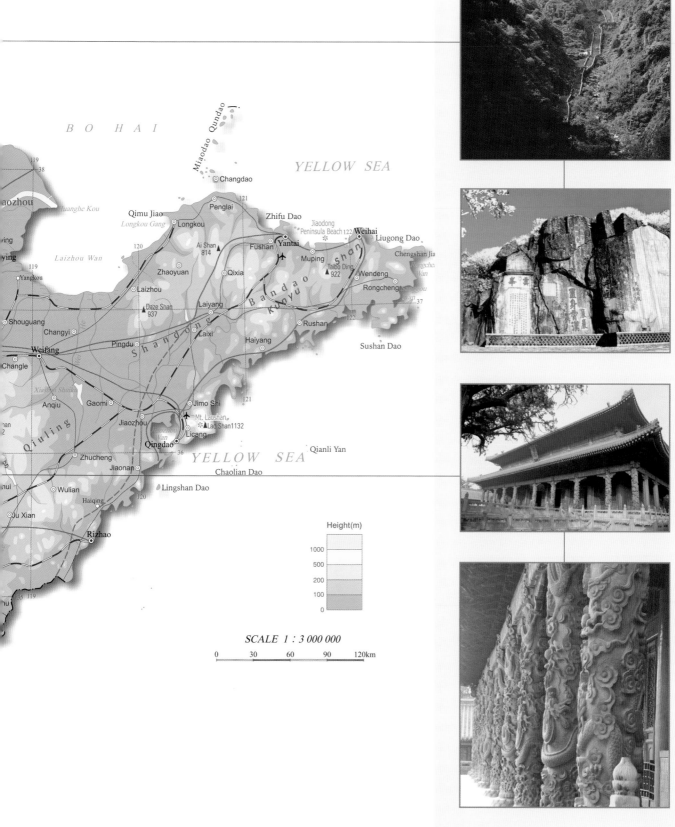

B O   H A I

YELLOW SEA

Miaodao Qundao

119
38

aozhou

Huanghe Kou

Changdao

121

Penglai

Qimu Jiao

Longkou Gang

Longkou

Zhifu Dao

Jiaodong
Peninsula Beach 122

Weihai

ying

120

Ai Shan
814

Fushan

Yantai

Liugong Dao

ying

119

Laizhou Wan

Zhaoyuan

Qixia

Muping

Taibo Ding
922

Chengshan Jia

Wendeng

Rongcheng

37

Yangkou

Shan

Bandao

Kunyu

Shouguang

Daze Shan
937

Laiyang

Shandong

Rushan

122

Changyi

Pingdu

Laixi

Haiyang

Sushan Dao

Weifang

Changle

Xiasho Shuiku

Anqiu

Gaomi

Jimo Shi

121

Qiuling

Jiaozhou

Mt. Laoshan
Lao Shan 1132

2

Licang

Qingdao

Van

Qianli Yan

36

YELLOW SEA

Zhucheng

Jiaonan

Chaolian Dao

nui

Wulian

Lingshan Dao

Haiqing

u Xian

Rizhao

135   119

hu

Height(m)

1000
500
200
100
0

SCALE 1 : 3 000 000

0   30   60   90   120km

Mount Taishan

☐ **Name:**

Mount Taishan

☐ **Geographical coordinates:**

36° 11' ~ 36° 31' N, 116° 50' ~ 117° 12' E

☐ **Date of inscription:**

December 11, 1987

☐ **Criteria for inclusion:**

I, II, III, IV, V, VI of cultural properties

III of natural properties

Tang Dynasty Inscriptions

⊙ Overview

Mount Taishan is situated in the central part of Shandong Province, with a main scenic area of 125 sq km and a forest coverage rate of 81%. Its main peak, Yuhuangding (Jade Emperor Summit), is 1,524 m above sea level. The mountain is mainly composed of "Taishan Rock", the oldest and most important example of ancient metamorphic rocks of Cambrian era in North China. The Cambrian earth section of the northern part of Mount Taishan is the standard earth section of Northern China Cambrian system (the middle and upper Cambrian system). Mount Taishan region is one of the cradles of Chinese civilization with lofty and respected position, enjoying the reputation of "Pillar under East Heaven" and "Head of the Five Mountains" and ranking top of all the famous mountains in China. The sacred Mount Taishan has been the place of worshipping heaven and offering sacrifices for successive emperors over the past 2,000 years. With its natural beauty, artistic glamour and excellent biological environment perfectly integrated, Mount Taishan represents a symbol of ancient Chinese civilization and beliefs.

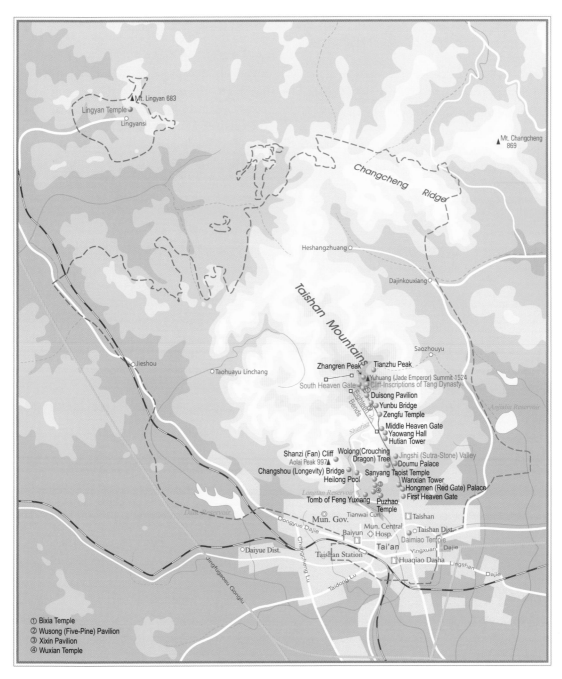

Mount Taishan

⊙ Description

Mount Taishan is magnificent, massive and stately, with high biodiversity and complicated geological conditions. Confucius said: "Only by ascending Mount Taishan will you find how dwarfish the world is". Mount Taishan has been enjoying the loftiest status among the five famous mountains in China. The Dawenkou-Longshan Culture dating from 4,000 ~ 7,000 years ago provides evidence of the prosperity in the early history of this region. The Confucianism founded by Confucius in this area during the Spring and Autumn Period had become the orthodox idea for running the country in several thousand years. In the pre-Qin days (before 221 BC) there were 72 monarchs coming to worship heaven and offer sacrifices at Mount Taishan; after Qin Dynasty, 12 emperors came

in person, leaving abundant cultural relics and developing the imperial worship culture which was unique in the world. The civil ethnical culture also has a long history. The emperors' worship to the heaven, the civil sacrifices of the common people and the carols of the literati make it a mountain of culture and a mountain of monarch. The mountain is honorably reputed as the "epitome of the Chinese cultural history" and has become the spiritual homeland of China.

Mount Taishan is a museum of stone inscriptions in nature. There are over 1,800 stone inscriptions scattered widely in the mountain, among which the most famous are the carved scripture of Northern Qi Dynasty in Jingshi Valley and the huge Inscriptions of

Taishan. There are 22 groups of ancient architecture complex on Mount Taishan. The Qi Great Wall to the north of Mount Taishan, dating from 2,500 years ago, is the oldest part of the Great Wall in China. The Daimiao Temple, initiated in the Han Dynasty (206 BC-220 AD), boasts its main building the "Songtiankuang Hall" as one of the three most famous palace buildings in ancient China. Bixia Temple, started in the Song Dynasty (960-1279), with rational structure and copper tile roof, is an excellent example of mountain architecture. In one word, the most distinctive characteristic of the ancient buildings on Mount Taishan is to make the best use of natural environments. The outstanding example of this is the South Heaven Gate, which reveals the extreme harmony between "ideology" and "environment". Also the colored sculptures and mural paintings of these ancient buildings are remarkably beautiful.

Mount Taishan has preserved many typical geological remains and landforms. The colorful scenes and wonderful sights were turned into breath-taking natural beauty, attracting literati to glorify over the centuries.

The favorable environments have provided an ideal habitat for animals and plants. There are 1,037 species of high-grade plants and 18,195 ancient trees, among which there are famous "Qin Pine", "Han Cypress", "Six-dynasty Pine", "Greeting Pine", "Tang Cypress" and "Song Gingko". They have all witnessed the emperors' worship to the heaven and offerings of sacrifices in ancient times. Among the aquatic lives red pigment fish is the most precious, used to be a kind of sacrifice, also one of the five most rare edible fish in China.

⊙ Highlights

Daimiao Temple The biggest ancient architecture complex existent on Mount Taishan, it is so named because Mount Taishan is also referred to as "Daizong". Mainly used for worshiping the mountain god, the temple is therefore called the "East Mountain God Mansion". Along its central axis sits the Zhengyang Gate, Peitian Gate, Ren'an Gate, Tiankuang Hall, Houqing Palace and Houzai Gate, representing the typical Chinese palatial architecture. The main building, Songtiankuang Hall, is one of the three most renowned palatial architectures in China, built for the purpose of worshiping gods of the mountain. Daimiao Temple is a key site of historical relics under state protection in China.

Jingshi Valley and Tang Rock Inscriptions On a large stone surface to the northeast of Doumu Palace are inscribed part of the Diamond Sutra written by a calligrapher in the Northern Qi Dynasty (550-577). Originally there were 2,500 characters, now there exist 1,067. These characters, each with a height of 50 cm, are gracefully written and regarded as "the eldest of big characters" and the treasure of Buddhism at Mount Taishan. On the Daguan Peak the stone inscriptions were carved on the cliffs, among which the most famous is Inscriptions of Taishan, written by Emperor Xuanzong in the 13th year of Kaiyuan in the Tang Dynasty (725). This imperial stone inscription is 13.3 m high and 5.5 m wide, totaling 1,000 characters. Both Jingshi Valley and Tang Stone Inscriptions are key sites of historical relics under state protection in China.

Jingshi Valley

Visiting place of Confucius

Tiankuang Hall, Daimiao Temple

Tiandi (Heaven-Earth) Square

Sister Pines

The Eighteen Bends Situated under the South Heaven Gate, it was called ring roads in the Han Dynasty and the present winding road took shape in the Tang Dynasty (618-907). It was so named because the road was winding up on the dangerous mountain slopes. Its vertical height is over 400 m with 79 winds, totaling 1,633 stairs. Above the Eighteen Bends is the South Heaven Gate, a symbol of Mount Taishan.

Imperial Path In history there were four imperial paths leading to the summit of Mount Taishan: the Zhou Imperial Path after King Wenwang, the Qin Imperial Path after the first Qin Emperor, the Han Imperial Path after Emperor Wudi, and the Tang Imperial Path after Emperor Gaozong. The Tang Imperial Path is today's main route up the mountain since the Tang Dynasty.

⊙ Information

■ **Transportation** *Tourists can take the flight to Jinan Yaoqiang Airport, then travel along the expressway to Tai'an. Beijing-Shanghai railway can get to Taishan Station directly. From Jinan to Tai'an there are trains at one-hour intervals and the bus service every 15 minutes.*

There are many paths up Mount Taishan. Tang Imperial Path: visitors can walk from the foot of the mountain to Daiding in 2 ~ 5 hours; or to the Middle Heaven Gate and take cable-car to Daiding. Tianwai Village tourist line: take a bus at Tianwai Village Square directly to the Middle Heaven Gate. Tianzhu Peak tourist line: start from the eastern suburb of Tai'an to walk northward along Taifo Road to Saozhou Valley at Aiwa Village. Lingyan Temple tourist area is 30 km from Tai'an City. Taohuayuan tourist line: start from Tai'an via national road 104 to the north for 5 km, then take Taohuayuan Tourist Road, take cable-car from Taohuayuan to the summit. Mountain winding tourist line goes on the southern side of Mount Taishan. From Tai'an Railway Station there are tourist buses to Tianzhu Peak and Taohuayuan.

■ **Accommodation** *Visitors can accommodate at four-star Huaqiao Hotel, three-star Taishan Hotel, Yuzuo Hotel, Shenqi Hotel, Dongdu Hotel, Hongmen Hotel, and one-star Xianju Hotel.*

■ **Food** *Local dishes feature Taishan tofu banquet and three-flavor soup (cabbage, tofu and water); local snacks are Taishan pan-cake and Dongping porridge.*

■ **Others** *Local products include Taishan Lingzhi (Ganoderma lucidum), Hongyu apricot, Feicheng peach, chestnut, walnut, tea, red pigment fish, Yanzi stone, Ningyang cricket, and medicinal herbs.*

Inquiry telephone: 0538-8272114, 8208583

Temple and Cemetery of Confucius and the Kong Family Mansion in Qufu

☐ **Name:**

Temple and Cemetery of Confucius and the Kong Family Mansion in Qufu

☐ **Geographical coordinates:**

35° 36' 42" N, 116° 58' 30" E

☐ **Date of inscription:**

December 17, 1994

☐ **Criteria for inclusion:**

I, IV, VI of cultural properties

Front hall of Kong Family Mansion

☉ Overview

It is due to the position and influence of Confucius in the 2,500-year history of China, that the Temple and Cemetery of Confucius and the Kong Family Mansion, situated in Qufu City, Shandong Province, enjoy great prestige in the world. Confucius (551-479 BC) was the great philosopher, politician and educator of ancient China. The Confucianism, centering on virtuous and benevolent governance, was widely accepted in feudal China and other Asian countries. Confucius has been therefore honored as "a model teacher for myriads of generations". In the 18th Century, Confucianism spread to Europe and had a substantial impact on the enlightenment movement. To show their respect and worship for Confucius and his thought, the governments of subsequent dynasties had built and preserved the grand Temple and Cemetery of Confucius and the Kong Family Mansion in Qufu, the hometown of Confucius.

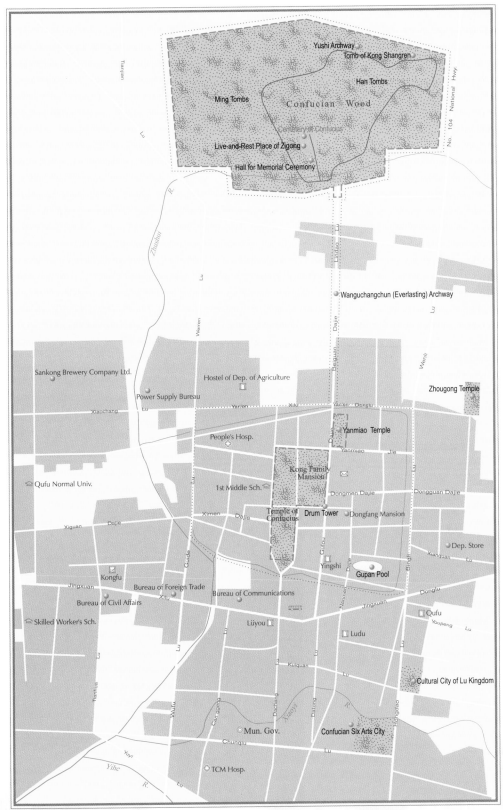

Qufu

⊙ Description

Confucian Temple is the place for worshipping Confucius. There are more than 2,000 Confucian Temples in Asia. The Temple of Confucius in Qufu is not only the principal one, but also the oldest, largest and most architecturally representative. Located in the center of Qufu City, the temple, which has gradually developed on the basis of Confucius' residence, is a massive, magnificent ancient building complex with the flavor of oriental architecture.

The Temple of Confucius houses over 1,000 steles dated from 149 BC to 1949 AD. They are not only precious resources for the study of the politics, philosophy and culture of various dynasties, the history of the Temple, but also the treasure of Chinese calligraphy. The Temple houses a large number of stone carvings, especially well-known are the Han Dynasty stone portraits, stone carvings depicting Confucius' deeds and stone-carved dragon columns of the Ming and Qing dynasties.

The Cemetery of Confucius, located on the southern bank of Sihe River in the north of Qufu City, is the burial ground of Confucius and his descendants. The Cemetery is the largest and longest-lasting family mausoleum in the world. Since the Han Dynasty, the descendants of Confucius have erected tombstones there. There are more than 4,000 tombstones of the Han (206 BC-220 AD), Song, Jin, Yuan, Ming, Qing (960-1911) dynasties and the Republic of China (1911-1949), making up the largest stele forest in China. The Cemetery is an open-air museum of tombs, buildings, stone carvings and steles, as well as a natural botanical garden.

The Kong Family Mansion was the official manor of Confucius' direct line of descent who were bestowed the title of Yan Shenggong by the emperor. Located to the east of the Temple of Confucius, the mansion also keeps documents and files of the Ming and Qing dynasties, which record the various activities in the mansion over 400 years. The 60,000-odd files are the largest and oldest private archives, and are of great value to the research of the history of Ming and Qing dynasties, especially the economy of that time.

The Temple and Cemetery of Confucius and the Kong Family Mansion were built over the feudal dynasties, strictly according to Confucian thought. With their neat format, orderly layout and rich commemorative significance, these complexes hold a special position among Chinese ancient temples, mausoleums and official mansions. They have also had great impact on commemorative buildings, gardens and residences in Chinese and oriental cultural spheres. In oriental countries there remain quite a few buildings with a strong style and favor completely different from those of the western culture. The existent Temple and Cemetery of Confucius and the Kong Family Mansion, last completed in the Ming and Qing dynasties by a large number of craftsmen, represent the unique artistic and aesthetic achievements of Chinese architecture at that time. The Temple of Confucius, in particular, reflects the style of Confucian architecture. Confucianism stressed "harmony", in politics, philosophy, ethics, as well as in aesthetics, which was an important characteristic of Chinese art. In the Temple of Confucius, buildings are set amid the green trees; the interior and exterior are interlinked; variations and coordination exist between different buildings and between the details and the whole of each building. The building complex of the Temple is undoubtedly a masterpiece and model of the architectural aesthetics of "harmony".

⊙ Highlights

Dacheng (Great Attainment) Hall This is the main hall of the Temple of Confucius. It was first built in the Song Dynasty during the year of Congning (1102-1107) and had been repaired and expanded in the following years. The existent building was last renovated in the Qing Dynasty. The hall, 24.45 m high and 45 m wide, with multiple-eave and nine-ridge, is resplendent and magnificent. The hall has 10 stone pillars, bearing exquisitely carved dragons. In the center of the hall is placed the picture of Confucius, flanked by the sculptures of Confucius' four disciples, and twelve great scholars.

Portrait of Confucius

Dacheng Hall, Temple of Confucius

Cemetery of Confucius Confucius was born in 551 BC and died in 479 BC at the age of 73. His disciples buried him at Sishang, north of the town of Lucheng. They guarded the tomb for three years before leaving. On the stone tablet in front of the tomb are seal calligraphy style carved characters, which translate as: "Tomb of The Greatest, Holiest, King of Culture". On the east side of the tomb of Confucius is the tomb of Kong Li, his son; and on the front is the tomb of Kong Ji, his grandson. This tomb pattern is called "carrying the son while holding the grandson", indicating a flourishing population and continuing family line.

Thirteen Stele Pavilions The pavilions are standing in two rows in the sixth courtyard of the Temple of Confucius. They were built to protect the imperial steles erected by the emperors. In the pavilions are 53 steles of the Tang, Song, Jin, Yuan, Ming and Qing Dynasties and the Republic of China, which record the development of Confucianism as well as the history and expansion of the Confucian Temple. The inscriptions were written in Chinese, Manchurian and Phags-pa Script. The two oldest buildings built in the Jin Dynasty (1195) and preserving the architectural style of that time, are the oldest buildings in the Temple.

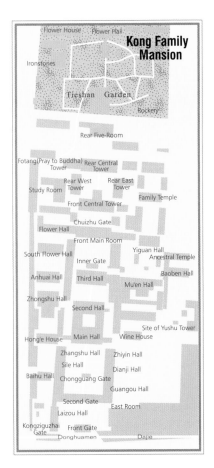

Kong Family Mansion

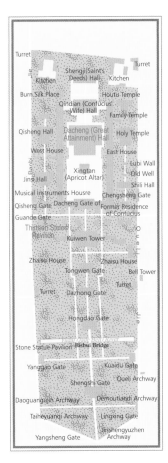

Temple of Confucius

Tomb of Confucius

⊙ Information

■ **Transportation** *National roads 327 and 104, Beijing-Fujian Expressway, Beijing-Shanghai Railway and Yanzhou-Shijiazhuang Railway run across the area.*

■ **Accommodation** *There are the three-star Queli Hotel, two-star Xingtan Hotel and Qufu Hotel, etc.*

■ **Food** *Local flavor dishes include Smoked Beancurd, Kong Family Hotpot and Steamed Duck.*

■ **Others** *Fragrant rice, Guodan apricot and mineral water are known as the "three treasures of Qufu". The Kong Family Mansion liquor, Kaidiao Wood Carving, woolen carpet, Dragon-head walking stick and Nishan Inkstone are the five specialties of central Shandong.*

Opening hours 8:00 ~ 17:00
Inquiry telephones: 0537-4412516, 4412444

HENAN PROVINCE

General Information

Henan, also called Yu in short, has its capital in Zhengzhou City. With an area of more than 160,000 sq km, it has under its administrative jurisdiction 17 prefecture-level cities, 21 county-level cities and 89 counties. The province has a population of 96.83 million and ethnic groups including Han, Hui, Mongol, Man, Miao and Yi.

Environment

Henan is located at the middle and lower reaches of the Yellow River. The terrain is descending from west to east, and the province is surrounded by mountains in the north, west and south. In the east are vast plains. Within the province are four river systems composed of the Yellow River, Huaihe River, Weihe River and Hanshui River. Its southern part and northern part are influenced by subtropical humid monsoon climate and warm temperate semi-humid monsoon climate respectively. The average temperature is -2 ~ 2°C in January and 26 ~ 28°C in July, with an average annual rainfall between 500 ~ 900 mm.

Places of Interest

Henan is one of the cradles of the Chinese civilization, and historical and cultural sites can be seen everywhere in the land of the central plains. There are 96 key sites of cultural relics under state protection, all of which are "National Treasures", and the province has the largest number of underground cultural relics across the country. Of the seven major ancient capitals in China, the ancient city of Anyang during the Yin and Shang dynasties, the ancient city of Luoyang for nine dynasties, and the ancient city of Kaifeng for seven dynasties are located within the territory of Henan. There are also the famous historical and cultural cities such as Zhengzhou, Nanyang, Shangqiu and Junxian. Luoyang has the Longmen Grottoes that is included in the World Heritage List, and the first Buddhist temple in China—the Baima (White Horse) Temple. In Kaifeng there are Iron Tower and Dragon Pagoda. The historical site of Yin Ruins and Wenfeng Tower are located in Anyang. In the province there are many landscapes of human culture and hundreds of tourist attractions such as Shaolin Temple, Guanlin, the Qingmingshanghe Garden, and the Baogong Temple.

Natural landscapes in Henan Province are mainly the Middle Sacred Mountain of Songshan and the natural landscape group of the Yellow River. Songshan Mountain, Longmen, Jigong Mountain, Shiren Mountain, Wangwu Mountain-Yuntai Mountain and Linlu Mountain are state-level scenic areas. The Hongqi (Red Flag) Canal, the Grand Canyon of Taihang Mountains, and the Baiyun Mountain have attracted large numbers of foreign and domestic tourists.

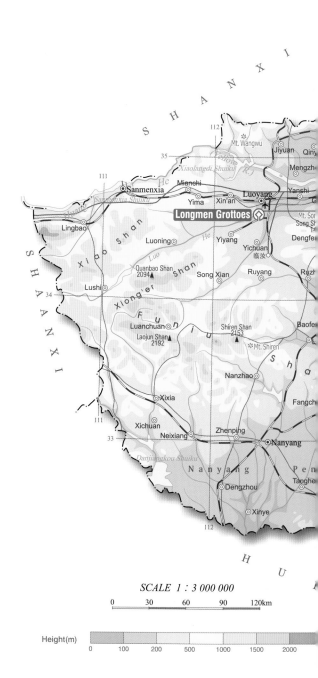

SCALE 1 : 3 000 000

Height(m)

Local Specialties

The tussah cocoon of Funiu Mountain, Xinzheng dates, Xinyang tippy tea, Luoyang tri-color painted earthware, Jun porcelain of Yuzhou, and Bianzhou embroidery of Kaifeng.

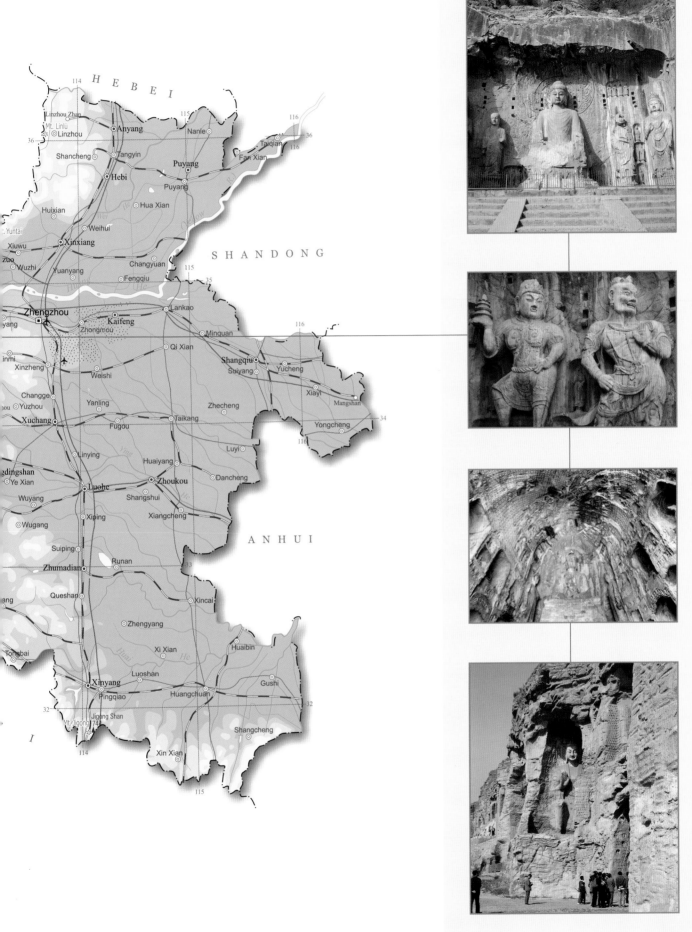

Longmen Grottoes

☐ **Name:**
Longmen Grottoes

☐ **Geographical coordinates:**
34° 33' N, 112° 28' E

☐ **Date of inscription:**
November 30, 2000

☐ **Criteria for inclusion:**
I, II, III of cultural properties

Binyang Cave

⊙ Overview

Located 12 km south of Luoyang, a Chinese city reputed for its history and culture, the Longmen Grottoes is an extremely important component part of the Chinese art of rock carving, and has made great contributions to the Chinese art of grotto sculpture. From the very beginning, the statuary art had developed a characteristic of its own and a trend of localization and popularization. As a typical example of the art of imperial rock carving, the Grottoes is a site of biggest concentration of statues produced by the nobilities of the Northern Wei and the Tang dynasties (316-907) to express their wishes and aspirations and carries a dense tint of the national religion.

The Longmen Grottoes also stands as the most splendid and magnificent chapter in the world art of rock carving from the end of the 5th Century to the middle of the 8th Century, and one of the existent treasure houses of ancient art in the world. Kept here are more than 2,300 grottoes, over 100,000 statues, and carved inscriptions totaling more than 300,000 Chinese characters. Usually regarded as a "stone history" covering various disciplines of study, the carved inscriptions here, totaling 2,840 pieces, rank first in the world in terms of their number.

The Longmen Grottoes is an integration of many Buddhist sects including the Avatamasaka Sect, the Zen Sect, the Sukhavati Sect, the Esoteric Sect, and the Faxiang Sect. This reflects its central position in the early period and heyday of

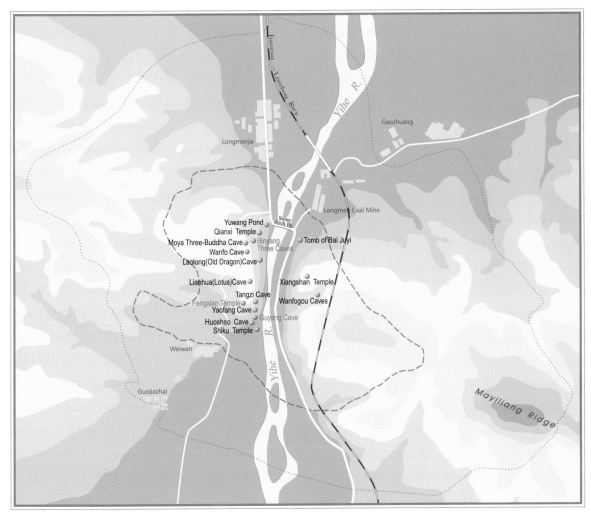

Longmen Grottoes

Tang Dynasty and provides material evidences for the study of the activities and course of development of the rites of different Buddhist sects.

⊙ Description

Located in an area flanked by two hills, and cut through in the middle by the Yihe River, the Longmen Grottoes was anciently known as Shique (buildings at the sides of ancient city gates or imperial palaces) for its natural shape. Because the area lies in the south of the capital, and ancient emperors usually likened themselves to the Son of the Heaven, it got its present name Longmen, meaning the "Dragon Gate". Longmen used to be a strategic pass and communication hub in ancient times. With green hills, clear waters, quiet environment, and comfortable climate, it has always been a resort patronized by scholars and men of letters. Also, the fine quality of the rock here is ideal for carving, so it was chosen as the site to build the grottoes.

The rocks of the area where Longmen Grottoes is situated are limestone formed by the orogenic movement in the Cambrian period (500 million years ago) or Carboniferous period (270 million years ago). The West Hill is 263.9 m above sea level and the East Hill is 303.5 m above sea level. When reaching the river, the hills

become precipitous and imposing. Into the hill face stretching for 1,000 meters along the river were carved grottoes sitting closely to each other like a honeycomb. Carving of grottoes at Longmen started around 493 AD, when Emperor Xiaowen of the Northern Wei Dynasty moved the capital to Luoyang. The carving continued for more than 400 years down through the dynasties of the Eastern Wei, Western Wei, Northern Qi, Sui, Tang and the Five Dynasties, to the Song dynasties, reaching its heyday between 5th-8th Century. The Longmen Grottoes is a typical example of the art of rock carving in the late early period and the middle period of Chinese history, and is world renown for its great number, big scale, delicate skill, diversified subjects, and rich in connotations. The statues carved in the Northern Wei and the Tang dynasties reached the peak of the art at that time, and differed themselves from those of other periods in terms of their unique imperial and localized style. It is also known as "the Forest of Ancient Steles" for the great number of carved inscriptions. The extensiveness of its coverage of various Buddhist sects and even Taoist themes is unusual for other rock carvings. Longmen Grottoes is incomparable for its time span of carving, advantageous location, and beautiful environment. The large number of material images and written evidences here have not only reflected, from different angles, the political, economic, religious, and cultural developments and

Fengxian Temple

changes in ancient China, but also contributed tremendously to the innovation and development of the Chinese art of rock carving. There are now more than 2,300 grottoes of different sizes lying in the two hills which house over 100,000 Buddhist statues, 2,800 carved inscriptions, and 70 stone-carved Buddhist pagodas. On the cliffs of the West Hill there are more than 50 large and medium-sized grottoes, with Guyang Cave, Binyang Middle Cave, Lianhua Cave, Huangpugong Cave, Weizi Cave, Putai Cave, Huoshao Cave, Cixiang Cave and Ludong Cave being the typical representatives carved during the Northern Wei Dynasty (386-534); the Qianxi Temple, Binyang Southern Cave, Binyang Northern Cave, Jingshan Temple, Moya Three-Buddha Cave, Wanfo Cave, Huijian Cave, the Fengxian Temple, Jingtu Hall, Longhua Temple, and Jinan Cave being the representatives carved in the Tang Dynasty (618-907). The grottoes in the East Hill, including 20 large and medium-sized ones such as Erlianhua Cave, Kanjingsi Cave, Dawanwufu Cave (also known as the Leigutai No. 3 Cave) and the Gaopingjunwang Cave, were all carved in the Tang Dynasty.

Luoyang has long been the center of Chinese Buddhism. Today there still exist over 10 locations of medium-sized and small grottoes around Longmen Grottoes. All these grottoes were carved under the influence of the Longmen Grottoes, but they compare unfavorably with Longmen Grottoes in terms of their time of carving, scale, number of artistic works, artistic achievements, and state of preservation. Thus Longmen Grottoes may be rated as the central grottoes of the grottoes in Central China.

⊙ Highlights

Fengxian Temple Initiated by Emperor Gaozong of the Tang Dynasty, Fengxian Temple was completed in the 2nd year of Shangyuan in the Tang Dynasty (675), with a donation from Empress Wu Zetian. It is the biggest among the grottoes at Longmen and most typical of the art of carving during the Tang Dynasty. Located in the temple are nine big statues including one Buddha, two Disciples, two Lokapalas, and two Vajras. The 17.14 m main statue, that of Vairocana, has a plump face looking solemn and graceful and moon-like brows above two eyes looking downward, the idealized image of a saint; Ananda wears gentle, quiet, meek and simplistic looks; Kasyapa has solemn, magnificent and self-restrained expressions; the Lokapalas look serious, powerful and strong; and the Vajras are firm, strong, and irritable. The Fengxian Temple, representing the greatest attainment in the art of statue carving during the Tang Dynasty, is a typical example of Buddhist art.

Guyang Cave Guyang Cave is the earliest grotto carved at Longmen and most rich in contents. Carved around 493 AD, it has been proved to be a cave of great merits built by Emperor Xiaowen of the Northern Wei Dynasty for his grandmother. Standing in the front wall are three statues built by Emperor Xiaowen, and covering the inner ceiling and other parts of the cave are shrines of different sizes and styles. Three lines of big shrines were well located in the southern and northern walls, with carvers' inscriptions attached to the shrines. Totaling over 800 in number, the cave ranks first in China in terms of carvers' inscriptions. Of the

Lokapala and Vajra

20 masterpiece inscriptions written in the Weibei style at the Longmen Grottoes, 19 lie in this cave. All the statues inside the cave are slender in figure, typical of the body shape in vogue during the late days of the Northern Wei Dynasty.

Binyang Middle Cave The Binyang Middle Cave and the two neighboring caves in the south and north form a group. It is a cave of great merits carved by Emperor Xuanwu of the Northern Wei Dynasty in the early 6th Century in memory of his father, Emperor Xiaowen. The carving started in 500 AD and was brought to an uncompleted end 24 years later, during which 802,366 laborers were involved. Of the three planned, only Binyang Middle Cave was completed. In the main wall of the cave were carved five statues. Also housed in the cave were the Bud-

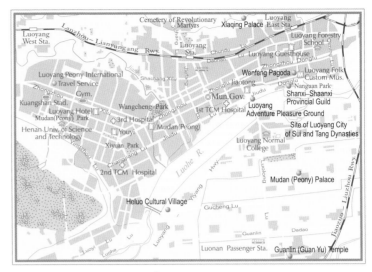

Guyang Cave

dha of the Past, the Buddha of the Present and the Buddha of the Future. One big relief stands on each side of the front wall of the cave, with the one in the north featuring Emperor Xiaowen and his retinues paying homage to the Buddha, and the one in the south featuring Empress Wenzhao and her girl attendants paying homage to the Buddha. Above each relief is the statue of Vimalakirti and that of Manjusri facing each other and a picture telling the story of the birth of the Buddha. The Binyang Middle Cave may be rated as an important representative of the Buddhist cave temples of the early 6th Century.

⊙ Information

■ **Transportation** *Longmen scenic area is easy of access. Visitors may take Bus No.81 at Luoyang Railway Station, Bus No.60 at Gushuixi, or Bus No.53 at Xiguan.*

■ **Accommodation** *Dongshan Guesthouse is a three-star garden-like hotel located in the Longmen scenic area, with a quiet and graceful environment and all facilities including villas, luxurious suites and standard guestrooms.*

■ **Food** *Zhenbutong Restaurant offers dishes of local flavors including Luoyang Shuixi (Water Banquet) and Jiangmiantiao noodle.*

■ **Others** *Trio-colored glazed pottery and duplicated bronzes are special local handicrafts.*

Opening hours: 7:00 ~ 18:00
Inquiry telephones: 0379-5980972; 5981299
Website: www.longmen.gov.cn

A Panorama of West Hil, Longmen

HUBEI PROVINCE

General Information

Hubei Province, also called E in short, has its capital in Wuhan City. With an area of more than 180,000 sq km, it has under its administrative jurisdiction 12 prefecture-level cities, 1 autonomous prefecture, 24 county-level cities, 37 counties, 2 autonomous counties and 1 forest district. The province has a population of 59.78 million and ethnic groups including Han, Tujia, Miao, Hui, Dong and Man.

Environment

It is located at the middle reaches of the Yangtze River and north of the Dongting Lake. The terrain of the province descends from west to east, featured with hills and hilly lands. The Hanjiang Plain lies in the southeast. The province has numerous lakes, thus known as the "province of a thousand lakes". It has a subtropical humid monsoon climate. The average temperature is 1 ~ 6°C in January and 24 ~ 30°C in July, with an average annual rainfall between 750 ~ 1,500 mm.

Places of Interest

"The land of rivers and lakes boast beautiful landscapes, and the province of scenic spots stands out abundant with historical sites." In Hubei, there are the Yellow Crane Tower that reminds visitors of the ancient verse "Only white clouds still float in vain from year to year"; the ancient zither-playing terrace where Yu Boya smashed his musical instrument in memory of his deceased bosom friend; Chibi, where Zhou Yu beat Cao Cao's troops with a overwhelming victory during the Three Kingdom Period; and Zigui, the hometown of the great Chinese poet Qu Yuan. The Zenghouyi bell set chimes represent the local culture of Hubei, and the Gezhouba Dam are triumphant songs of the new times. Jiangling, Wuhan, Xiangfan, Suizhou and Zhongxiang are China's famous historical and cultural cities. The ancient architectural complex on the Wudang Mountains and the Xianling Tomb of the Imperial Tombs of the Ming and Qing Dynasties are listed in the World Heritage List.

The East Lake of Wuhan, Wudang Mountain, Dahong Mountain, Longzhong, Jiugong Mountain and Lushui are state-level scenic areas. Hundreds of lakes with Yunmeng Lake as the best representative, the far-reaching peaks of the Wudang Mountain, the age-old primitive forests of Shennongjia and the mysterious wildlife world are the best places for sci-

② Imperial Tombs of the Ming and Qing Dynasties

entists to conduct scientific research and for curious tourists to seek adventures.

Local Specialties

Wuchang fish, lotus seed of Honghu Lake, osmanthus flower of Xianning, raw lacquer of Lichuan, the Chinese wood oil of Laifeng, navel oranges of Zigui, sweet oranges of Yichang and sesame candy of Xiaogan.

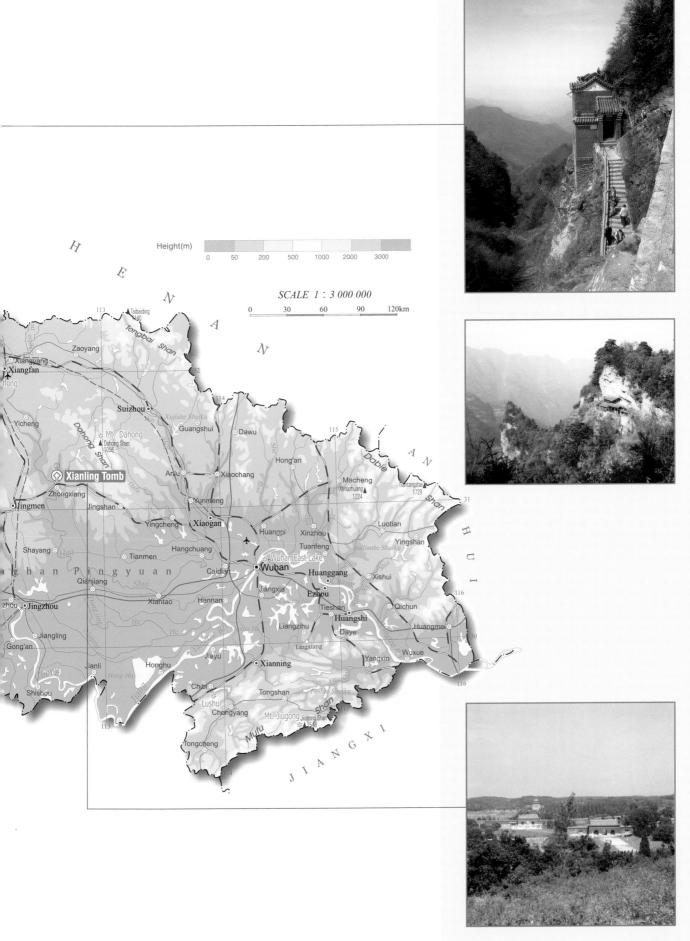

SCALE 1 : 3 000 000

Height(m)

0   50   200   500   1000   2000   3000

0   30   60   90   120km

H
E
N
A
N

Taibaiding
1140
Tongbai Shan

Zaoyang

Xiangyang
Xiangfan
hong

Yicheng

Suizhou

Guangshui   Dawu

Xujiahe Shuiku

Mt. Dahong
Dahong Shan
1056

Dabie Shan
A
N
H
U
I

Hong'an

Macheng
Ximazhuang
1224

Tiantangzhai
1729

31

Zhongxiang

Anlu   Xiaochang

Xianling Tomb

Jingmen   Jingshan

Yingcheng   Xiaogan

Yunmeng

Luotian

Xinzhou

Tuanfeng   Yingshan

Huangpi

Bailianhe Shuiku

Shayang

Tianmen

Hangchuang

Wuhan East Lake
Wuhan

Qianjiang
Caidian

Jiangxia

Huanggang

Xishui

116

Xiantao

Hannan

Ezhou

ghan Pingyuan

Tieshan

Qichun

zhou Jingzhou
He

Liangzihu
Huangshi

Daye   Huangmei

30

Jiangling

Gong'an

Jianli   Honghu

Hong Hu

Jiayu

Lingxiang

Xianning

Yangxin   Wuxue

116

Shishou

Chibi

Lushui

Tongshan

Fushui Shuiku

Chongyang   Mt. Jiugong Jiugong Shan
1543

Mufu   Shan

113

Tongcheng

J I A N G X I

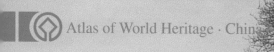
Ancient Building Complex in the Wudang Mountains

☐ **Name:**

Ancient Building Complex in the Wudang Mountains

☐ **Geographical coordinates:**

32° 22' 30" ~ 32° 35' 06" N,

110° 56' 15" ~ 111° 15' 23" E

☐ **Date of inscription:**

December 15, 1994

☐ **Criteria for inclusion:**

I, II, VI of cultural properties

Taihe Palace

⊙ Overview

Wudang Mountains, also known as Taihe Mountains, is situated in Shiyan City of Hubei Province, with an area of 400 km in diameter. The building complex had been planned and constructed under the direct command of emperors. Management of the architectural complex, in particular, came under the direct control of officials designated by emperors in the Ming Dynasty. Thus, the mountains offer important material evidence for the study of the politics of the Ming Dynasty and the evolution of Chinese religions. It is the most extraordinary Taoist temple existent in China in terms of size, rank, and numbers of statues and sacrificial vessels. The layout of the constructions has been planned in a harmonious way with local surroundings, setting a fine example of *fengshui* practices. The Golden Hall, with its bronze statues and tables, represented major development in China's science and technology as well as metallurgy in the 15th Century.

Turtle and snake, Golden Hall

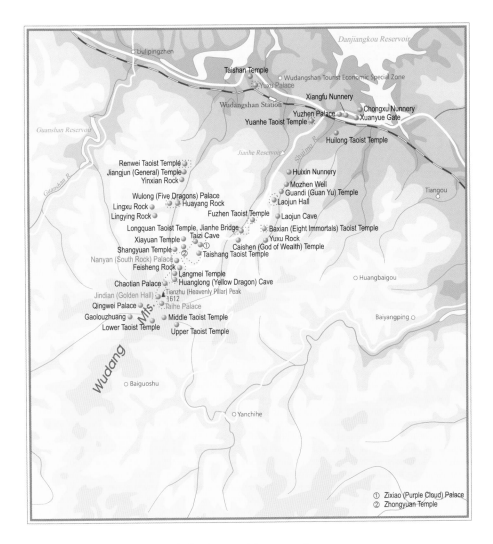

Map labels:
- Danjiangkou Reservoir
- Liulipingzhen
- Taishan Temple
- Wudangshan Tourist Economic Special Zone
- Yuxu Palace
- Xiangfu Nunnery
- Wudangshan Station
- Yuzhen Palace
- Chongxu Nunnery
- Yuanhe Taoist Temple
- Xuanyue Gate
- Guanshan Reservoir
- Huilong Taoist Temple
- Jianhe Reservoir
- Shuima R.
- Huixin Nunnery
- Renwei Taoist Temple
- Jiangjun (General) Temple
- Yinxian Rock
- Mozhen Well
- Guandi (Guan Yu) Temple
- Tiangou
- Guanshan R.
- Wulong (Five Dragons) Palace
- Huayang Rock
- Laojun Hall
- Lingxu Rock
- Lingying Rock
- Fuzhen Taoist Temple
- Laojun Cave
- Longquan Taoist Temple, Jianhe Bridge
- Baxian (Eight Immortals) Taoist Temple
- Xiayuan Temple
- Taizi Cave
- Yuxu Rock
- Shangyuan Temple
- ①
- Caishen (God of Wealth) Temple
- ②
- Taishang Taoist Temple
- Nanyan (South Rock) Palace
- Feisheng Rock
- Langmei Temple
- Huangbaigou
- Chaotian Palace
- Huanglong (Yellow Dragon) Cave
- Jindian (Golden Hall)
- Tianzhu (Heavenly Pillar) Peak
- 1612
- Qingwei Palace
- Taihe Palace
- Baiyangping
- Gaolouzhuang
- Middle Taoist Temple
- Lower Taoist Temple
- Upper Taoist Temple
- Wudang Mts.
- Baiguoshu
- Yanchihe
- ① Zixiao (Purple Cloud) Palace
- ② Zhongyuan Temple

Wudang Mountains

Description

Being an eastern branch of the Daba Mountains, Wudang Mountains is situated in the Qinling Mountains. Its main peak towers 1,612 m above sea level like a pillar holding up the sky, surrounded by 72 peaks and 24 creeks and rivers. Xu Xiake, a famous geographer of the Ming Dynasty, praised the place as being more of a feast to the eye than the Five Sacred Mountains of China.

The ancient architectural complex of Wudang Mountains was first built in the reign of Zhenguan in the Tang Dynasty (627-649) and expanded in the Song Dynasty. Kublai Khan, Emperor of the Yuan Dynasty (r.1260-1294), ordered to have the scope of architecture expanded for the purpose of gaining support from the masses. After Zhu Di, son of Zhu Yuanzhang, succeeded the throne, large construction took place from the 10th to 21st year of Yongle in the Ming Dynasty (1412-1423). Hence, a Taoist architectural complex comprising nine palaces, thirty-six halls and seventy-two temples was built. The emperor was so obsessed with Taoism that he also dispatched officials here to practice Taoism. In the 31st year of the of Jiajing (1552), another round of renovation and ex-

Zixiao Palace

Zixiao Palace

Golden Hall

pansion were undertaken. And a new marble archway was built. At the same time, Wudang Mountains was conferred the title "Grand Taihe Mountain" by the emperor. Since then, it became an imperial temple. For more than 200 years, every emperor of the Ming Dynasty, following the ancestors system, conducted conscientious maintenance and protection over the palaces.

What remained of the ancient architectural complex today are over 200 buildings, including six palaces of Taihe, Nanyan, Zixiao, Yuzhen, Yuxu and Wulong, the Taoist temples of Yuanhe and Fuzhen, and numerous nunneries, shrines and rock temples, with a floor space of 50,000 sq m and a total area of 100 ha.

There are over 10,000 pieces of cultural relics in the palaces and temples in Wudang Mountains, of which, more than 3,000 pieces are listed as the ones under Grade I state protection, including statues, stone tablets, scriptures, carvings, murals, color paintings, and Taoist musical instruments and sacrificial vessels. Sixty-two scenic spots featuring primarily ancient building complex and their sites are scattered in the vast scenic area, which covers 31,200 ha.

Nanyan scenery

⊙ Highlights

Zixiao (Purple Cloud) Palace Located under the Zhanqi Peak at an altitude of 804 m, it is one of the best-preserved palaces in Wudang Mountains. The palace was built in the reign of Xuanhe (1119-1125) in the Northern Song Dynasty. In the 10th year of Yongle in the Ming Dynasty (1412), over 160 structures were built, including Xuandi Hall and the gate, corridors and stele pavilions. An additional 860 rooms were built in the 31st year of Jiajing (1552) upon the instruction of Emperor Shizong of the Ming Dynasty.

Golden Hall Situated on top of the Tianzhu Peak, it has an altitude of 1,612 m. Built in the style of an imperial palace in the 14th year of Yongle (1416), the building facing the east was designed to stress the supremacy of religious authority. It is the oldest bronze hall existing in China.

Nanyan (South Rock) Palace Standing at an elevation of 964.7 m above sea level, the palace was first built in the Tang Dynasty and underwent expansion in the 10th year of Yongle of the Ming Dynasty (1413) when the emperor ordered the construction of over 460 rooms. In the 32nd year of Jiajing (1553), the palace was further expanded upon the mandate of the emperor, increasing the total number of rooms to more than 680. The rooms, built against the mountain, were combined harmoniously with the environment.

Yuxu Palace Legends had it that Zhang Sanfeng, a renowned Taoist of the late Yuan Dynasty, once lived here. The palace was the headquarters for the expansion of the architectures in the reign of Emperor Yongle of the Ming Dynasty. The biggest palace in Wudang Mountains, it was built as a virtual replica of the imperial palace. In the reign of Emperor Wanli (1575), the eastern and western auxiliary palaces were expanded. The whole palace had more than 2,000 rooms.

Statue in the Golden Hall

Luocheng City of Yuxu Palace

⊙ Information

■ **Transportation** *Air flights connect Wudang Airport with Beijing, Guangzhou, Xi'an and other major cities. A railway leading from Wuhan to Chongqing also cuts across the mountain. Trains from Beijing, Shanghai, Guangzhou, Xiamen, Fuzhou, Qingdao, Wuhan, Zhengzhou, Xi'an, Luoyang, Zhanjiang, Huaihua and other cities also stop here. Provincial road 316 and national road 209 also pass the place, and the Shiyan-Xiangfan section of Yinchuan-Wuhan expressway has been completed.*

■ **Accommodation** *Wudangshan Hotel, Baihui Villa, Dianli Hotel, Xuanwu Hotel, Guoshui Hotel are among the relatively well-*

equipped hotels. Up in the mountain, in the area around Wuyaling there are many hotels and hostels. One can also stay in the temple up in the mountain to gain a glimpse of the life of monks.

■ **Food** *Taoist cuisine is unique and worth a try. There is a street in imitation of ancient times, where snack stores line up together, offering a variety of delicacies.*

■ **Others** *Local products include Wudang tea, mushrooms, kiwi fruit, Ginkgo, Wudang Sword.*

Inquiry telephones: 0719-5689187, 5668567, 5665396, 5665639

Overlooking the front gate

HUNAN PROVINCE

General Information

Hunan Province, also called Xiang in short, has its capital in Changsha City. With an area of 210,000 sq km, it has under its administrative jurisdiction 13 prefecture-level cities, 1 autonomous prefecture, 16 county-level cities, 65 counties, and 7 autonomous counties. The province has a population of 65.64 million and ethnic groups include Han, Tujia, Miao, Dong, Yao, Bai, Hui and Zhuang.

Environment

Located on the southern side of the middle reaches of the Yangtze River. The province is a U-shaped basin surrounded by mountains in the east, south and west. The hilly and mountainous areas account for more than 80% with lakes making up less than 20%. Scattered with numerous lakes, the province is best known as "the land of fish and rice". It has a subtropical humid monsoon climate. The average temperature is 3 ~ 8°C in January and 27 ~ 30°C in July, with an average annual rainfall between 1,250 ~ 1,750 mm.

Places of Interest

Hunan Province has a long history with rich human and cultural resources. The tombs of Chinese forefathers Emperor Yandi and Emperor Shundi are worshipped by their offspring. The plain feather-like silk gown unearthed from the Mawangdui Tomb of the Han Dynasty and the bamboo slips of the Three Kingdoms Period uncovered at Zoumalou are famous both at home and broad. The Shaoshanchong village is the birthplace of Mao Zedong, and the water of the Dongting Lake nourished Qu Yuan, Cai Lun, Tan Sitong and Qi Baishi. Famous cities like Changsha, Yueyang and Fenghuang have a history as fine as poems, paintings and essays, as well as ever-lasting songs.

Hunan has a vast area that bring together great mountains and beautiful rivers and lakes. The Hengshan Mountain, Wulingyuan in Zhangjiajie, Yueyang Tower, Dongting Lake, Shaoshan, Yuelu Mountain, Langshan Mountain, Mengdong River and Taohuayuan have been designated as state-level scenic areas. Wulingyuan has been included in the World Heritage List. Diversified tourist events such as the International Dragon Boat Festival in Yueyang, the International Firecracker Festival in Changsha, the International Forest Conservation Festival in Zhangjiajie, and the International Month of Rafting on the Mengdong River have been a plus for the scenic areas.

Local Specialties

Royal Junshan tea, China fir in western Hunan, Xiang Embroidery of Changsha, Liling chinaware, Chinese linen of Liuyang, dry hot pepper of Baoqing, firecrackers of Liuyang, and bamboo products of Yiyang.

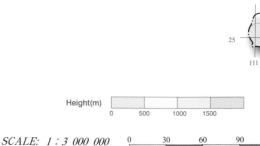

Height(m)

SCALE: 1 : 3 000 000

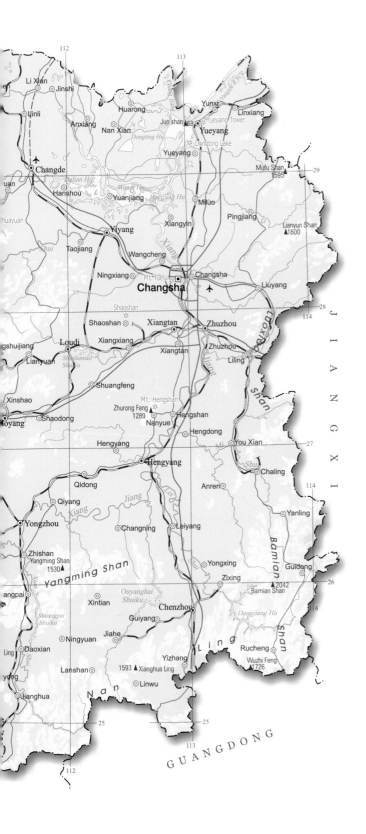

Wulingyuan Scenic and Historic Interest Area

☐ **Name:**

Wulingyuan Scenic and Historic Interest Area

☐ **Geographical coordinates:**

29° 16' 25" ~ 29° 24' 25" N,
110° 20' 30" ~ 110° 41' 15" E

☐ **Date of inscription:**

December 14, 1992

☐ **Criterion for inclusion:**

III of natural properties

Tianzishan

⊙ Overview

Wulingyuan, located at the upper and middle reaches of Lishui River in the northwest of Hunan Province, is a part of the Wuling Mountains. It covers a total area of 397 sq km, with the core scenic area of 264 sq km. It is renowned throughout the world for the unique landform of narrow sandstone pillars and peaks. The highest peak in the scenic area is 1,264.5 m, while the lowest measures 269 m. The relative height difference is about 1,000 m. With precipitous cliffs, deep valleys, clear creeks, lush forests and mysterious caves, the resort commands a breathtaking view. The region is a habitat of many ancient and rare plants, as well as some plants which are unique to China, hence it is praised as "Memento of the Earth". Wulingyuan is a state-level scenic area in China.

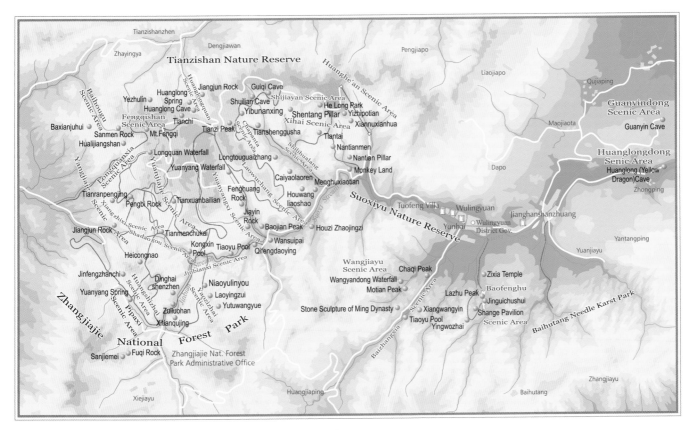

Wulingyuan

⊙ Description

Situated in humid monsoon climate region in the northern meso-subtropical zone, Wulingyuan is endowed not only with sandstone peaks and pillars, but also with spectacular karst landscapes, which is the epitome of karst landscapes in South Asia and East Asia. Heavy rainfall and high humidity result in wonderful phenomena of seas of clouds.

There are 3,103 precipitous sandstone peaks in Wulingyuan, of which 243 are higher than 1000 m. The mountains rise up from the ground in such an abrupt way that they look like pillars up-holding the sky.

Wulingyuan is bestowed with numerous creeks and ravines, where the scenery is beautiful, with birds chirping and flowers blossoming. There are 32 gullies longer than 2000 m, totaling 84 km in length, the famous ones being the Ten Mile Gallery, Jinbian Creek, and Heicao Gully.

Wulingyuan is rich in karst caves, including Huanglong Cave, Guanyin Cave, Xiangshui Cave, Guiqi Cave, Feiyun Cave, Jinluo Cave. Major scenic zones and spots are Huangshizhai, Yuanjiajie,

Zhangjiajie

Houhuayuan, Wulongzhai, Yangjiajie, Nantianmen, Xihai, Helong Park, Dianjiangtai, Shentangwan, Xianren Bridge, Baofeng Lake, and Huanglong Cave.

Wulingyuan has a complete ecological system, characterized by the rich resources of endangered animal and plant species. It is an important area in China where rare plants and animals gather. The region has a forest coverage rate of 92%, with distinct vertical zonation, complete plant communities, and stable ecological balance. Two second growth forests have be conserved, which reflect the original state of the ancient plant communities of the Yangtze River Valley. The old maidenhair tree, 50 m in height and 1.6 m in diameter, is renowned as a living fossil of the natural heritage. Surveys show that the resort has over 3000 species of higher plants including over 700 species of woody plants in 250 genera and 107 families, and over 450 species of flower plants. The unique-shaped Wuling pine, a specific plant, is widely distributed in the region. A total of 35 species of seed plants are among China's first list of rare and endangered plants under state protection. There are 119 species of vertebrates in 20 genera and 20 orders, of which 30 species are listed under state protection. Wulingyuan is thus praised as a "Natural Museum" and a "Natural Botanic Garden".

Sea of clouds

Highlights

Zhangjiajie National Forest Park It has a total area of 48 sq km, with a forest coverage rate of 97%. Zhangjiajie is noted for its oddly shaped peaks, serene waterscape, and beautiful woods. The forest park contains some 517 species of woody plants in 98 families, and its gymnosperm species account for half of the world's total. The key scenic spots are Huangshizhai, Jinbian Creek, Yaozizhai, Shadao Gully, Pipa Creek, and Yuanjiajie.

Suoxiyu With a total area of 147 sq km, it was so named because the Suoshui River flows through the core part of the area. This nature reserve boasts rich scenic resources such as karst caves, lakes, waterfalls, forests, sea of clouds, rare animals and birds, and rich vegetation resources. The scenic spots of Huanglong Cave, Baofeng Lake, Macaque Park, West Sea, Ten Mile Gallery and Baizhang Gorge are treasures of Wulingyuan.

Mirage

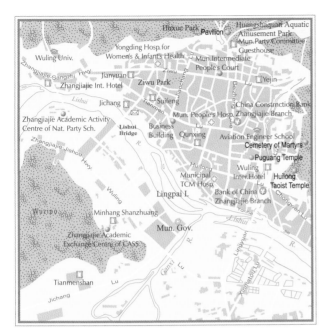

Morning glow at Xihai (West Sea)

Zhangjiajie

Tianzishan This nature reserve covers a total area of 67 sq km, and boasts a touring route that totals 40 km around the mountain. Yubi Peak is the most remarkable of its numerous towering peaks. There are also patches of primitive forest. The main peak, 1,262.5 m above sea level, is an ideal place for watching the sunrise and enjoying the natural surroundings.

Yangjiajie With a total area of 34 sq km, it is best known for the Longquan (Dragon Spring) Waterfall, reputed as "the First Wonderful Spring on Earth". Yangjiajie embodies the beauties of Zhangjiajie and Tianzishan. There are some 1,000 peaks scattered with creeks, ravines, springs and waterfalls as well as pools. The place also abounds with animal and plant resources.

☉ Information

Transportation *Zhangjiajie has air flights reaching over 20 cities of China. There are daily flights to Beijing, Shanghai, Guangzhou, Chengdu and Changsha. Railways connect Zhangjiajie with over 10 major cities. A highway links the downtown area with the scenic areas. Within the scenic areas there are eight pedestrian routes; there are also two roads in the park, one connects Suoxiyu with Zhangjiajie , and the other connects Helong Parkof Tianzishan with the Rear Garden of Yangjiajie.*

Accommodation *In the scenic areas there are seven hotels with star levels, as well as many family hotels.*

Food *The Tujia people's cuisine carries distinct features, with traces of Hunan cuisine. Local flavor dishes are preserved pig heads, loaches boring into tofu, etc.*

Others *Local specialties are kiwi fruit and preserved ham. Inquiry telephones: 0744-8380193*

A landscape painting

CHONGQING MUNICIPALITY

General Information

Chongqing, also called Yu in short, is a municipality directly under the central government. Chongqing has an area of 82,300 sq km, and has under its administrative jurisdiction 15 districts, 4 county-level cities, 17 counties and 4 autonomous counties. The municipality has a population of 31.14 million and ethnic groups including Han, Tujia, Miao, Hui, Mongol and Yi.

Environment

It is located in the southeast of the Sichuan Basin. In the east, west and south are mountainous areas, and in west and southwest are hilly areas and flat land. The trunk stream of the Yangtze River cuts through the whole territory. It has a middle subtropical humid monsoon climate. The average temperature is about 5°C in January and 27°C (29°C around Chongqing city proper) in July, with an average annual rainfall between 900 ~ 1,400 mm.

Places of Interest

Chongqing is a famous city with rich cultural and historical significance, boasting a 3,000-year history. The Baodingshan stone carving in Dazu is a treasure representing the late period art of stone grottoes and has been listed as the world cultural heritage. The Ghost City of Fengdu, Shibaozhai in Zhongzhou, Taibai Rock in Wanzhou, the Temple of Zhangfei in Yunyang and White Emperor City in Fengjie represent the best scenic spots of the Three Gorges area. The Longgupo site of Mount Wushan, the Red Crag Village and the Gele Mountain demonstrate the Bayu Culture and the spirit of Red Crag revolutionaries.

The mountains and rivers of Chongqing are famous for their natural beauty. There are the magnificent Three Gorges on the Yangtze River, the beautiful scenes of steep valley along the Greater and Lesser Ninghe rivers in Mount Wushan, the mysterious Sky Hole and Grand Crevice in Fengjie, the primitive forests on the Simian Mountain of Jiangjin, Furong River, south and north hot springs, Jinyun Mountain, Stone Forest of Wansheng in southern Chongqing, and Jinfo Forest Park in Nanchuan. All these scenic spots constitute an unmatched picturesque landscape. The night view of the mountain city of Chongqing is surely the best of all. Its fascinating stunning beauty remains ever-fresh in the memories of tourists.

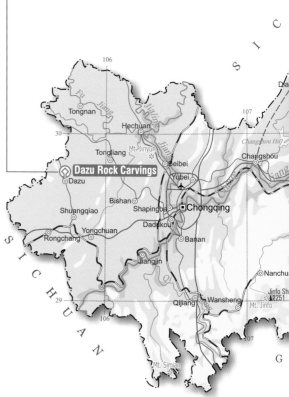

Local Specialties

Pomelo shaddock of Dianjiang, Hechuan red oranges, Fuling preserved pickle, Yongchuan fermented soya beans, Dazu bamboo knitting, Jiangjin oranges, Sichuan satin, Rongchang chinaware and Liangshan bamboo curtains.

SCALE 1 : 2 500 000

0   25   50   75   100km

Height(m)

100   200   500   1000   1500   2000

Dazu Rock Carvings

☐ **Name:**

Dazu Rock Carvings

☐ **Geographical coordinates:**

29° 22' 28" ~ 29° 51' 49" N,

105° 28' 06" ~ 106° 01' 56" E

☐ **Date of inscription:**

December 1, 1999

☐ **Criteria for inclusion:**

I, II, III of cultural properties

Nirvana of Sakyamuni

☉ Overview

Located in the junction area of the hills of Central Sichuan and the folded zone of East Sichuan and influenced by the lithology and water erosion, Dazu County has a typical hilly terrain composed of undulating ridges, peaks and terraced land.

Dazu Rock Carvings is the general name of the grottoes within Dazu County, Chongqing Municipality. Of these grottoes, 75 housing a total of over 50,000 statues have been declared sites of cultural relics under state protection, and the grottoes of Beishan, Baodingshan, Nanshan, Shimenshan and Shizhuanshan are the most typical examples. Carving of the statues started in the early Tang Dynasty and the Five Dynasties and flourished in the Southern and the Northern Song Dynasties. Dazu Rock Carvings are the last monumental work of China's rock carving art. As an artistic masterpiece, Dazu Rock Carvings are of superb artistic, historical and scientific value. The Buddhist, Taoist and Confucianist statues give true expression to the philosophical thinking and the local conditions and customs of the Chinese society at that time. The statuary art and the religious and philosophical thinking developed at Dazu Rock Carvings have exerted important influences on later generations.

⊙ Description

Taking root in the fertile land of the centuries-old local culture and absorbing the essence of the grotto art of preceding times, Dazu Rock Carvings opened a new chapter in the grotto art through innovation. Carrying a distinctive national, customary and life-copying tint, they set a typical example of grotto art in Chinese style. Dazu Rock Carvings, together with Mogao Caves, Yungang Grottoes and Longmen Grottoes, build up the complete history of grotto art in China.

Avalokitesvara Cave, Shimenshan

Dazu Rock Carvings have made important contributions to the creation and development of grotto art in China. In terms of sculpturing, realism and exaggeration were applied to what is difficult to record and express, so that the works become lifelike both in form and content. The subjects, meanwhile, taken from but not limited to classics, are both panoramic and innovative. As to the layout, the carvings show a wonderful integration of art, religion, science and nature. Aesthetically, they are mysterious, natural and graceful, catering fully to the aesthetic demand of traditional Chinese culture. For presentation, the old formulas applied to some religious sculptures had been cast off and given place to new ones characterized by personification of deities and unity between deities and human beings, characteristics that are extremely Chinese.

Dazu Rock Carvings are typical example of life representation of grotto art. Richly expressive of worldly beliefs and full of sim

✺✺ Dazu Rock Carvings ✺✺

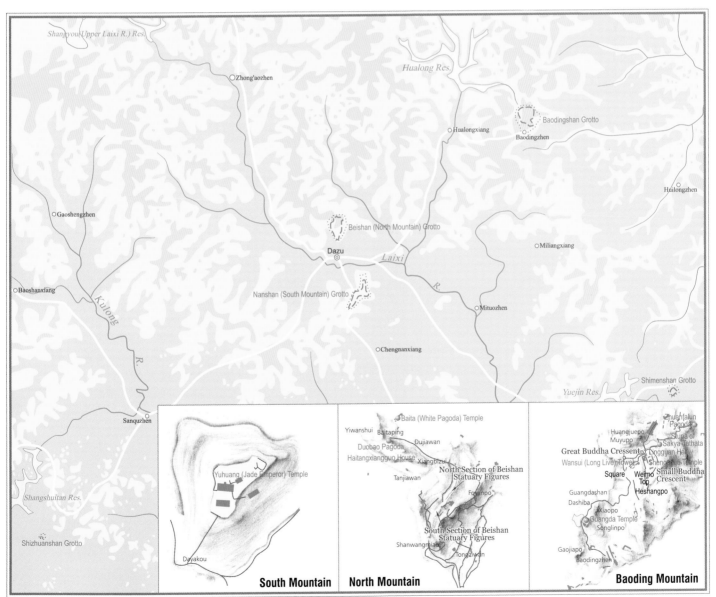

Beishan Grotto

the deity instead of a particular religion and diversification of religious beliefs are important changes that have taken place in the long progression of popular religious beliefs in China. On the one hand, mutual integration took the place of confrontation during the course of development of Confucianism, Taoism and Buddhism--three pillars of traditional Chinese culture. One expression of this trend is the practice of grotto carving, an art of Buddhist origin, in Taoism and Confucianism, and the placement of the statues of the founders of these three cultures in the same cave, on an equal footing. Some caves at Dazu house Confucianist, Taoist or Buddhist statues separately, some house combination of Buddhist and Taoist statues or combination of Confucianist, Taoist and Buddhist statues, indicating that Confucius, Lao Zi and Sakyamuni were all held in esteem as the greatest sages. The ideological trend of blending the three different schools of thought had taken a solid root, and the boundaries of the three had become increasingly undetectable among the common believers during 10th-13th Century. On the other hand, the rich thematic contents of the rock carvings at Dazu provide a positive proof that the gods held in esteem in Indian Buddhism and the immortals held in esteem in the early days of Taoism had come to integrate with the deities held in esteem among common believers in China during this period of time, indicating the trend of diversification of religious beliefs. The great development of and changes in the religious beliefs of ordinary Chinese as recorded in Dazu rock carvings became the foundation for the common beliefs of successive generations, exerting profound and far-reaching influences.

⊙ Highlights

Baodingshan Grotto Carved by Zhao Zhifeng, a reputed monk of his time, through more than 70 years (1174-1252) of painstaking efforts, this is a work of Buddhist art full of human appeal. It is a large place where rites of the Esoteric Sect of Chinese Buddhism were performed, with nearly 10,000 Buddhist statues of different sizes. Massive in scale and rich in content, these statues were created according to the principle of instilment of rationalities, stimulation of emotions, allurement with promises of happiness and warning of disasters and hardship. Embodying scientific principles in the plastic art, it is a synthesis of the art of grotto carving.

Beishan Grotto This grotto was first carved by Wei Junjing, prefect of Changzhou and military commander of four local prefectures, in the 1st year of Jingfu in the Tang Dynasty (892) and

plistic flavor of life, they cut a unique figure in the art of grotto carving. In terms of content and expression, they tried to integrate daily life and aesthetic appeal. The figures are quiet and gentle in look and gorgeous in dress. Their bodies, meanwhile, are graceful but not obsequious, charming but not seductive. The Buddha, the deities, the arhats, the warriors and the diverse attendants were all depiction of various kinds of real human beings. This was when the art of grotto carving in China completed its course of localization.

Dazu Rock Carvings have added a new chapter to the history of the Esoteric Sect in Chinese Buddhism. The Esoteric Sect became popular in China along the Yellow River Valley in the early 8th Century and gradually died out in the early 9th Century when it was introduced to Japan. The large numbers of statues and inscriptions in Beishan and Baodingshan tell irrefutably, however, that instead of dying out, the Esoteric Sect had its heyday in Sichuan during 9th-13th Century. At the end of the 9th Century (the late Tang Dynasty), Monk Liu Benzun from west Sichuan founded the Esoteric Sect of his own style and named himself the chief abbot of the Yoga Sect, taking great pains to preach and carry forward Buddhism. By the 12th Century and the middle of the 13th Century (the middle of the Southern Song Dynasty), Zhao Zhifeng, a reputed monk, succeeded Liu and preached Buddhist doctrines at Dazu under the banner of "the Esoteric Sect as handed down through six generations". He also created the rock carvings in Baoding Mountain, a rare place where rites of the Esoteric Sect were performed, complete in system and with characteristics of its own, thus extending the history of the Esoteric Sect by 400 years and writing another page into the history of the Esoteric Sect in Chinese Buddhism.

Dazu Rock Carvings vividly reflect the important development of and changes in the popular religious beliefs in China. Belief in

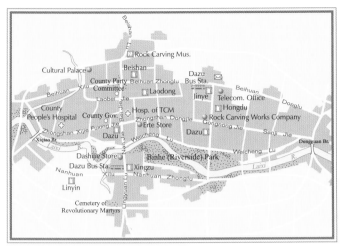

Ritual site of Liu Benzun

ᘏᕽᕽᕽ Dazu ᕽᕽᕽᘏ

expanded by local officials, civilians and Buddhist monks. It got its present-day scale under the reign of Shaoxing (1131-1163) in the Southern Song Dynasty. Stretching for about 500 m like a new moon along the mountain, the shrines sit close to each other like in a honeycomb. Divided into two sections, one in the south and another in the north, and serialized from 1 to 290, the statues are known for their delicacy, exquisiteness and gracefulness. Of the statues, those of the Goddess of Mercy (Avalokitesvara) with all their unique characteristics make a big number. As a place of gathering of the beautiful goddess, Beishan Grotto is known as "China's Exhibition Hall of the Statues of the Goddess of Mercy".

Nanshan Grotto and others All the statues at Dazu, be they Confucianist, Buddhist, or Taoist, are excellent and different from those in grottoes of earlier times. The Taoist statues of the Song Dynasty, as represented by those in Nanshan Mountain, are a group of Taoist statues most delicate in carving and most complete in deity representation among the stone carvings in China at that time. The typical group of Buddhist and Taoist statues standing together in Shimenshan grottoes and the typical group of Confucianist, Buddhist and Taoist statues standing together in Shizhuanshan grottoes, in particular, are of the highest artistic attainment in rock carving and very rare in China. Most of all, the statue of Confucius standing in the spotlight in Shizhuanshan grottoes is extremely precious.

⊙ Information

■ **Transportation** *Located in Dazu County in the west of Chongqing Municipality, Dazu Rock Carvings is 83 km to the west of Chongqing City and 271 km to the east of Chengdu. Access to Dazu is easy by railways and expressways. From Chongqing tourists may take a bus at Caiyuanba or Chenjiaba, departing every 30 minutes and taking about 1.5 hours to arrive at Dazu. For tourists starting from Chengdu, there will be a 3.5-hour bus ride departing from Hehuachi. Those taking the train from Chengdu or Chongqing may get off at Youting Station and change to a coach running 32 km to Dazu. Once in Dazu, a bus or taxi may be taken to the scenic spots in Beishan and Nanshan (1 km from the county town) or Baodingshan Grotto (11 km from the country town).*

■ **Accommodation** *There are over 50 hotels in Dazu County, with a total of over 5,000 beds. Apart from the three-star Dazu Hotel, visitors may also put up at other hotels of different architectural style and functionalities, namely Longshuihu Hotel, Wudu Longshuihu Villa, and Lianyi Hotel. Hehua Villa and Piba Hotel offer unique services in rustic way.*

■ **Others** *Local products include small metals, stone carved Buddhist statues, wood carved Bodhisattva statues, bamboo woven articles, winter bamboo shoots, and local wines. Various kinds of festivals are also celebrated here, including the Incense-Burning Festival on the 19th day of the 2nd month of Chinese lunar calendar, the Dragon Boat Contest on the 5th day of the 5th month of Chinese lunar calendar, and lantern and dragon dances in the Spring Festival.*

Opening hours: 8:00 ~ 18:00
Inquiry telephone: 023-43734666

Part of Baodingshan Grotto

SICHUAN PROVINCE

General Information

Sichuan Province, also called Chuan or Shu in short, has its capital in Chengdu City. With an area of 480,000 sq km, it has under its administrative jurisdiction 18 prefecture-level cities, 3 autonomous prefectures, 14 county-level cities, 120 counties and 4 autonomous counties. The province has a population of 84.74 million and ethnic groups including Han, Yi, Zang (Tibetan), Qiang, Miao and Hui.

Environment

It is located in the southwest of China at the upper reaches of the Yangtze River. The east is Sichuan Basin and further inward is the Chengdu Plain. The highland area of West Sichuan and the Qionglai Mountains are part of the eastern rim of the Qinghai-Tibet Plateau, and the southern part is the northern range of the Hengduan Mountains, where there are numerous valleys and vast forests. In the east is the sub-tropical humid monsoon climate, while in the west is the temperate zone sub-tropical plateau climate. The average temperature is 8 ~ 10°C in January and 12 ~ 26°C in July, with an average annual rainfall between 500 ~ 1,500 mm.

Places of Interest

"The vast fertile fields and rich reserves of resources make the so-called Land of Abundance or Tianfu". It has been 2,000 years since Sichuan got the reputation of the Land of Abundance. Numerous cultural relics uncovered at the relic site of Sanxingdui in Guanghan have proved that the Bashu culture has been deep rooted here since more than 4,000 years ago. A lot of great men that remain eternally well-known in history come from Sichuan. Li Bai set out on a journey to remote areas with his sword on his back. Du Fu recited poems in his thatched cottage. Zhuge Liang worked hard until the last minute in his life. Li Bing and his sons constructed Dujiangyan Irrigation System that earns them eternal fame. Chengdu, Langzhong, Yibin, Zigong, Leshan, Dujiangyan and Luzhou have become famous historical and cultural cities of China.

Emei Mountain, Huanglongsi-Jiuzhaigou, Qingcheng Mountain-Dujiangyan, Shudao Path of Jianmen, Gongga Mountain and the Bamboo Sea in southern Sichuan are the state-level scenic areas. Mount Emei, Mount Qingcheng, Huanglong Valley and Jiuzhaigou have been included in the World Heritage List. Hailuo Gully, Lugu Lake, Siguniang Mountain, Xichang Satellite City, the southern Sichuan tourist zone and the Ertan scenic spots are all famous tourist destinations. It is true that Sichuan is abundant of scenic spots, each standing out in picturesque beauty.

Local Specialties

Sichuan embroidery, Wuliangye spirits, Jiannanchun spirits, Luzhou Laojiao spirits, Dengying beef slices, and Tianfu peanuts.

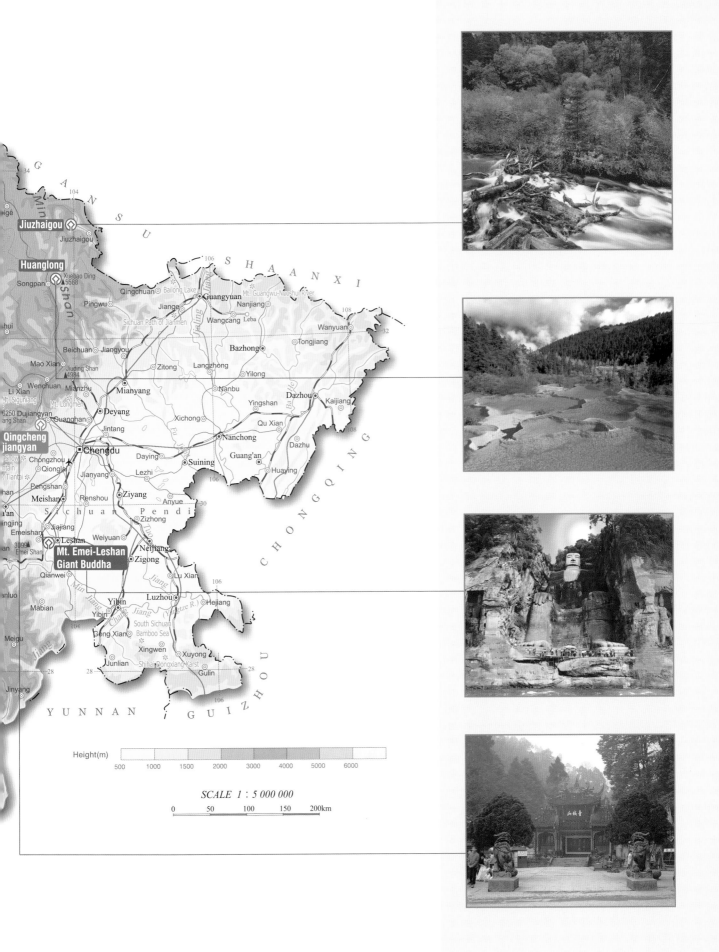

Height(m)

| | 500 | 1000 | 1500 | 2000 | 3000 | 4000 | 5000 | 6000 |

SCALE 1 : 5 000 000

0   50   100   150   200km

Jiuzhaigou Valley Scenic and Historic Interest Area

☐ **Name:**

Jiuzhaigou Valley Scenic and Historic Interest Area

☐ **Geographical coordinates:**

32° 54' ~ 33° 19' N, 103° 46' ~ 104° 05' E

☐ **Date of inscription:**

December 1, 1992

☐ **Criterion for inclusion:**

III of cultural properties

Shuzheng Waterfall

⊙ Overview

Jiuzhaigou, located at the northern slope of Ga'erna Peak in the southern section of Minshan Mountains in the northwest of Sichuan Province, is a big valley at the upper reaches of Jialing River, a tributary of the Yangtze. Measuring over 60 km, the valley covers an area of 651.34 sq km, and a total of 720 sq km with the inclusion of peripheral areas, such as Ganhaizi, etc. Seldom seen in the world, it is the only nature reserve in China featuring groups of mountain lakes, waterfalls and karst landscape. The place is inhabited by giant pandas and other rare animals. There are 2,061 species of tracheophyte, including 74 higher plants under state protection, and 310 species of vertebrates, including 47 rare animals under state protection. Jiuzhaigou Valley is listed as a national nature reserve, as well as a state-level scenic area.

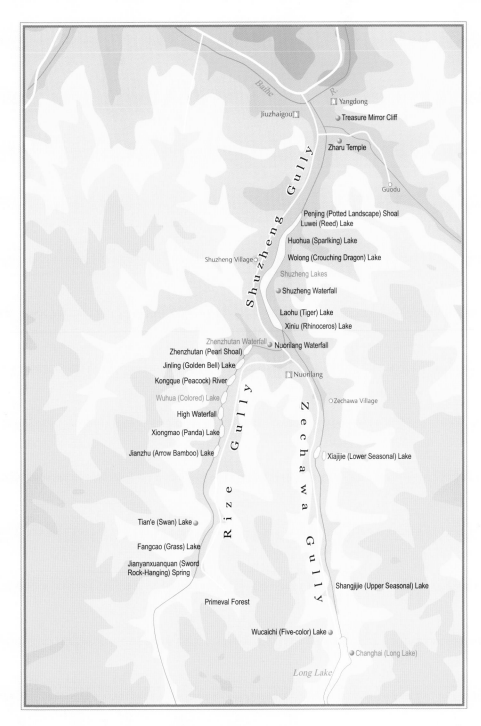

Map labels:
- Baihe R.
- Yangdong
- Jiuzhaigou
- Treasure Mirror Cliff
- Zharu Temple
- Guodu
- Shuzheng Gully
- Penjing (Potted Landscape) Shoal
- Luwei (Reed) Lake
- Huohua (Sparlking) Lake
- Wolong (Crouching Dragon) Lake
- Shuzheng Village
- Shuzheng Lakes
- Shuzheng Waterfall
- Laohu (Tiger) Lake
- Xiniu (Rhinoceros) Lake
- Zhenzhutan Waterfall
- Nuorilang Waterfall
- Zhenzhutan (Pearl Shoal)
- Jinling (Golden Bell) Lake
- Kongque (Peacock) River
- Nuorilang
- Zechawa Village
- Wuhua (Colored) Lake
- High Waterfall
- Rize Gully
- Zechawa Gully
- Xiongmao (Panda) Lake
- Jianzhu (Arrow Bamboo) Lake
- Xiajijie (Lower Seasonal) Lake
- Tian'e (Swan) Lake
- Fangcao (Grass) Lake
- Jianyanxuanquan (Sword Rock-Hanging) Spring
- Shangjijie (Upper Seasonal) Lake
- Primeval Forest
- Wucaichi (Five-color) Lake
- Changhai (Long Lake)
- Long Lake

Jiuzhaigou

☉ Description

Lying in the transition zone between Qinghai-Tibet Plateau and Sichuan Basin, Jiuzhaigou has various geological features, which give rise to a vast expanse of karst landform in calcareous deposits. The place, literally meaning "Nine Village Valley", is named after the nine Tibetan villages scattered in the valley, including Zaru, Heye, Shuzheng, and Zechawa, etc.

The Y-shaped main valley of Jiuzhaigou is comprised of three gullies: Shuzheng Gully, Rize Gully and Zechawa Gully. Scattered among the lofty ridges and towering mountains are more than 100 barrier lakes of varying size. In the verdant gullies there are 114 lakes, 17 waterfalls, 5 calcareous deposits, 47 fountains, and 11 sections of rapids. Rivers flow through the valley over a

Giant cypress at Changhai Lake

Zhenzhu Shoal

fall of nearly 2000 m, among the 12 snow-capped peaks. Firs, spruces, larches maples, and many other trees also grow here in abundance, presenting distinctive landscapes in different seasons.

Water is the soul of Jiuzhaigou. Lakes, springs, waterfalls, shoals and creeks decorate the mountains and valleys, reflecting the beautiful scenery in the clear water. Within a day, a lake may turns form blue to green according to the change of weather, sunlight, and angle of rays, creating an intriguing sight. There is a saying that goes: "one won't bother to see water after returning from Jiuzhaigou". In the eyes of the local Tibetans, Jiuzhaigou is their sacred mountains and sacred lakes, and they aspire to build it into an ideal paradise with their primitive and plain ideology.

⊙ Highlights

Changhai Lake Located at the end of Zechawa Gully, it has an elevation of 3,060 m, and covers an area of 928,440 sq m. A typical barrier lake formed by glaciation, Changhai is the biggest lake in Jiuzhaigou. Here one can still see visible remains of glaciers. A giant cypress, which local Tibetans worship as sacred, stands by the lake.

Wuhua (Colored) Lake Located at the end of Kongque (Peacock) River of the Rize Gully, the lake is said to have the best of the views of Jiuzhaigou. The trestle over the west side of the lake and the spot named Tiger Mouth at the highway are the best positions to marvel at the beauty of the lake.

Fairyland on Earth

"Crocodile in the lake"

Zhenzhutan (Pearl Shoal) Waterfall The waterfall is located at the middle section of Rize Gully and is not far from Wuhua Lake. At the upper reaches of the waterfall is a shallow shoal of pale yellow calcareous deposits. Rapid currents rush through the shoal, throwing up bubbles like thousands of peals, then plunge straight down and give birth to the spectacular view of the waterfall.

Shuzheng Lakes Located at the middle section of Shuzheng Gully, neighboring Shuzheng Village, 19 lakes of varying size interconnect with one another, forming a group of terraced lakes.

A stream in Jiuzhaigou

Jianzhu Lake

Wuhua Lake

⊙ Information

■ **Transportation** *There are flights from Chengdu and Chongqing to Jiuzhaigou. Buses depart for Jiazhaigou everyday from Xinnanmen Terminal and Chadianzi Terminal of Chengdu. There are also buses to Jiuzhaigou from Mianyang and Leshan.*

■ **Accommodation** *There are Jiuzhai Tiantang International Convention and Resort Center, five-star Jiuzhaigou Sheraton Hotel, four-star CTS Hotel, Gesang Hotel, Jinlong Yugang Hotel, three-star Jiuzhaigou Hotel, Jiulong Hotel and two-star Jiuxin Hotel and Jiu'an Hotel, and Tibetan style Heye Hotel, Guibinlou Hotel and Yueliangwan Villa.*

■ **Food** *The Nuorilang Reception Center can accommodate 4,000 at the same time. Local snacks are ghee tea, yak meat, and noodles.*

■ **Others** *Local products include angelica, caladium, ox horn combs etc., and Tibetan decorative items make nice tourist souvenirs.*

Inquiry telephone: 0837-7739753
Website: www.jiuzhaigouvalley.com

Huanglong Scenic and Historic Interest Area

☐ **Name:**

Huanglong Scenic and Historic Interest Area

☐ **Geographical coordinates:**

32°40' N, 103° 34' E

☐ **Date of inscription:**

December 1, 1992

☐ **Criterion for inclusion:**

III of cultural properties

Calcareous tufa streams

⊙ Overview

Huanglong Scenic Area is located in Songpan County of Aba Tibetan-Qiang Autonomous Prefecture in the northwest of Sichuan Province. Lying to the northeast of Xuebaoding, the main peak of Minshan Mountain, the scenic area covers an area of 1,340 sq km, with a core area of 700 sq km. The lowest spot has an elevation of 1,700 m, and the highest, 5,588 m. The scenic area is composed of Huanglong Valley, Danyun Gorge, Muni Valley, Xuebaoding, Xueshanliang, Hongxin (Red Heart) Crag, Western Valley, etc. It is a comprehensive scenic area integrating large open karst landscapes and other natural scenery as well as folk customs of ethnic groups. Karst landscapes of Huanglong Valley, a classic representative of the kind in the world, are immense in scope and well preserved. It is one of the first state-level scenic areas in China.

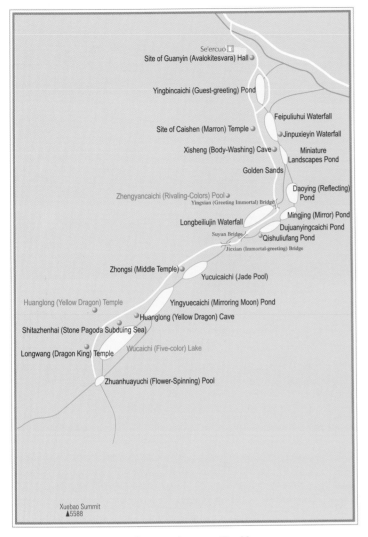

Se'ercuo
Site of Guanyin (Avalokitesvara) Hall

Yingbincaichi (Guest-greeting) Pond

Feipuliuhui Waterfall
Site of Caishen (Marron) Temple
Jinpuxieyin Waterfall
Xisheng (Body-Washing) Cave
Miniature Landscapes Pond

Golden Sands

Daoying (Reflecting) Pond

Zhengyancaichi (Rivaling-Colors) Pool
Yingxian (Greeting Immortal) Bridge
Mingjing (Mirror) Pond
Longbeiliujin Waterfall
Dujuanyingcaichi Pond
Suyun Bridge
Qishuliufang Pond
Jiexian (Immortal-greeting) Bridge

Zhongsi (Middle Temple)
Yucuicaichi (Jade Pool)

Huanglong (Yellow Dragon) Temple
Yingyuecaichi (Mirroring Moon) Pond
Huanglong (Yellow Dragon) Cave
Shitazhenhai (Stone Pagoda Subduing Sea)
Wucaichi (Five-color) Lake
Longwang (Dragon King) Temple

Zhuanhuayuchi (Flower-Spinning) Pool

Xuebao Summit
▲5588

ᘒᘒᘒ Huanglong Gully ᘒᘒᘒ

Calcareous tufa streams

Hongxin (Red Heart) Crag
To Jiuzhaigou Valley
Huanglong Administrative Office
Longdishui (Dragon Dripping Water)
Huanglongxiang
Longdishui
Xueshanliang Ridge
Huanglong Gully
To Big Grassland
Zhangjia Gully
Danyun Gorge
Chuanzhusi
Huanglong Gully
Zhangjia Gully
Shijiabao
To Pingwu
Xuebaoding
West Gully
Songpan
Xuebaoding (Snowy Peak)
To Chengdu
Muni Gully

Huanglong

⊙ Description

Huanglong, or the Yellow Dragon, was so named after its general shape, while its Tibetan name means "golden lake". The extensive Minshan Mountain, vast primitive forest and unique customs of local ethnic groups attract thousands of visitors every year. The place is best known for its karst caves, colored pools, snow-capped mountains, gorges, ancient temples and unique folk customs.

Huanglong has the biggest and most well preserved open karst landscape in the world. Here numerous karst ponds, karst rivers and karst caves together make up the large exposed pale yellow calcareous deposits that resemble a golden dragon at a bird'-eye view.

Danyun Gorge, Western Valley and Longdishui (Dragon Dripping Water) are the best of the landcapes typical of the area. Here dark forests cover both sides of deep gorges, waterfalls tear through grotesque stones and thunder down into the unknown world. Strange stones, precipitous peaks, flowers and birds, insects and fish, clouds and red leaves make a natural scroll of Chinese painting of mountains and waters.

Huanglong is also a paradise for the local Tibetan, Qiang, Hui

Xueshanliang

Red Heart Crag

and Han peoples. Here one can experience the folk customs of these peoples all in one place: dance the Tibetan and Qiang Guozhuang, taste their ghee tee and visit their White Pagoda Temple.

There are three temples in the Huanglong Scenic Area, each located at an interval of five km from one another. According to historical record, Ma Chaojin, a general of the Ming Dynasty, built Huanglong Temple in commemoration of the Yellow Dragon of the Minjiang River, who contributed greatly to Dayu in his endeavor to control the flood. In the temple a statue of Taoist sage named Huanglong Zhenren has been worshipped. In the mid 6th month of every lunar calendar year, a temple fair is held, whereby tens of thousands of local people sing and dance throughout the nights.

Huanglong is a gigantic gene bank. Due to the primitive ecology and rich content of oxygen, the area is compared to a natural oxygen bar. Incomplete statistics show that here live nearly 1,700 species of animals and plants, including pandas, golden hair monkeys, Chinese caterpillar fungus, *Frillaria thunbergli*, mushrooms, etc.

⊙ Highlights

Xueshanliang (Snow Ridge) The towering snow peak, precipitous cliffs and sea of clouds make up a spectacular landscape.

Xuebaoding(Snow Peak) Rising 5,588 m above sea level, the main peak of Minshan mountain looks like a jade pyramid-divine, noble and solemn. Around the peak are hundreds of mountain lakes and dozens of glaciers.

Colored Ponds

Red Heart Crag It is a great mountain made up of dark rocks, with a red heart-shaped patch on the mountain cliff, hence the name. In the rugged mountain are scattered many clear lakes. When the sun sets, the Red Heart Crag turns golden, the "heart" is mirrored in the lakes, projecting a scene of fairyland.

Huanglong Colored Ponds They are the largest, the most complete and most unique karst landscape in the world, showing the mastermind of the Nature.

⊙ Information

■ **Transportation** *Air flights now link Chengdu and Chongqing to Jiuhuang Airport. Railways connect Chengdu with Beijing, Shanghai, Guangzhou, Chongqing, Xi'an, Kunming, Urumqi and Lanzhou. The easiest way to Huanglong is to arrive Chengdu by air, then reach Huanglong via Chuanzhusi-Jiuzhaigou Highway, or directly fly from Chengdu to Jiuhuang Airport. Huanglong is located 35 km east of Songpan County and borders Jiuzhaigou with one mountain, but buses have to take a roundabout route of 100 km from Jiuzhaigou to Huanglong.*

■ **Accommodation** *Near the scenic area there are Huanglong Mountain Villa, Minyuang Mountain Villa, and Songpan Huanglong Hotel.*

■ **Food** *Huanglong Dujuanlin Tourist Service Center is located in the scenic area, serving Chinese food, snack foods and drinks.*

■ **Others** *It is suggested that tourists should bring their own instant food because eateries are rare in the scenic area.*

Website: www.huanglong.com

Xuebaoding

Rivaling Colors Pool, Huanglong

Mount Emei Senic Area, including Leshan Giant Buddha Scenic Area

☐ **Name:**

Mount Emei Scenic Area, including

Leshan Giant Buddha Scenic Area

☐ **Date of inscription:**

December 6, 1996

☐ **Criteria for inclusion:**

IV, VI of the cultural properties

IV of the natural properties

Golden Summit, Mt. Emei

Mount Emei

☐ **Geographical coordinates:**

29° 16' 30" ~ 29° 43' 42" N, 103° 10' 30" ~ 103° 37' 10" E

⊙ Overview

Mount Emei lies in the central south of Sichuan Province, on the zone of transition from Sichuan Basin to Qinghai-Tibet Plateau. The highest peak, Wanfoding (Ten Thousand Buddha Peak), is 3,099 m above sea level. The protected zone covers an area of 154 sq km. Mount Emei is known as "Beauty under Heaven" for its natural scenery and is famed as a "Holy Land of Buddhism". This is the area where a brilliant history and culture was created by the people of ancient times. In the 1st Century AD, one of the earliest Buddhist temples in China was built on the top of Mount Emei. As more and more temples were built on the mountain, Mount Emei gradually becomes one of the holy mountains of Buddhism in China. Located at the junction of multiple natural elements, the mountain has typical topographical features and a well-protected ecological environment. Thanks to its location in the zone of conjunction and transition of world biota, the area is rich in biological resources with distinct regional features, and various rare and endangered species.

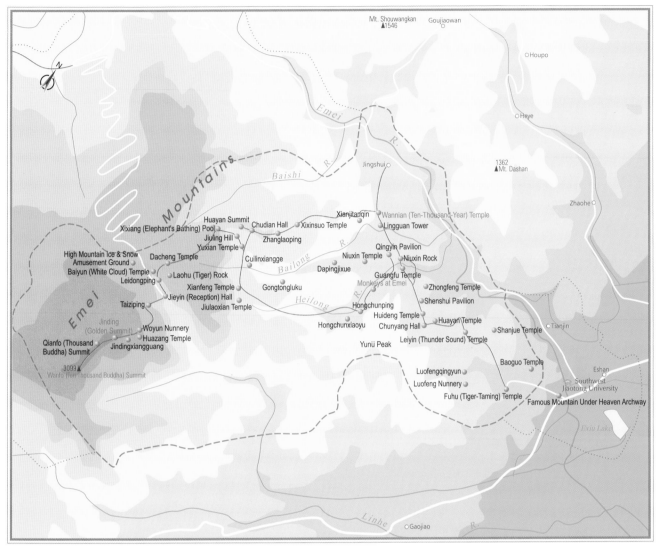

Mt. Shouwangkan ▲1546 Goujiaowan
Houpo
Emei R.
Heye
Baishi R.
Jingshui
1362 ▲Mt. Dashan
Zhaohe
Mountains
Xianjitanqin
Wannian (Ten-Thousand-Year) Temple
Huayan Summit
Chudian Hall
Xixinsuo Temple
Lingguan Tower
Xixiang (Elephant's Bathing) Pool
Zhanglaoping
Jiuling Hill
Qingyin Pavilion
Yuxian Temple
Niuxin Temple
Niuxin Rock
High Mountain Ice & Snow
Amusement Ground
Dacheng Temple
Cuilinxiangge
Dapingjixue
Baiyun (White Cloud) Temple
Laohu (Tiger) Rock
Guangfu Temple
Leidongping
Xianfeng Temple
Gongtongluku
Monkeys at Emei
Zhongfeng Temple
Taiziping
Jieyin (Reception) Hall
Heilong R.
Hongchunping
Shenshui Pavilion
Jiulaoxian Temple
Hongchunxiaoyu
Huideng Temple
Huayan Temple
Emei
Jinding (Golden Summit)
Woyun Nunnery
Chunyang Hall
Shanjue Temple
Tianjin
Huazang Temple
Leiyin (Thunder Sound) Temple
Qianfo (Thousand Buddha) Summit
Jindingxiangguang
Yunü Peak
Baoguo Temple
Eshan
3099▲
Wanfo (Ten Thousand Buddha) Summit
Luofengqingyun
Southwest Jiaotong University
Luofeng Nunnery
Fuhu (Tiger-Taming) Temple
Famous Mountain Under Heaven Archway
Exiu Lake
Linhe R.
Gaojiao

Mount Emei

◉ Description

With unique geological features, Mount Emei has a comparatively complete sedimentary formation preserved since Pre-Cambrian Period, providing precious geological data, typical examples and sufficient bases for research of the earth crust and biological evolution. In addition, a variety of majestic and spectacular landforms formed in the neotectonic movement endow Mount Emei with an aesthetic image, scientific value and a special and higher status in mountainous scenic spots of the world.

Mount Emei is characterized as being majestic, beautiful, mysterious and wonderful.

Majestic: Mount Emei rises high from the ground on the southwest periphery of Sichuan Basin, with a relative height difference of 2,600 m. The three main peaks of the mountain stand side by side and soar mightily into the sky.

Beautiful: Mount Emei is located at the junction of multiple natural elements, with a distinct vertical zonation of vegetation and a wide variety of vegetation species. Percentage of vegetation coverage is above 95%.

Mysterious and Wonderful: Mount Emei, home for the preaching rites of Samantabhadra, is shrouded in a mysterious religious atmosphere by virtue of the strength of its Buddhist culture. Propagation of mythic legends and literary art also adds an illusory and mysterious color to the mountain. Mount Emei has many marvelous spectacles, such as Buddhist Halo, Devine Lights, sea of clouds

Supine Buddha, Leshan

and sunrise on the Golden Summit, Cloud in Leidong, and Dawn Rain at Hongchun.

Mount Emei is rich in botanic species and has typical vegetation of the subtropical zone. There are more than 3,200 species in 242 families of known higher plants, and over 100 species of specific higher plants. Mount Emei also has a great quantity of ancient and endangered species, of which 31 are in the list of state-protected plants.

Mount Emei is also a gene bank of animal species, with distinct and typical characteristics known as the "Four Abundances": abundant in ancient, rare and endangered species, unique species, model species, and Oriental region species.

Highlights

Four Wonders on the Golden Summit The main peak of Mount Emei-Golden Summit, 3,077 m above sea level, is the best spot for viewing the four spectacular sights—sunrise, sea of clouds, Buddhist Halo, and Devine Lights.

Clusters of Temple Building Complex on Mount Emei Mount Emei is a famous Buddhist mountain, known as the place for Samantabhadra's preaching rites. Mount Emei is one of the four holy mountains of Buddhism in China, the other three being Mount Putuo in Zhejiang, Mount Wutai in Shanxi and Mount Jiuhua in Anhui. Over 100 monasteries and temples have been built successively on the mountain, housing thousands of monks. Nowadays, about 30 structures still remain, including Feilai Hall, a key site of cultural relics under state protection.

Bronze and Iron Statues of Buddha in Wannian Temple Wannian Temple, a beamless brick structure, houses 306 bronze and iron statues of Buddha in total, cast in the 5th year of Taiping Xingguo in the Song Dynasty (980). Among them, there is a bronze statue of Samantabhadra on an elephant, standing 7.85 m high and weighing 62 tonnes. The statue is cast in the shape of the Samantabhadra sitting on a lotus flower throne, which is fixed on the back of a 6-tusked white elephant. This statue is a key cultural relic under state protection.

Natural Ecological Monkey Zone at Qingyin Pavilion Located between Qingyin Pavilion and Hongchunping, it is the largest natural ecological monkey zone in China, inhabited by more than 200 Tibetan macaques, which are listed as Grade II wildlife under state protection.

Information

■ **Transportation** *It takes about 1.5 hours from Chengdu Shuangliu International Airport to the foot of Mount Emei by car, or 20 minutes from Emei railway station by train. By water, one can take a boat along the Yangtze River and Minjiang River to Leshan City and then head for Mount Emei. Buses departing from Xinnanmen in Chengdu reach the foot of the mountain in 1.5 hours via Chengdu-Leshan Expressway and Leshan-Emei Expressway. At the tourist passenger center there are sightseeing buses to each scenic spot.*

■ **Accommodation** *In Baoguo Temple Scenic Spot there are four-star Hongzhushan Hotel, Emeishan Grand Hotel, Emeishan Hotel, three-star Fenghuanghu Hotel, Xiongxiu Hotel; In Golden Summit Scenic Spot there is the three-star Jinding Hotel; in the downtown area of Emeishan, there are four-star Huasheng Hotel, two-star Dianli Hotel and Jiataimei Hotel.*

■ **Food** *There is a "Gourmands' Street" in the downtown area of Emeishan and a "Street of Famous Snack Food" in Baoguo Temple Scenic Spot.*

■ **Others** *Local specialties include Bamboo-leaf Green Tea, Erui Tea, Xianzhi Bamboo-leaf Tip Tea, gastrodia tuber, Ginseng, Ciliatenerve Knotweed Root, Notoginseng, hemsleya root, Chinese caterpillar fungus, snow-preserved konnjaku, and bamboo shoots. Mount Emei Clever Monkey Series are unique tourist handicraft articles.*

Opening hours: open all the year round.
Inquiry telephones: 0833-5533355, 5590528, 5590529
Website: www.ems517.com

Sea of clouds, Mt. Emei

Leshan Giant Buddha

☐ **Geographical coordinates:**
29° 31' ~ 29° 35' N, 103° 43' ~ 103° 47' E

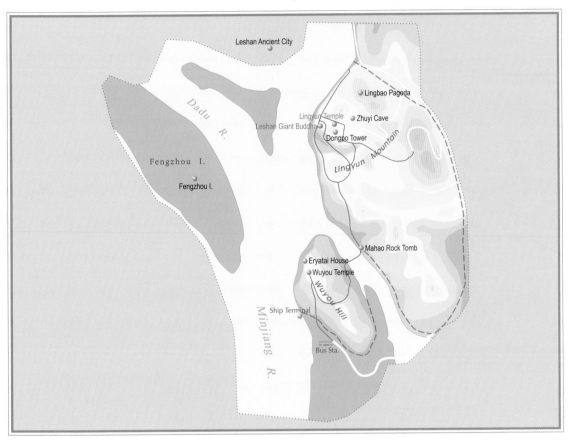

Leshan Ancient City

Lingbao Pagoda

Dadu R.

Lingyun Temple
Zhuyi Cave
Leshan Giant Buddha
Dongpo Tower
Lingyun Mountain

Fengzhou I.

Fengzhou I.

Mahao Rock Tomb
Eryatai House
Wuyou Temple
Wuyou Hill

Ship Terminal

Minjiang R.

Bus Sta.

Leshan Giant Buddha

⊙ Overview

Carved out of solid rock on the west cliff of the Qiluan Peak of Lingyun Mountain at the confluence of Minjiang, Dadu and Qingyi rivers, Leshan Giant Buddha is an ancient sitting sculpture of Maitreya, and is also known as Jiazhou Grand Buddha or Lingyun Grand Buddha after the place where it is located. Construction of the Statue of Buddha began in the 1st year of Xuanzhong in the Tang Dynasty (713 AD), and was completed in the 19th year of Dezhong (803 AD), taking 90 years in all. Listed as a key site of cultural relics under state protection, it is the largest stone statue in ancient China and the largest stone-carved sitting Buddha in the world.

Bronze statue of Samantabhadra

Leshan Giant Buddha

the finger 8.3 m long, the instep 8.5 m wide, instep-to-knee 28 m high, and there are 1,021 coiled buns of hair on his head. A scientific water drainage system is hidden on the inside from the back wall of the neck all the way to the feet of the Buddha.

The construction of the statue was initiated and engineered by a monk called Haitong, who was born in Guizhou and built a thatched cottage in Lingyun Mountain. Each flood season, the tempestuous floodwater from the three rivers joined at the foot of Lingyun Mountain, like thousands of horses galloping ahead and storming the mountain wall, which often overturned boats and caused tragedies claiming lives and causing damage. For this reason, the Monk determined to carve a sculpture of Maitreya from the cliff, with an aim to halt the fierceness of floodwater and calm the floodwater by relying on the unbounded supernatural power of Maitreya. Consequently, Monk Haitong traveled all over the country and experienced innumerable trials and hardships to collect alms for the construction of the Buddha. In order to protect the alms from being taken by corrupt officials, he gave up his eyes, which became the most tragic and stirring scene in the construction history of the Giant Buddha.

The project was such a huge and difficult one, that Monk Haitong did not live to see its completion. Subsequently, Zhangqiu Jianqiong and Wei Gao, governors of Xichuan of Jiannan Prefecture, raised funds and continued the construction of the Statue of Buddha until it was successfully completed. On the cliff of the right side of the statue, there is a steep trestle road built simultaneously with the Statue, with nine zigzags from top to the foot of the mountain. Walking on the zigzags, tourists would have a soul-stirring sensation as if climbing the cliff in a desperate situation. *Notes on the Construction of Maitreya Stone Sculpture in Lingyun Temple of Jiazhou* recorded the process from beginning to end, and the original stele is still visible on the cliff on the right riverside of the Statue.

Qingyi Mountain

Description

Carved from a mountain, Leshan Giant Buddha sits at the confluence of the three rivers, facing the west with a solemn expression and imposing presence, looking down at Jiazhou and overlooking Mount Emei from a distance. The statue of Buddha, sitting 71 m as high as Lingyun Mountain, is strong and tall, with an elegant and sober facial expression and well-proportioned figure: the head is 14.7 m high and 10 m wide; the nose is 5.6 m long, the ear 7 m long, the eyebrow 5.6 m long, each eye 3.3 m long, the mouth 3.3 m long, the neck 3 m high, the shoulder 28 m wide,

Oriental Buddhist capital

Wuyou Temple

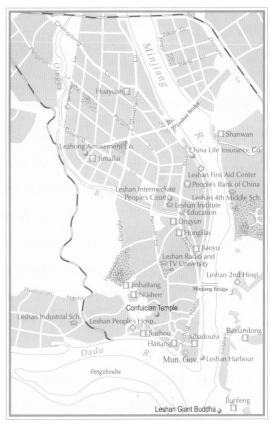

The construction of Leshan Statue of Buddha successfully paints a picture of the cultural and economic prosperity at the height of the Tang Dynasty, and the figure reflects the artistic style of statues in the Tang Dynasty: round and full face type, towering hairline, slender eyes and thin lips, smooth folds on the clothing, solemn and quiet facial expression, as well as a natural, graceful and peaceful posture. The whole statue is included wonderfully into the natural mountain, forming the grand image of "the Buddha is a mountain, and the mountain is a Buddha".

⊙ Highlights

Qingyi Mountain It was said that "the landscapes under heaven lie in Chengdu, Chengdu's scenic spots lie in Jiazhou, and Jiazhou's famous scenery is Lingyun". Lingyun Mountain, where Leshan Giant Buddha is located, used to be named Qingyi Mountain or Jiuding Mountain. Amid luxuriant forests, slender bamboo and rich species of flowers are redwall buildings, painted eaves and red cliffs.

Lingyun Temple It is comprised of ancient buildings with great weight and majesty; towering Lingbao Pagoda of Tang Dynasty which is a 13-storey square brick pagoda with closely adjacent eaves; tranquil and elegant Dongpo Tower set off among bamboo and trees; and Mahao Rock Tombs of the Han Dynasty displaying numerous valuable portraits and unearthed relics.

Mahao Rock Tombs

✿ Leshan ✿

Huge Supine Buddha The adjacent Wuyou Mountain, Lingyun Mountain and Dongyan Mountain give the silhouette of a "huge supine Buddha", which can be called a natural wonder and acclaimed as the peak of perfection. Around Leshan Giant Buddha are numerous cultural and scenic spots, such as Wuyou Temple, Mahao Rock Tombs, and Heavenly-Buddhist Kingdom. These scenic spots and Leshan Giant Buddha add radiance and beauty to each other.

⊙ Information

▨ **Transportation** *Special tourist lines include Leshan Passenger Transport Center-Emeishan City, Leshan Harbor-Baoguo Temple of Mount Emei, Leshan Harbor-Leshan Giant Buddha-Wuyou Temple. There are buses shuttling between scenic spots of Mount Emei and Leshan Giant Buddha. Bus Lines No. 3, 7, 8, 13 operating in Leshan City and ferryboats on Minjiang River can reach Leshan Giant Buddha.*

▨ **Accommodation** *Three-star hotels include Jiazhou Hotel, Shanwan Hotel and Jinhaitang Hotel; two-star hotels are Jiurifeng Hotel, Baxiandong Hotel, Jiajiang Hotel.*

▨ **Food** *Local delicacies include Jiangtuan Fish steamed in clear soup, Dongpo Cuttlefish, duck breast with tender ginger, Pearl Fish, tofu jelly with beef, Qiaojiao Beef, Stuffed Pearl Rice Balls, and stuffed glutinous rice cake wrapped in leaves.*

▨ **Others** *Inquiry telephone: 0833-2302131*
Website: www.leshandafo.cn

Mt. Qingcheng and the Dujiangyan Irrigation System

☐ **Name:**

Mt. Qingcheng and the Dujiangyan Irrigation System

☐ **Geographic coordinates:**

30° 52' 29" ~ 31° 01' 48" N, 103° 25' 45" ~ 103° 38' 15" E

☐ **Date of inscription:**

November 29, 2000

☐ **Criteria of inclusion:**

II, IV, VI of cultural properties

Dujiangyan

Mt. Qingcheng

⊙ Overview

Located 10 km southwest of Dujiangyan City, Sichuan Province, and 49 km northwest of Chengdu, the provincial capital, Mt. Qingcheng, a famous and historic mountain, is one of the holy birthplaces of Chinese Taoism as the Tianshi Sect of Chinese Taoism was founded there and is known as the fifth among the ten most famous Taoist mountains in China. As early as the 2nd century BC, it was appointed by emperor of the Qin Dynasty to be one of the 18 sacred mountains or places for holding imperial sacrificial ceremony. In 143 AD, Zhang Ling founded the Tianshi Sect and formulated 24 rules in a hut at Chicheng Cliff on the Mountain. It reached the height of its prosperity in the 7th Century with 7 Taoist sects, around 40 temples and 2,400 statues of deities. In 1982, it was included among the first state-level scenic areas of China.

Triple Pool Spring

⊙ Description

Mount Qingcheng

Mt. Qingcheng is situated on the juncture of Qionglai Mountain and Chengdu Plain. Lying against Minshan Mountain and overlooking Chengdu Plain, it is surrounded by verdant mountain peaks with a shape like the outline of a city wall; therefore it gains its name "Qingcheng", which means "Green City" in Chinese. It is also well known for its natural ecological beauty, steep ravines, peculiar old trees and odd stones, and has been reputed to be "the greenest and serenest place in the world" since the Tang Dynasty. Its protected zone covers 1,522 ha and has 36 peaks (the highest being 2,434 m above sea level), 8 large caves, 72 small caves, and 108 scenes. There are also 11 Taoist temples and some 40 ancient buildings of various types, characterized by Taoist culture and folk customs of the western region of the ancient Shu Kingdom (modern Chengdu).

The Mountain has since ancient times attracted distinguished and refined scholars, intellectuals, generals of all ages who either traveled, composed, relaxed or delivered sermons there. There appeared successively many famous Taoists such as Fan Changsheng and Du Guangting. Meanwhile, Qingcheng Alchemy, Qingcheng Theory of *Yi Jing* (the Book of Changes), architecture, martial art, music, medicine, and health care became typical of Chinese Taoist culture. Composed and passed on by Zhang Kongshan, a Taoist monk from Mt. Qingcheng, a piece of music named *Running Water* performed with an ancient Chinese stringed instrument, was recorded on a golden record in 1977 and is currently traveling through space aboard the American spacecraft Voyager II.

Macha, Dujiangyan

Main hall of Tianshi Cave

Shangqing Palace

⊙ Highlights

Tianshidong (Master) Cave First built in 730 AD, the current architecture—an intact ancient tempe complex—came into being after reconstruction in the 16th Century and renovation in 1920. Behind the halls, Hunyuanding is where Zhang Ling once built a cottage and preached Taoism; inside the halls a 6th Century stone statue of Master Zhang can be found, together with many well-preserved precious cultural relics such as the Decree of Pardon stele by Emperor Shenwu in the 9th Century, statue of Fu Xi, Shen Nong and Xuan Yuan (regarded as three ancestors of the Chinese people). In the temple there is a 1,800-year-old gingko tree with massive stalactites descending from the trunk.

Jianfu (Building Fortune) Palace Located below Zhangren Peak, first built in 730 AD and rebuilt in 1888, it is one of the key Taoist temples on the Mountain. Inside the temple, there is a famous long couplet composed of 394 characters and engraved on a piece of board in the 17th Century as well as the dressing table of Qingfu princess of Ming Dynasty.

Shangqing (Supreme Purity) Palace Situated on the slopes of the first peak of the Mountain, it was initially built in the 4th Century and reconstructed in 1869. Inside the halls, there are many steles, tablets and inscriptions written by famous people; outside the palace, there are ancient relics such as Guanri (Sun Viewing) Pavilion, Shengdeng (Sacred Light) Pavilion, Laojun (Lao-tzu) Pavilion, Paoma (Running Horse) Terrace, and Qigan (Flag Post) Rock.

Dujiangyan

⊙ Overview

Dujiangyan Irrigation System is the oldest, most magnificent and only remaining water conservancy project in the world, with a characteristic of water diversion without damming. It is such a wonder in the history of global water conservancy projects and breaks Chinese and even world records not only because it is the only one in existence, but also because it still functions efficiently and provides continuing benefits for the local people despite being built in about 256 BC, over 2,260 years ago, while other ancient irrigation systems are all disused or have simply disappeared.

A panorama of Dujiangyan

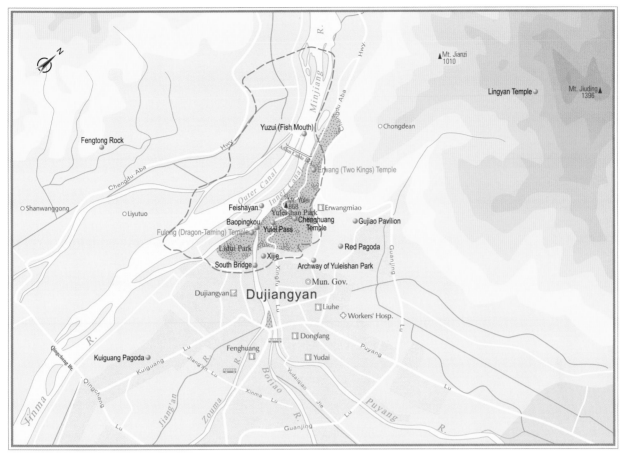

Dujiangyan

Integrating the forces of man, landform and water together, it is the only ancient ecologic irrigation system without damming in the world and without precedent in the history of international science and technology.

⊙ Description

Dujiangyan has a long history of aquatic culture, aquatic science, aquatic technology and ancient architecture. 2,260 years ago, Li Bing, the governor of Shu Prefecture of the Qin Kingdom and an outstanding expert in the field of water conservancy, led and organized the construction of the irrigation system by referring to water-control experiences of predecessors. Conforming to the order of nature; he chose the most appropriate location for the system by skillfully taking advantage of the special landform of water outlet and natural fall of Minjiang River and scientifically applying mechanics theory of crook circulation. Li adopted many techniques and rules to integrate dyke, water division, flood discharge and silt discharge into a whole system. The Irrigation System successfully solved the most difficult problems in water conservancy projects; exerted the ecological advantages of long dyke and low weir and overcame a great deal of harm which could be caused by silt if a high dam and big reservoir had been built. It converted the damage into benefits for people in West Sichuan. From then on, there has been no flood and drought, no shortage of water; Chengdu Plain has hence become "the Land of Abundance", a famous granary in China. The concept and experiences followed in the Irriga-

tion System are the successful application of systems engineering by the Chinese people. There is no doubt that it is a worldwide model of best utilization of water resources.

Dujiangyan Irrigation System consists of two major sections: diversion works and irrigation area. The diversion works comprises three main parts including a fish-mouth-like water-dividing dyke, Feishayan Spillway for discharging redundant water and silt, and a bottleneck-like water intake, as well as subsidiary works like Baizhang Dyke, Shunshui Dyke, and Y-shaped Dyke. Yuzui (Fish Mouth) is constructed in the middle of the watercourse of Minjiang River for the purpose of dividing the river into two parts, the inner canal and the outer canal. Under the influence of circulation, water with less silt concentration is drawn in by the inner canal and therefore can be used for gravity irrigation; the outer canal contains more silt and hence plays a role of flood and silt discharge. Located between the Y-shaped Dyke and Lidui (isolated mound), Feishayan is built for discharging superfluous water and a small amount of silt of the inner canal into the outer canal. Baopingkou (Bottleneck) is a water intake, artificially dug and shaped like a bottleneck, acting as the throat of the inner canal, with the function of controlling water inflow rate and ensuring water use for irrigation. Being on the left side of the inner canal and rear of the Fish Mouth, "Baizhang Dyke" is mainly for redressing the flow of water to maintain stabilization of inlets of inner and outer canals after division by the Fish Mouth and appropriately dividing water and silt. Lying on the left bank of the inlet of the inner canal, "Shunshui Dyke" is chiefly for adjusting the direction of water flow at the intake section of the inner canal so as to reduce the threat to Feishayan Spillway. Located next to the spillway and on the left side of the isolated mound, the Y-shaped Dyke assists flood discharge. Through rational and correct design,

Feishayan Spillway

the three major parts interact with each other in smooth coordination, forming an integrated and scientific system, which jointly performs comprehensive functions of water division, water blocking, flow control, flood discharge and silt discharge into full play.

⊙ Highlights

Erwang (Two Kings) Temple Facing the Dujiangyan Irrigation System across the river, Erwang Temple, a key site of cultural relics under state protection, was first built in the 5th Century and rebuilt in the 17th Century, exclusively for commemorating Lin Bing, his son, and others who dedicated to water-control throughout the past dynasties. The stone inscriptions including "Three-character Principle", "Six-character Rule" and "Eight-character Maxim" inside the halls are especially precious as they provide valuable water control experiences for the later generations.

Fulong (Dragon-taming) Temple Located on Lidui (Isolated

Erwang Temple

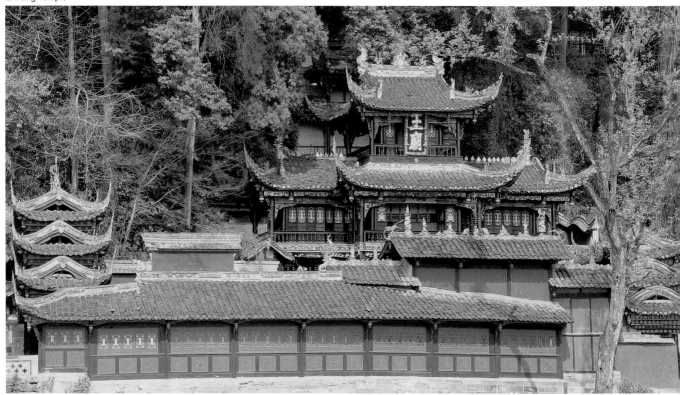

Mound), a key site of cultural relics under state protection, was first built in the 5th Century and reconstructed in the 18th Century. It is made up of three main halls, each with a unique style, possessing important reference for research on ancient architecture. There are valuable cultural relics such as a stone statue of Li Bing made in the 2nd Century and an iron tripod with flying dragon of the 14th Century.

Anlan (Billow Calming) Cable Bridge Lying beneath the Erwang Temple and spanning Minjiang River, the bridge, a key site of cultural relics under state protection, was originally built in the 7th Century. With a full length of 260 m, it was built with bars and cables made of bamboo. In 1962, the bamboo cables were replaced by wire ropes. The bridge is named "Anlan" (Billow Calming) because people on both sides of the river can get through safely in spite of the raging waves underneath the bridge. Historically, it was of great significance for linking both banks of Minjiang River and is valuable for research on ancient bridges of China.

Fulong Taoist Temple

⊙ Information

■ **Transportation** *Dujiangyan City is about 60 km away from Chengdu Shuangliu International Airport, and it is a 45-minute ride via the expressway. Leaving from the passenger transport station at Chadianzi, Chengdu, it takes about 30 minutes by bus via the expressway. From the city proper to each scenic spot, it takes about 10 minutes by public bus or taxi.*

■ **Accommodation** *Four-star hotels include Jinye Hotel, Guoyan Hotel, Hexiang Hotel; three-star hotels include Qingcheng Hotel, Lingyan Hotel and Erwangmiao Hotel.*

■ **Food** *Local delicacies and teahouse are available at Yinqiao Hotel, and hotpot is offered at Xiaotian'e Hotel.*

■ **Others** *Dujiangyan is one of the main regions for growing Chinese medicinal herbs and plants. It boasts abundant resources of animal and plants with various species and huge quantities; the most famous are Rhixoma Ligustici, gingko, Cortex Phellodendri, Euonymus Japonicus, Officinal Magnolia, and "Four Qingcheng Taoist Specialties" (chicken stewed with gingko, pickles, sweet alcohol and tea) which was once a tribute to the emperors. Dujiangyan also produces kiwi fruit and is well known for its root carvings.*

Inquiry telephones: 028-87120836 (Dujiangyan);
028-87288159 (Mt. Qingcheng)

Anlan Cable Bridge

YUNNAN PROVINCE

General Information

Yunnan Province, also called Yun or Dian in short, has its capital in Kunming City. With an area of over 380,000 sq km, it has under its administrative jurisdiction 8 prefecture-level cities, 8 autonomous prefectures, 9 county-level cities, 79 counties and 29 autonomous counties. The province has a population of 41.41 million and ethnic groups including Han, Yi, Bai, Hani, Zhuang, Dai, Miao, Hui, Lisu, Lahu, Va, Naxi, Jingpo, Zang (Tibetan) and Blang.

Environment

Yunnan is located on the southwest border of China, neighboring Myanmar, Laos and Vietnam. Its terrain descends from northwest to south, 93% or more are hilly areas and plateaus, and 6% are basins spread between the mountains. It has a central and southern sub-tropical humid monsoon climate. The average temperature is 8 ~ 12°C in January and 18 ~ 24°C in July, with an average annual rainfall between 600 ~ 2,300 mm.

Places of Interest

With snow-capped mountains, grassland, rivers and tropical forests under the blue sky, Yunnan is like multi-colored, kaleidoscopic brocade depicting numerous splendid landscapes. There are the green, dense rubber forests of Xishuanbanna and the crystal-clear ice-eroded lakes on the Qianhu (Thousand Lake) Mountain; the towering magnificent Yulong Snow Mountain, Haba Snow Mountain, Moirig Snow Mountain, the Nujiang River, Lancang River and Jinsha River converge here to form a unique wonder of nature--Three Parallel Rivers. Dali, Stone Forest, Dianchi Lake in Kunming, Cangshan Mountain and Erhai Lake, Ruili River-Daying River, Jiuxiang and Jianshui are like exotic flowers embroidered on the brocade, so bright yet so natural.

In the tranquil dwelling houses in the ancient city of Lijiang, the Naxi people are playing the slow, melodious music left over by their ancestors. The Dai girls are presenting a colorful picture with their graceful dances. Kunming, Dali, Lijiang, Jianshui and Weishan witness the combination of legends, songs and dances, painting and ancient music. Twenty-five ethnic groups live together in harmony, which present a diversified multi-ethnic picture.

Local Specialties

Dali stone carving, Gejiu tinware, Dai brocade, Banna carpets, Pu'er tea, Dian black tea, Xuanwei hams, root of pseudo-ginseng, tuber of elevated gastrodia, and Chinese caterpillar fungus.

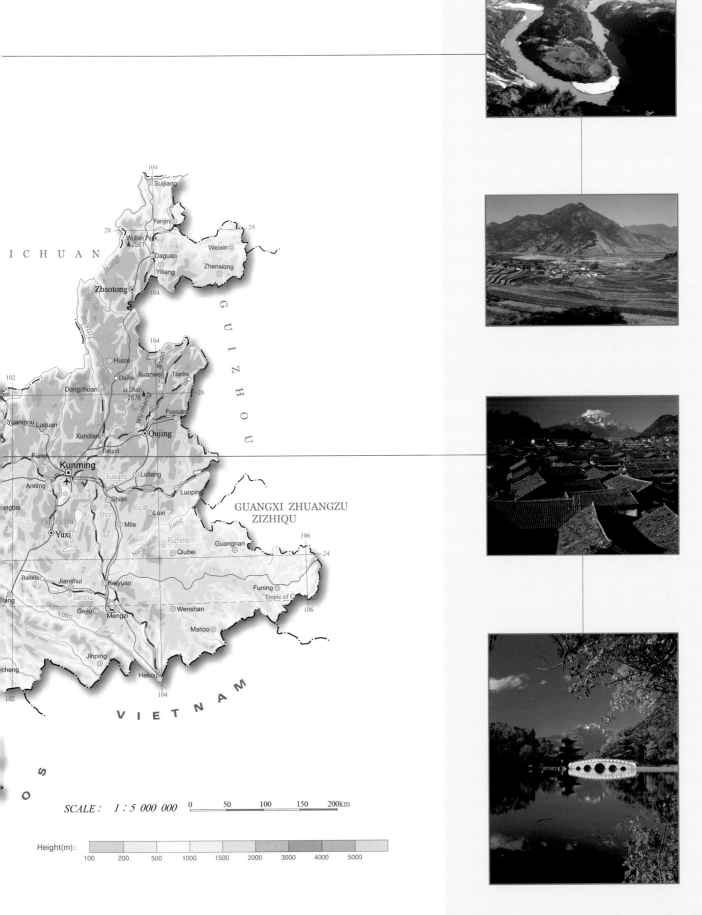

SCALE : 1 : 5 000 000

Height(m):

Old Town of Lijiang

☐ **Name:**

Old Town of Lijiang

☐ **Geographical coordinates:**

26° 52' N, 100° 14' E

☐ **Date of inscription:**

December 4, 1997

☐ **Criteria for inclusion:**

II, IV of cultural properties

Entrance to the old town

⊙ Overview

A famous historical and cultural city in China, Lijiang is located in the middle of Lijiang Basin, 2,400 m above sea level, on the northwestern Yunnan plateau. With a history of over 800 years, the mountain-surrounded town is an outstanding example of ethnic urban construction that bears a distinctive characteristic and style of Chinese vernacular dwellings. Featuring a layout blending local ethnic flavor with nature, Lijiang is an ancient town that preserves the most intact ethnic characteristics in China. The town was an important passage on the "southern silk road" and the "tea-horse ancient road". In the town, one can still feel the harmonious coexistence of Han, Tibetan and Dongba cultures. Lijiang stands against Shizi Mountain in the west, Xiangshan Mountain and Jinhong Mountain in the north, and faces an open basin in the southeast. The northwestern cold current is blocked by the mountains as the sunlight from southeast can be best used. Yuquan (Jade Spring) River splits into three and enters the town, creating a beautiful scene where streams wind through streets and neighborhoods and willows droop by every household.

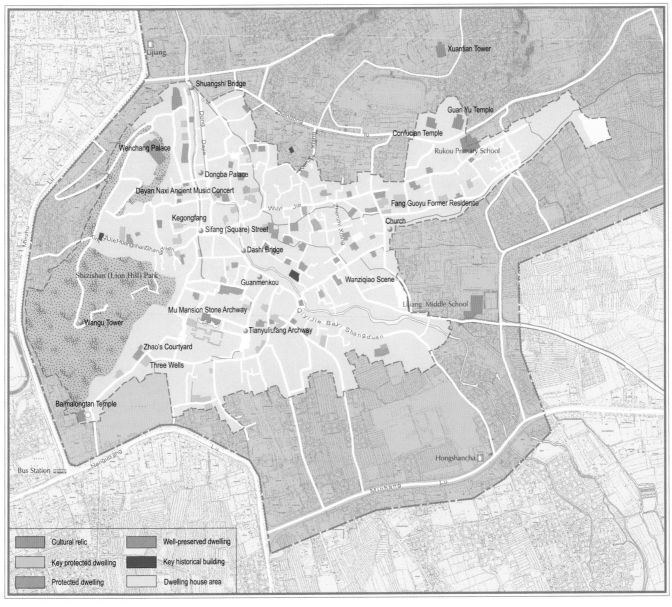

Old Town of Lijiang

⊙ Description

The Old Town of Lijiang takes up a unique place among Chinese famous cities as an ethnic town with a long history. Simple and natural, it gathers the beauty of a water town and mountain city. From the urban layout to construction, the city blends the gist of Han, Bai, Tibetan and Yi ethnic groups and presents the unique style of the Naxi nationality.

The old town fully demonstrates the achievements of architectural diversity in China's urban construction. Located in the basin area on the plateau and far from the inland area, the town was not affected by the "chessboard" design notion in the Central Plains area. There is no regular road network, nor tall city wall. The Yulong Snow Mountain, Shizi Mountain and Jinhong Mountain serve as its protective screens. The houses were well-arranged along the three streams and against the mountains. It is different from any other old town.

The Old Town of Lijiang is one type of the Chinese vernacular

dwellings that bears distinct style. The construction and layout of the town were not designed in a unified way but according to the tradition and natural conditions. One can find wisdom in plain design and pursuit for natural beauty. The old town is therefore an extremely important heritage in the history of Chinese culture and architecture.

The Old Town of Lijiang is a unity of natural beauty and man-made beauty, and is a nice blend of art and utility. The exquisite and harmonious vernacular dwelling in the old town is the cultural and artistic crystal of Naxi people who have absorbed the wisdom of other ethnic groups.

The Old Town of Lijiang, with rich traditional ethnic culture, has witnessed the flourishing and development of Naxi people, making up important historical evidence for the study of human cultural development. The vernacular dwelling decorations, gardens, couplets and stone tablets with inscriptions reflect Naxi

people's cultural taste and the connotations and flavor of local religions, aesthetics and literature. It is indeed a beautiful chapter in the history of human civilization.

The Old Town of Lijiang is located 2,400 m above sea level in the Jinsha River Basin, on the transitional zone between Qinghai-Tibet Plateau and Yunnan-Guizhou Plateau. High in northwest and low in southeast, the area has complicated geological conditions and various landforms. Mountains, plateaus and river valleys coexist at different altitudes. It has a typical vertical climate zone affected by South Asia plateau monsoon climate, with distinctive dry and humid seasons and little temperature change, and it is like spring all the year round. Special geographical and climate conditions foster abundant scenic, biological and water-energy resources. The Yulong Snow Mountain in the north, 5,596 m above sea level, provides water that flows across every street and lane, creating a scene of riverside town.

⊙ Highlights

Sifang (Square) Street It is a square market in the center of the old town. The street was in the shape in the late Ming Dynasty (1368-1644). It was an important town in West Yunnan and a transfer point for Sino-Indian trade. The street witnessed the booming commercial and cultural exchanges with foreign countries. There are four main streets extending

from Sifang Street to east, west, south and north, linking more lanes and streams. In the past, business people gathered here to sell handicraft and native products, and after the market fair was closed, residents would open the sluice to wash the streets covered with unique cobblestones. Today, Sifang Street is the place where community activities, especially the folk dances, are held.

Dashi (Big Stone) Bridge The style of bridges varies with water systems. Zhonghe River makes up the largest water system, dividing the town into two parts. Its numerous bridges are solid and steady, mostly long and wide stone arch bridges, including Dashi Bridge. Located 100 m to

Dashi Bridge

the east of Sifang Street, the bridge was built by a local headman. It is also called Yingxue (Snow Reflection) Bridge after the reflection of Yulong Snow Mountain in the water under the bridge. A double-arch stone bridge built with stone tablets, it is over 10 m long and 4 m wide. The slope of the surface is not steep for the convenience of transportation. As it is in the center of the old town where Mishi Lane, Wuyi Street and Sifang Street meet, the bridge has supported the business and cultural exchange in the past centuries, and is regarded as the No. 1 bridge in the old town.

Zhao's Courtyard It is a traditional vernacular dwelling at No. 58 Guangbi Lane, Guangyi Street. The courtyard is a key site of cultural relics under state protection. In the 1920s, many businessmen gathered in the town and built houses. Zhao's courtyard was first built in 1925 by the best architects in the neighboring areas. The main frames of the courtyard buildings were somewhat damaged later, and the courtyard buildings had been renovated by the owner since 1933. The compound is composed of two rows of

courtyards and a garden. The buildings bear a strong style of Naxi vernacular dwelling: white walls, blue tiles, wooden exterior and harmonious coloring, while its harmonious coexistence with surrounding environment is highlighted. It is close to the tranquil Baima Longtan Temple in the south and the grand Mu's Mansion in the east. In front of the gate is the age-old site of the "Three Wells".

⊙ Information

■ **Transportation** *There are flights everyday to Lijiang from Shanghai, Guangzhou, Chengdu and Kunming. Sleeping shuttle buses and daytime shuttle buses run frequently between Lijiang and Kunming, Dali, Xamgyi'nyilha and Ninglang. The scenic spots in the old town are all within walking distance.*

■ **Accommodation** *The town has a five-star hotel, Guanfang Hotel, and a four-star hotel, Yulong Garden Hotel. Other hotels include Adange Hotel, Senlong Hotel, Jiannanchun Hotel and Guanguang Hotel. There are also 130 ethnic vernacular hotels such as Fuxiang, Gucheng, Luyuan, Mulaoye and Lijiangyuan.*

■ **Food** *There are about 110 restaurants in the town. Gucheng Restaurant is built in a Naxi-style courtyard. Haji Beef Restaurant is a Muslim restaurant. Dashiqiao Snacks offers Lijiang rice cakes and bean jelly. Xuelou Restaurant offers "three-tea" banquet.*

■ **Others** *Visit the Dongba sacrificial rituals; learn to write Dongba pictographic characters; visit traditional paper mill and winery; attend the traditional dance party at night in Sifang Street; and listen to ancient Naxi music at the Ancient Music Palace. The native specialty products are Lijiang liquor, Wumuchun tea, Chinese caterpillar fungus and wild fruit oil. The handicraft products include Dongba batik, tapestry and wood ware.*

Website: www.lijiang.com.cn

Lijiang

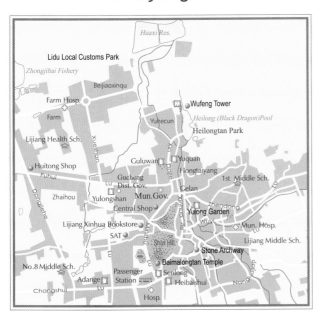

Three Parallel Rivers of Yunnan Protected Areas

Dulong Wonder Field

Shiguzhen at the first bend of Changjiang River

☐ **Name:**

Three Parallel Rivers of Yunnan Protected Areas

☐ **Geographical coordinates:**

25° 30' ~ 29° 00' N, 98° 00' ~ 100° 31' E

☐ **Date of inscription:**

July 3, 2003

☐ **Criteria for inclusion:**

I, II, III, IV of natural properties

⊙ Overview

The Three Parallel Rivers is situated at the juncture of three geographical realms of East Asia, South Asia and Qinghai-Tibet Plateau. Amid the high and steep mountains, Nujiang River (the upper reaches of Salween River), Lancang River (the upper reaches of Mekong River) and Jinsha River (the upper reaches of Yangtze River) flow from north to south for nearly 170 km, forming a unique natural wonder of the world--three parallel rivers. The total area covers 17,000 sq km and is composed of eight sections. This area has witnessed major stages and events in the evolution of the earth. It is an outstanding example featuring various alpine landforms, rich and unique landscapes, diversified animals and plants, and different ethnic cultures. It is one of the world areas with richest biodiversity, and also the important gene bank of animals and plants in China.

⊙ Description

1. The Three Parallel Rivers area is a typical example reflecting the main stages of the earth's evolution. Geologically, it is a southeastern extension of the Qinghai-Tibet Plateau and the main body of Hengduan Mountains. It is the most compressed huge compound orogenic belt, a key area that reflects the major events in the evolution of the earth, and the area of special geological structure formed by strong crust deformation and uplifting.

There are a rich variety of rocks in the area, and the geological remains are intact. It reflects the evolution of oceanic crust and change in the sedimentary facies from deep-sea basin to bench terrace. It also provides rich information about the geological activity deep in the crust and the process of polymetamorphic evolution and superimposed deformation during the orogenic movement.

This is a typical area of various types of alpine landforms and their evolution. There is a large area of eroded granite peak clusters, alpine karst landscapes, and *Danxia* landform (characterized by red cliffed scarp).

2. The Three Parallel Rivers area reflects the important constant evolution of the bio- and ecosystem. Here can be found the climate types equivalent to the northern hemisphere's southern subtropical zone, mid-subtropical zone, northern subtropical zone, warm temperate zone, temperate zone, cold temperate zone and frigid zone. It is an epitome of the biological environment of the Eurasian Plate. Meanwhile, it is an area that has seen the most intense differentiation of biological species and groups since the Cenozoic Era. It is the main north-south passage and shelter for the species on the Eurasian Plate and has the richest biomes on the continent. The area is almost the epitome of the biological and ecological environment of the northern hemisphere as it has all the types of northern hemisphere biomes except desert and ocean.

3. The Three Parallel Rivers area, which boasts remarkable biodiversity, is home to a number of endangered species. It is the representative and core area of Hengduan Mountains Biological Zone, ranking first among the 17 "key areas" of biodiversity protection in China. It is also one of the regions in the world with richest biodiversity, as well as the main center of animal and plant differentiation and origination in Eurasia.

The Three Parallel Rivers area has been the shelter of the rare and endangered animals and plants and one of the world's most famous sources of animal and plant specimens.

4. The Three Parallel Rivers area is of unique geological and biological value and natural esthetic value. It carries outstanding cultural connotations. The variable vertical climates, colorful landforms, biodiversity and unique ethnic cultures have made the area an ideal place of scientific exploration and sightseeing for people of different backgrounds.

⊰⊙⊱ Three Parallel Rivers ⊰⊙⊱

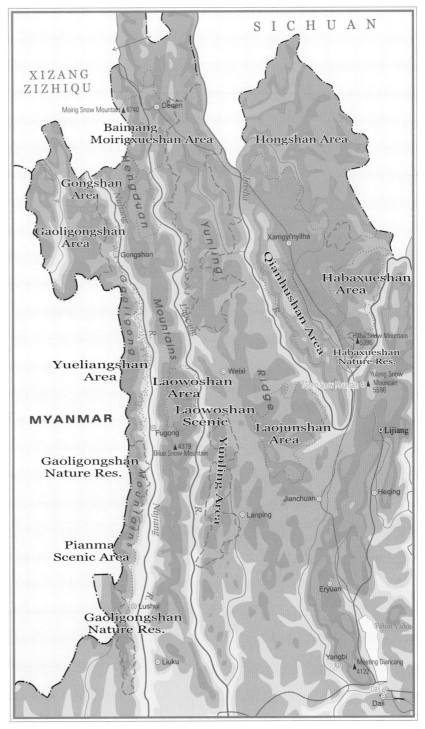

⊙ Highlights

Moirig (Meili) Snow Mountain Scenic Area Located in the upper reaches of Lancang River, the mountain indicates the border of Yunnan and Xizang (Tibet), linking Adongge Mountain in the north and Taizi Snow Mountain in the south and covering 1,587.5 sq km. In the mountain, there are many snow peaks higher than 5,000 m above sea level. The main peak Kawagebo is 6,740 m above sea level. The area has Mingyong Glacier, a modern oceanic glacier with the lowest ice tongue of the same latitude in the world. In the area are gathered the most typical and richest landscape types of Three Parallel Rivers, including snow peaks, low-altitude modern glaciers, dry-hot river valley landforms and human dwelling environments.

Moirig Snow Mountain

Laojun Mountain Scenic Area The area extends to the boundary between Lijiang and Lanping in the west, to the northern boundary of Liming Township in the north, to the boundary between Lijing at the foot of Laojun Mountain and Jianchuan in the south, and to Taohua in the east. It also includes Ludian, a new main part of the scenic area in the north. The area covers 1,045 sq km. Laojun Mountain is an important part of the Three Parallel Rivers, characterized by China's top *Danxia* landform, world-significant biodiversity, alpine glacial erosion lake and alpine meadow. Therefore, the area is of great value in geological and zoological study, biodiversity and ecological preservation, historical and ethnic culture research and landscape aesthetics.

Qianhu (Thousand Lakes) Mountain Scenic Area It is located in the western part of Xiaozhongdian Township, Xamgyi'nyilha (Shangri-La) County, Deqen Prefecture, covering a total area of 985.4 sq km and standing 2,400 ~ 4,200 m above sea level. There are more than 100 alpine glacial erosion lakes of varying sizes. The best-known lakes are Bigu Tianchi and Sanbihai. The area bears the unique scenic value with its alpine forests and lakes. There exists a complete and unique alpine ecological system, featuring alpine meadow, azalea forest and spruce and fir forests as well as rare animals and plants, yellow azalea and black-neck cranes. This is a part of the Three Parallel Rivers area that display typical alpine biodiversity.

Yueliang (Moon) Mountain Scenic Area It is located at Lishadi Township of Fugong County, on the west bank of Nujiang River Canyon and extends to Gaoligong Mountains. The highest peak is 4,069 m above sea level, and the lowest point is at the surface of Nujiang River, 1,200 m above sea level. Covering 445.5 sq km, the area is scattered with numerous large rivers, canyons and brooks. The Nujiang River Canyon is known for its height, depth, steepness and beauty. The weather changes with the height, and the landscape changes vertically with the varying climate. This is a typical area to showcase canyon, geological remains and karst caves.

Mt. Qiangui, Laojun Mountain

Information

■ **Transportation** *To Laojun Mountain, visitors may start from Lijiang, via Shigu to Liming by minivan, taxi or shuttle bus; to Qianhu Mountain, from Xamgyi'nyilha (Shangri-la) county town via national road 214 by shuttle bus; to main scenic area of Moirig Snow Mountain, from Xamgyi'nyilha county town via Benzilan, Dongzhulin Temple, Baimang Snow Mountain and Deqen county town by bus, by horse or on foot; to Gongshan and Shiyueliang, from Kunming via Baoshan (Dali) to Liuku by bus, by horse or on foot, then, from Liuku to Shiyueliang via Fugong, Shangpa Town, Lishadi, or, from Liuku to Gaoligong Mountain via Gongshan to Dulong River.*

First bend of Lancang River

■ **Accommodation** *To Laojun Mountain of Lijiang, visitors can stay at Qunlong Villa, Liming Hongshi Hotel Street and the ancient city of Lijiang; to Qianhu scenic area of Xamgyi'nyilha, at Guanguang Hotel, Huantai Hotel and Longfengxiang Hotel in Deqen; to Moirig Snow Mountain of Xamgyi'-nyilha, at Taizifeng Hotel, Caihong Hotel, Adunzi Hotel and Gesang Hotel; to Gongshan and Shiyueliang, at Youdian Hotel, Nujiangzhou Hotel, Wazhaka Villa and Wenmian Dulong Villa.*

■ **Others** *Local special products include: Snow Tea, Chinese caterpillar fungus, beimu (Fritillaria thunbergii), white kidney beans, walnut kernel, Chinese red pepper, tianma (Gastrodia elata) in Laojun Mountain; leather products, pottery, woolen products, wooden products, traditional carvings, cushions and Zhuoli hat in Qianhu Mountain; wooden products, silverware, Nixi earth pottery, Tibetan medicine, wild herbs and wild fungus in Moirig Snow Mountain; Chinese caterpillar*

fungus, Dulong carpet, Nu carpet, bamboo products, Dilitu, Qiben and Chu Wine in Gongshan and Shiyueliang.

Inquiry telephones: 0888-5151990, 5158111 (Lijiang);
0887-8225753, 8225390 (Xamgyi'nyilha);
0887-8414209, 8413451 (Deqen);
0886-3512285, 3413875 (Fugong)

Kunming

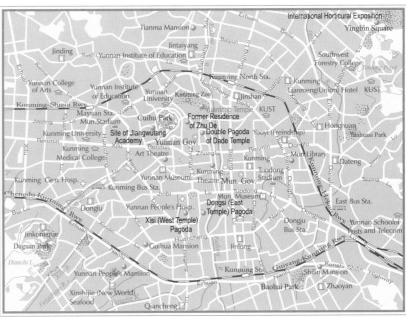

XIZANG (TIBET) AUTONOMOUS REGION

General Information

Tibet Autonomous Region, also called Zang in short, has its capital in Lhasa City. With an area of more than 1.2 million sq km, it has under its administrative jurisdiction 1 prefecture-level city, 6 prefectures, 1 county-level city and 71 counties. The autonomous region has a population of 2.55 million and ethnic groups including Zang (Tibetan), Han, Hui, Monba and Lhoba. The Tibetan accounts for more than 93% of the total population.

Environment

It is located at the southwestern border of China, neighboring with India, Nepal, Sikkim, Bhutan and Myanmar. The Qinghai-Tibet Plateau forms the main body of the territory, with an average elevation of more than 4,000 m above sea level, also known as "the Roof of the World". It has a plateau climate. The average temperature is -10° ~ 4°C in January (about 6°C in Shannan region), and around 15°C in July, with an average annual rainfall between 50 ~ 500 mm (more than 2,000 mm in Shannan region).

Places of Interest

It is widely said that only when one reaches the sacred mountain can he finds how humble human beings are; only when he sees the sacred lake can he understand what piety is; only when he manages to reach the remote Medog can he get the true meaning of a narrow escape; only when he stands gazing at Qomolangma Peak can he be endowed with a heart that accommodates the entire world. The charm of Tibet as a land of profound sacredness sitting close to heaven cannot be felt without a tour there in person.

Lhasa, Xigaze and Gyangze, as famous cities of cultural and historical value, are telling the profound history of Tibet. The Potala Palace, the Jokhang Lamasery, and the summer palace Norbulingka, as part of the world cultural heritage, represent the far-reaching culture of Tibet. The Yalong River, Namtso, the Tashilumpo Monastery and the Yarlung Zangbo Grand Canyon, as the scenic spots and historical sites, are scrolls of beautiful paintings depicting the mountains and rivers of the plateau.

Like an untapped virgin land, the snow-capped plateau, which is full of towering mountain peaks, rivers and lakes, unveils a unique, mysterious quality of glamour.

Local Specialties

Tibet carpets, Tibet boots, Nyingchi winter peaches, musk, angelica, hairy deerhorn, gastrodia tuber, saffron crocus, and Chinese caterpillar fungus.

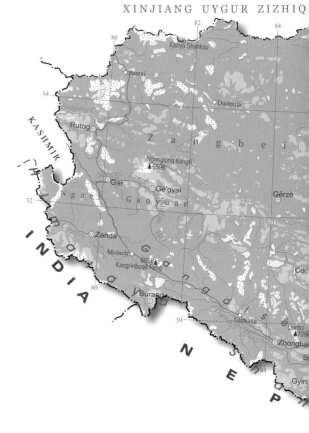

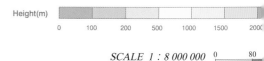

Height(m)

0 100 200 500 1000 1500 2000

SCALE 1 : 8 000 000 0 80

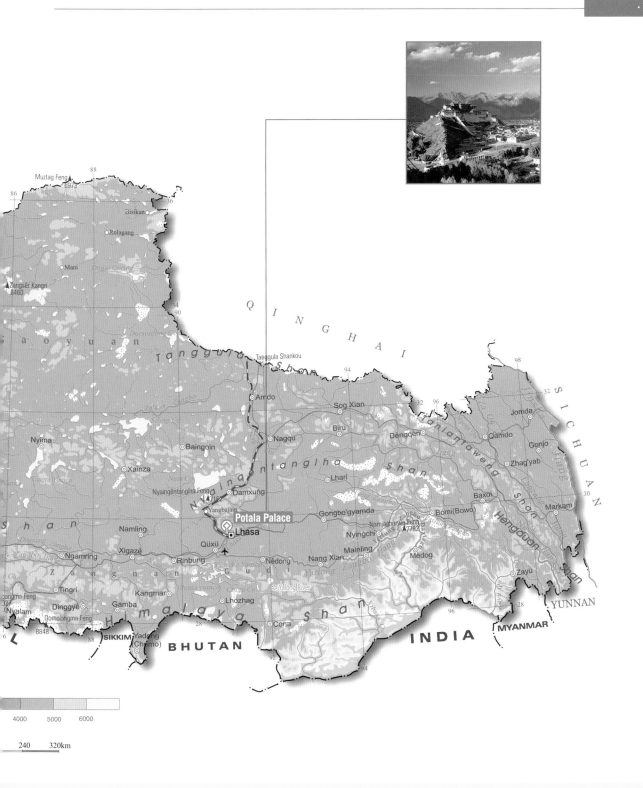

Muztag Feng
6973

88

86

36

Bisikan

Rolagang

Mani

Ongai Congo

Zangsêr Kangri
6460

Q I N G H A I

a o y u a n

Dorsondon

T a n g g u l a   S h a n

Tanggula Shankou

34

90

94

S I C H U A N

Amdo

Sog Xian

32

Jomda

96

32

98

Nyima

Biru

Dêngqên

Qamdo

Gonjo

T a n i a n f a w e n g

Nagqu

Zhag'yab

Baingoin

Xainza

Lhari

N a i n q ê n t a n g l h a   S h a n

Gonjo

Zhag'yab

Nyainqêntanglha Feng
7162

Damxung

Baxoi

Markam

30

Yangbajain

Gongbo'gyamda

Bomi(Bowo)

H e n g d u a n   S h a n

Potala Palace

Lhasa

Namjagbarwa Feng
7782

Namling

Nyingchi

Xigazê

Rinbung

Nang Xian

Mainling

Mêdog

Ngamring

Nêdong

Gudi

Yarlung

Z a n g n a n

Yalong River

Zayü

28

Tingri

Kangmar

Lhozhag

YUNNAN

Dinggyê

Gamba

H i m a l a y a   S h a n

27

Nyalam

Qoinolangma Feng

Cona

96

8848

88

SIKKIM

Yadong (Chomo)

B H U T A N

28

92

I N D I A

MYANMAR

94

4000 5000 6000

240 320km

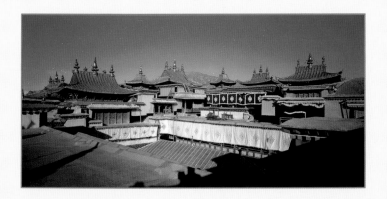

137

Historic Ensemble of the Potala Palace, Lhasa

☐ **Name:**

Historic Ensemble of the Potala Palace, Lhasa

☐ **Geographical coordinates:**

29° 39' N, 91° 08' E

☐ **Date of inscription:**

December 15, 1994

☐ **Criteria for inclusion:**

I, IV, VI of cultural properties

Roof of Jokhang Temple

◉ Overview

The Potala Palace, constructed during the period of Tibetan King Songtsang Kampo in the 7th Century, is located on the top of the Red Hill in Lhasa, a city on the "roof of the world". Its elevation is more than 3,700 m above sea level. With a construction space totaling 138,025 sq m and a height of 117 m, the building is the largest and most complete ancient Tibetan castle-style palace complex now existing in Tibet. Its unique architectural style and shaping incorporate architectural features of the Tibetan, the Han, the Indian and the Nepalese, and the palace is considered a shining pearl in the world history of architecture. In terms of its palace layout, civil engineering, metallurgy, sculpture, frescoes and collection of various cultural relics, it manifests the hard work and wisdom of the ancient Tibetan people and the great achievements of the Tibetan architectural arts. It is virtually the epitome of the history of Tibet, and is a valuable evidence for the study of the history, culture and arts of the Tibetan people and the accomplishments of multicultural integration.

⊙ Description

Constructed against the hill terrain, the Potala Palace combines the traditional earth-stone-wood structure of the Tibetan people with the castle style architecture, including the palaces, the memorial hall, the hall of the Buddha, the Scripture hall, monks' dormitories and courtyards. The foundation was built on the rocks, and it seems as if the palace is rising into the sky and the view is grand, magnificent and imposing. The architecture is composed of the palaces, the hall of the Buddha and the memorial hall, and was designed and constructed according to the layout of Buddhist altar city. The main structures include the White Palace and the Red Palace.

The White Palace is so named because its exterior is painted white. The "Z" shaped path on the slope at the foot of the palace leads to the flat square called Deyangxia (east courtyard) at the front gate. The main building of the palace is located at the west side of the courtyard. The main hall is East Great Hall, the site where the Dalai Lamas held grand ceremonies. The sleeping chambers of the Dalai Lama are on the top part of the palace, including the homage hall, the meeting hall, the scripture hall and the bedroom. The furnishings of the sleeping chambers are arranged as they were in history.

The Red Palace, located west of the White Palace, is so named because its exterior is painted red. Located at the center of the Potala Palace above the Red Hill, with seven golden tops on the roof, it makes the Potala Palace grand, solemn and magnificent. Inside the Red Palace, the memorial hall contains stupas of the

Roof of the Potala Palace

Dalai Lamas throughout the dynasties, and there are also Buddhist pagodas and scripture rooms of various descriptions.

Tens of thousands of fine frescoes in various halls, vestibules, passages and corridors are the works by outstanding painters and artists from Tibet. Their themes and contents are diversified. Some reflect the origin of the mankind, historical figures and stories; some depict religious legends and Buddhist stories; and some others involve the architecture, folk customs, sports and recreational life. These frescoes, made with meticulous techniques and in bright colors, are masterpieces of the Tibetan painting.

The Potala Palace has a rich collection of various cultural relics, including sculptures, silk paintings, ceramics, jade wares, religious objects, canopies, curtains and numerous classic books, on the subjects of astronomy, medicine, arts, history and Buddhism, etc.

Statue of Maitreya, Potala Palace

⊙ Highlights

The Sacred Avalokitesvara Hall It is the oldest and most sacred hall of the Buddha in the Potala Palace. This hall enshrines the freedom of the mind Avalokitesvara, the Buddha worshipped by Tibetan King Songtsang Kampo and the Dalai Lamas. The Buddha statue is 0.93 m high and 0.1 m wide. It is said that the statue was sculpted in the 7th Century by Buddhist disciples out of sandalwood grown in southern Nepal. In the period when the Tubo King Lang Darma (r.838-842) purged Buddhism, this statue was moved to the Phabongkha Lamasery in northern Lhasa, and was later moved to the Ramoche Lamasery in Lhasa. In 1618 when Gemabapengcuolangjie led the army and controlled Tibet, Jixuedibasuolanglangjie from Lhasa borrowed the Mongolian army from Qinghai to fight back. As a reward, he gave this Buddhist statue to Hong Taiji, the commander of the Mongolian army. In 1645 when the Potala Palace was reconstructed, Talaigunji, empress of Mongolian Khan Gushihan, presented this statue to the 5th Dalai Lama Ngawang Losang Gyatso, who enshrined the statue in the Avalokitesvara

Hall. This Buddha statue became the main Buddha worshipped in the Potala Palace, and has been worshipped ever since by all disciples and believers.

Stupa of the 5th Dalai Lama The 5th Dalai Lama Ngawang Lobsang Gyatso (1617-1682) was born in the Shannan area of Tibet and died in the Potala Palace at the age of 66. His stupa, located at the center of the memorial hall in the Red Palace, is the first stupa of the Potala Palace. Facing the east, it is a 14.85-m-high wood-structured stupa covered with 3,721 kg of gold plate. The stupa was inlaid with 18,852 jewels, including pearls, turquoises, corals, lazurites, diamonds, rubies and sapphires. In addition, a 5 cm treasured pearl grown in the brain of elephant, bestowed to the 5th Dalai Lama by Emperor Shunzhi, was also inlaid in this stupa. Other valuable cultural relics housed in the stupa include a mandate left behind by Songtsang Kampo, a collection of the "Annotated Shilun Scripture" inscribed on shells, a collection of "One-hundred-thousand-character Eulogy Scriptures" written with nose blood by Lianhuasheng and his concubines Yixijiecuo and Chisongdezan, a piece of thumb relic from Sakyamuni, and a piece of tooth relic from Tsongkhapa (1357-1419).

Norbulingka

☐ **Name:**
The Potala Palace (extension)—Norbulingka
☐ **Date of inscription:**
December 1, 2001

Lhasa

⊙ Overview

After the 7th Dalai Lama Kelsang Gyatso began to construct the Wuyao Potrang Palace in 1751, Norbulingka had become an important residence of the Dalai Lamas throughout the dynasties. And it is now one of the important sites where the people hold festival and celebration activities and events. Norbulingka is considered a multi-functional museum, featuring the garden structures, palace buildings, plateau animals and plants, historical relics, cultural relics and ethnic customs, and it reveals the unique physical, historical and human characteristics of Tibet. It is a masterpiece combining architectural arts, religious arts and garden arts of Tibet. Its architectures are mainly in Tibetan style, incorporating the characteristics of palace and garden architecture of other ethnic groups such as the Han.

⊙ Description

As the ancient and new architectures in Norbulingka are in perfect harmony, they also demonstrate their own unique features. Frescoes inside the palaces and halls are everywhere, and their themes include the human evolution, historical events, Buddhist legends and fable stories of Tibet to reflect the traditional cultural features of the Tibetan people.

Since the 7th Dalai Lama, Norbulingka had become the residence of the successive Dalai Lamas and was also named as the Summer Palace. From the 3rd month to the 9th month on the Tibetan calendar each year, the Dalai Lama would move from the Potala Palace to live in Norbulingka, and all major agencies of the Tibetan local government would also move here. Norbulingka, just as the Potala Palace and the Jokhang Temple, had exerted an important influence on the history, society and culture of Tibet.

Norbulingka reflects the achievements in landscape gardening, architecture, painting and sculpture by the Tibetan ethnic group, and bears striking influences of the Han culture and cultures of other ethnic groups. It is the most typical villa-styled structure combining garden with palace-styled architectures, the largest and best-constructed garden in Tibet, and a precious historical, cultural and garden heritage.

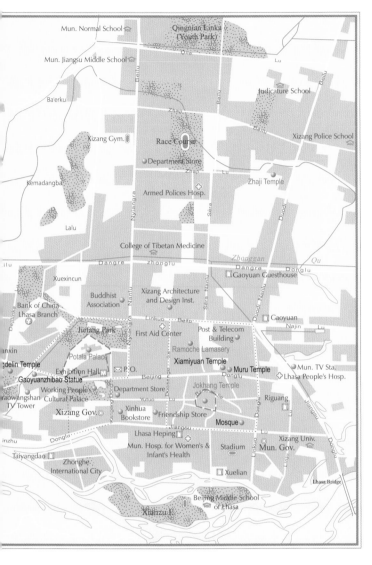

cient trees aged more than 200 years, and is therefore reputed as a garden of plateau plants.

The Norbulingka Zoo occupies over 4,000 sq m of land and has 130 animals in 14 species. Most of them are wildlife indigenous in the Qinghai-Tibet Plateau, such as white-lipped deer and brown bear, animals under Grade II state protection.

⊙ Highlights

Kelsang Potrang It was constructed in 1755 by the 7th Dalai Lama and was named after him. The palace is a three-storey structure, its walls were laid with squared stones, the upper part of the stonewall is covered with thick beima grass, and the surface of the grass layer is decorated with gold-gilded Buddhist patterns. Dharma-cakra, treasure bottle and other objects are erected atop of the roof.

Chensel Potrang

Norbulingka now houses about 20,000 pieces of cultural relics. In the garden, there are trees under Grade I and Grade II state protection, including Himalayan cypress, cedar, monterey cypress, shiny-leaved yellow horn, tropical plants of bamboo and silk tree as well as rare flower hydrangea. In addition to various rare flowers and plants indigenous in Tibet, Norbulingka also boasts an-

Chensel Potrang It began to be constructed in April 1922 at the order of the 13th Dalai Lama Thubten Gyatso after he visited Beijing in 1908 and toured the imperial palaces and gardens. This three-storey Tibetan building is known for its wood sculptures. There are frescoes on every block of its wall, and religion is the main theme, including stories and portraits of the historical figures.

Interior of Norbulingka

Norbulingka

Many of the frescoes bear the style of the Han people.

Tagten Migyur Potrang It began to be constructed in 1954 and was completed in 1956. The two-storey palace was constructed for the 14th Dalai Lama. Also called the new palace, it is composed of over 30 rooms and halls, including the divine hall, the meditation room, the scripture room, the living room, the bedroom and the washing room. This palace not only has the architectural characteristics of temples and monasteries, but also bears the artistic styles of palaces and villas, and it is therefore grander and more elegant than other palaces.

Jokhang Temple

☐ **Name:**

The Potala Palace (extension)—Jokhang Temple

☐ **Date of inscription:**

November 30, 2000

⊙ Overview

Jokhang Temple, constructed during the period of Songtsang Kampo in the 7th Century, is located at the Barkhor Street in the old city of Lhasa and is considered one of the Tibetan Buddhism's most sacred temples, covering an area of 13,000 sq m. The temple

still preserves the special features of the typical Tibetan ancient architecture and historical center, and it is a masterpiece of unique architectural arts and religious arts. Its construction and architectural styles are unique, and it integrates the architectural features of the Tibetan and the Han as well as those of India and Nepal.

Statue of Sakyamuni, Jokhang Temple

⊙ Description

Facing the east, the four-storey high Jokhang Temple with a golden top looks great and magnificent. The buildings are basically arranged along an axis and consist of four sections: vestibule, courtyard, the Hall of the Buddha, and the monks' rooms and warehouses. The Hall of the Buddha is located at the rear section; the spacious courtyard surrounded by corridors is located in front of the Hall of the Buddha; and outside the courtyard stands the vestibule. About 10 m from the front gate, there are the stele marking the meetings between the officials of the imperial court of the Tang Dynasty and the Tibetan regional government, the stele depicting the persuasion for smallpox inoculation, and the Tang Dynasty willow (Princess Willow).

The buildings of the Jokhang Temple are wood-stone structured. The walls were all laid with stones and painted white, on which black-framed Tibetan squared windows were opened. The vestibule of the front gate is in the recessed shape. The vestibule house is high: the right side is one storey higher than the other sides, covered with gold-gilded Manni wheel; on the back wall is a huge fresco of the four maharajas; the front eaves are canopies made of yak wool or cotton cloth, and the golden shining divine wheels, divine animals and huge religious objects are erected on the bronze grass surface. The vestibule house

Jokhang Temple

has two gates, and the center is a walk-through hall where the four maharajas are standing on two sides. Behind the vestibule house there is an open courtyard. Behind the courtyard, a closed compound was constructed, at the center is a small yard surrounded by several Buddhist halls.

The Jokhang Temple houses 3,299 statues of Buddha, Bodhisattvas, divine guardians and historical figures, made of different materials in different periods since the 7th Century, from India, Nepal, the inner land and Tibet, 1,324 *tangkhas*, 595 stupas and 150 pieces of religious objects. In addition, there are 108 volumes of the grand scriptures written in red ink, presented by chieftain Muzeng of Yunnan during the Ming Dynasty. In the Temple, a horse-head-shaped kettle is also kept, which is said to be the wine kettle used by Songtsang Kampo.

Inside the Hall of Buddha there are plenty of murals, of them the 1000-m-long "Princess Wencheng Entering Tibet" and the "Construction of the Jokhang Temple" are of high historical and artistic values.

⊙ Highlights

Sakyamuni Hall Inside the hall, the Sakyamuni statue, 1.5 m high, was said to be brought into Tibet by Princess Wencheng from Xi'an. The bronze statue, gilded with gold, depicting a kindly image of Sakyamuni, is a rare piece of artistic treasure.

Hall of Group Statues The statues were modeled on real figures, leaving much room for artistic creation. The group statues are vivid, including the militant and brilliant Fa Wang (Dharma Raja), the wise and quick-witted Princess Wencheng, the steady and virtuous Princess Khribtsun, the experienced and astute Blon-stong-btsan-po and the scripture-reading Tunmisangbuzha. During the Tubo Dynasty (629-846), the lintels and doorframes of Buddhist halls were finely made, decorated with various religious figures, animal

and plant images. The layout pattern and images of these decorations reflect the artistic styles of Nepal and ancient India.

⊙ Information

Transportation *Air routes link Tibet with Chengdu, Beijing, Shanghai, Chongqing, Xi'an, Xining, Guangzhou, Qamdo, Kunming and Kathmandu. The Gongga Airport is located 100 km south of Lhasa and it is a two-hour journey by car between the airport and downtown Lhasa. Lhasa is also a terminal of long-distance buses, and public transport in the city is very convenient.*

Accommodation *Lhasa Holiday Inn is the best hotel in Tibet. Barkhor Hotel, one of the "top 10 mountain hotels in the world", is characterized by its Tibetan atmosphere.*

Food *Restaurants are mainly Tibetan and Sichuan cuisines, several also serve Nepalese and Indian food. The canteens of many hotels and hostels at Beijing Road serve Western food. The Gangji Restaurant facing the Jokhang Temple Square mainly serves Tibetan food, and visitors could enjoy the street view while having their meals. The Xueshengong, in front of the Potala Palace, is another place where visitors could have a taste of genuine Tibetan food.*

Others *Local special products include butter, cheese, Chinese caterpillar fungus, Saussurea involucrata, silk painting and Tibetan knife.*

Opening hours: Potala Palace 9:00 ~ 17:00; Jokhang Temple 8:00 ~ 13:00, 14:00 ~ 19:00

Inquiry telephones: Potala Palace 0891-6822753, 6822896; Norbulingka 0891-6822644, 6832625, 6822233; Jokhang Temple Monastery 0891-6321398, 6336858

SHAANXI PROVINCE

General Information

Shaanxi Province, also called Qin, has its capital in Xi'an City. With an area of over 190,000 sq km, it has under its administrative jurisdiction 10 prefecture-level cities, 3 county-level cities, and 80 counties. It has a population of 36.11 million and ethnic groups including Han, Hui, Man and Mongol.

Environment

It is located in the hinterland of China, at the lower reaches of the Yellow River. Northern Shaanxi is in the central part of the Yellow Plateau. Guanzhong, known as an 800-mile Qin Plain, is featured with an alluvial plain as a result of the impact of the Weihe River. Between the Qinling Mountains and Bashan Mountains in southern Shaanxi is the valley of the Hanshui River. The climate varies from north to south, ranging from the semi-arid monsoon climate of the temperate zone, through the semi-arid and semi-humid monsoon climate of the warm temperate zone, to the sub-tropical humid monsoon climate. The average temperature is 0°C or above in January in southern Shaanxi, and at around 24°C in July, with an average annual rainfall between 400 ~ 1,000 mm.

Places of Interest

"The 5,000-year history is mirrored in Xi'an." Shaanxi is one of the most important cradles where the Chinese civilization was concentrated. As early as 1 million years ago, the Lantian Man settled down and lived there. Altogether 13 dynasties in history had chosen it as their capitals one after another. In this "natural history museum", there are not only the relics of the ancient Chang'an City, the legendary tomb of Emperor Huangdi, Empress Wu Zetian's Tomb, the Qianling Tomb, Maoling Tomb and the Tomb of Wudi of the Han Dynasty, but also the Banpo Village Site, the Forest of Steles, the Famen Temple, Huaqing Hot Springs, and Dayan (Big Wild-goose) Pagoda. The once deep-buried terracotta warriors and horses are one of the world's great wonders. The northern Shaanxi Plateau has given birth to some of China's famous cities of historical and cultural values, such as Xi'an, Yan'an, Xianyang and Hanzhong. Moreover, it has cultivated the typical Loess Plateau arts and customs, the classic, sonorous *Xintianyou* folksong, the energetic and brisk waist-drum dancing, delicate paper cutting, and the novelty-rich Chinese Peasant Painting.

The natural landscape of Shaanxi is equally unmatched. There are the West Sacred Mountain of Huashan, Lishan Mountain in Lintong, Tiantai Mountain in Baoji, Maosoleum

of Emperor Huangdi, Qiachuan in Heyang, and the torrential Hukou Waterfall of the Yellow River, which expresses one's feelings—"See how the Yellow River's water pours down from heaven".

Local Specialties

Xifeng spirits, Yaozhou celadon porcelain, Lintong Pomegranate, Shangluo walnuts, tri-colored painted earthenware, and paper cutting in northern Shaanxi.

Height(m)

| 100 | 200 | 500 | 1000 | 1500 | 2000 | 3000 |

SCALE 1 : 4 000 000   0   40   80   120   160km

Mausoleum of the First Qin Emperor

□ **Name:**

Mausoleum of the First Qin Emperor

□ **Date of inscription:**

December 11, 1987

□ **Criteria for inclusion:**

I, III, IV, VI of cultural properties

Bronze chariot

⊙ Overview

The burial place of China's first ruler of feudal dynasty, Mausoleum of the First Qin Emperor is one of the biggest imperial tombs in the world and the richest in content. The discovery of its sacrificial pit—the Qin Terracotta Warriors and Horses—constitutes a major discovery in the archaeological history, and the Qin terracotta is praised as the "Eighth Wonder of the World". Comparable with the Pyramid of Egypt and sculptures of ancient Greece and Rome, it is universally acknowledged that the pits are the treasured wealth of human civilization. The remains of the Qin Terracotta Warriors and Horses and its unearthed cultural relics have provided extremely valuable objects to explore into the military affairs, politics, economy, culture and art of the Qin Dynasty in the 2nd Century BC. The terracotta warriors and horses reproduced the way of life as it was. With bright colored drawings in minute details, each warrior figure carried a distinct personality of its own, with different gestures and facial expressions. It was a treasure house of China's ancient colored sculptures. In recent years, more sacrificial pits were excavated, adding to our knowledge about the Mausoleum.

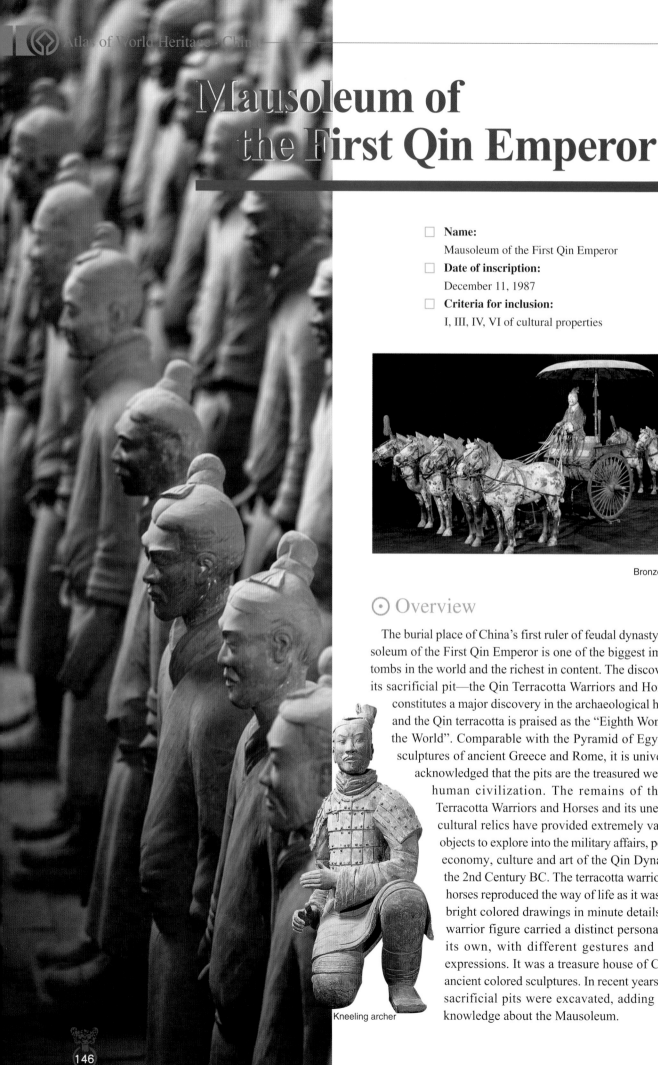

Kneeling archer

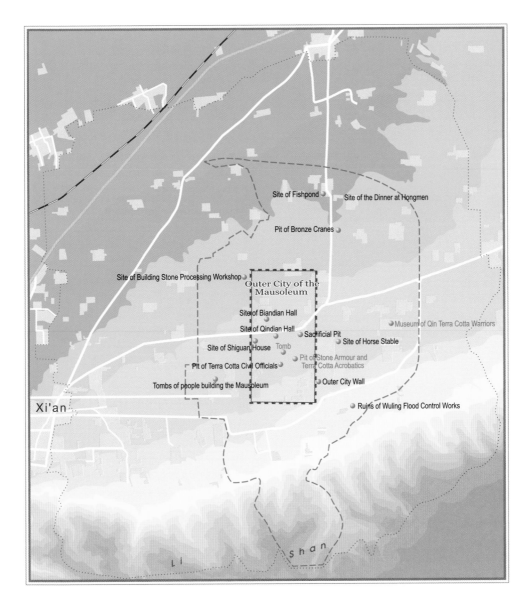

Site of Fishpond
Site of the Dinner at Hongmen
Pit of Bronze Cranes
Site of Building Stone Processing Workshop
Outer City of the Mausoleum
Site of Biandian Hall
Site of Qindian Hall
Sacrificial Pit
Museum of Qin Terra Cotta Warriors
Site of Shiguan House
Tomb
Site of Horse Stable
Pit of Terra Cotta Civil Officials
Pit of Stone Armour and Terra Cotta Acrobatics
Tombs of people building the Mausoleum
Outer City Wall
Xi'an
Ruins of Wuling Flood Control Works
Li   S h a n

Mausoleum of the First Qin Emperor

⊙ Description

The Mausoleum of the Frist Qin Emperor is located at the northern foot of Lishan Mountain, 5 km east of the Lintong District of Xi'an. Facing Lishan Mountain to the south and Weihe River to the north, it commands a spectacular natural view. Construction of the mausoleum started in 246 BC and was forced to be completed in haste in 208 BC due to peasant uprisings. Thus the mausoleum was built over a span of 39 years. According to historical records, as many as 720,000 laborers were mobilized at the peak of its construction.

The designing thought of the mausoleum was to reproduce the real world for the deceased in the underground world and the mausoleum was built to mirror the urban plan of Xianyang, capital of the Qin Dynasty. Two rounds of walls were built in the mausoleum, signifying the two walls guarding the imperial city and palace. With the burial mound as the center, the mausoleum was divided into the Underground Palace, the Inner City, the Outer City and

suburban areas. Many structures for the purposes of conducting sacrificial rituals and construction of the subordinate tombs were scattered between the imperial palace and the inner city. They include residences for the emperor and his entourage as well as the subordinate tombs of his empresses and concubines. These facilities prove that they are equivalent to the imperial palace of the First Qin Emperor. Between the Inner City and the Outer City are parks and animal farms as well as residences of officials. To date, pits of stables, pits of rare birds and animals, a pit of civil officials, a pit containing stone armor and helmets and a pit containing terracotta acrobats have been excavated. Such facilities were meant for the pleasure of the emperor when he was away from the imperial palace. Areas beyond the Outer City were facilities that were meant to build, manage and protect the imperial palace. Among the discoveries in this area are a quarry site, pits of terracotta warriors and horses, pits of bronze waterfowls, pits of small stables,

Qin Terracotta Museum

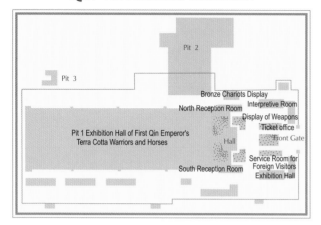

Pit 2

Pit 3

Bronze Chariots Display
Interpretive Room
North Reception Room
Display of Weapons
Ticket office
Pit 1 Exhibition Hall of First Qin Emperor's
Terra Cotta Warriors and Horses
Hall
Front Gate
Service Room for
Foreign Visitors
South Reception Room
Exhibition Hall

numerous subordinate tombs and graveyards of tomb builders, as well as kilns for bricks and tiles. To block off floods from Lishan Mountain, a 40-m wide dyke was built at the point where the southern part of the mausoleum area joins the mountain. It is believed that over 600 subordinate pits and tombs in different sizes are located around the mausoleum. So far, 50,000 pieces of cultural relics have been unearthed.

Located 1,500 m east of the mausoleum, the pits of terracotta warriors and horses belong to the outer ranges of the sacrificial burial system of the First Qin Emperor Mausoleum. In 1974, the pits were discovered by accident when local farmers were sinking a well. At present three subordinate pits in varying sizes and content have been discovered. They simulated the military alignment in a lifelike manner and served as the imperial army for the underground imperial palace.

In December 1980, two colored bronze chariots with horses were unearthed at the western side of the burial mound of the mausoleum. They are the earliest and biggest of their kind discovered so far in China. Being the most complex in structure and most exquisite in production techniques, the chariots were praised as the "Crown of Bronze-ware" of ancient China. They provided valuable objective materials for the study of Qin history and metallurgy, as well as ancient chariot rank system.

From 1998 till now, within the inner and outer cities of the First Qin Emperor Mausoleum, pits containing stone armor and helmets, pottery civil officials, terracotta acrobats and bronze waterfowls, as well as other articles, have been unearthed. Their discovery has not only enriched the connotation of sacrificial burial system of the mausoleum, but also offered more clues for the study of the social outlook of the Qin Dynasty and the layout of the mausoleum.

⊙ Highlights

Burial Mound and Underground Palace of the First Qin Emperor Mausoleum Located in the southern part of the inner city, the burial mound is a dome-like structure that measures 51 m in height and has a girth of 1,700 m at the bottom. Under the burial

mound is a massive palace. According to *Shi Ji* (the Historical Records), the tomb was lavishly equipped: "It was filled with mercury as the symbol of rivers and seas and was stuffed with various handicrafts and treasures." The Historical Records also noted that to protect the palace from harassment, the artisans building the tomb were sealed inside and no one ever managed to get out. To prevent the tombs from thefts and burglaries, bows and arrows were made so that thieves approaching the tomb could be shot and killed. Up till now the burial mound and the underground palace have been kept intact.

Pits of Terracotta Warriors and Horses The three pits were underground tunnels made of wood and mud. Judging from the shape and structures of the pits as well as the equipment of the terracotta warriors and horses, Pit 1 represented the principal body of the army, which were infantries with chariots; Pit 2 housed an army mixed with infantry, cavalry and soldiers in chariots; Pit 3 was the headquarters that commanded the armies in Pit 1 and Pit 2. The three pits have a combined area of 22,780 sq m. The pits contain over 7,400 life-size pottery warriors and horses, over 100 chariots and more than 40,000 bronze weapons.

Pits of Stone Armors In 1998, within the confines of the inner and outer walls of the Qin Mausoleum, a pit similar in structure with the pits of Qin terracotta warriors and horses was discovered. With an area of 13,000 sq m, the pit housed many stone armor and helmets. Each armor was made of several hundred stone pieces, with the thinnest being 2～3 mm. Discovery of the numerous stone armors constitutes an unprecedented event in the archaeology of China and the world, which is of significant value to the study of the history of military, and science and technology.

Cavalry soldiers

Full view of Pit 1

Side view of Pit 1

⊙ Information

■ **Transportation** *The Xianyang Airport of Xi'an has more than 80 domestic routes and 6 international routes. All major cities in China are connected with Xi'an by railways. Taxis and buses can reach the Mausoleum of First Qin Emperor and the Qin Terracotta Warriors and Horses Museum via expressways and special routes.*

■ **Accommodation** *There are the five-star hotels of the Hyatt Regency, Shangri-La Golden Flower, and Sheraton Xi'an; four-star hotels of the Royal Xi'an and Grand New World; three-star hotels of the Bell Tower, Xi'an Renmin Mansion and Shenzhou Mingzhu, to name a few.*

■ **Food** *Famous restaurants include Lao Sunjia Restaurant, Xi'an Restaurant, Defachang Jiaozi Restaurant and*

Tongshengxiang Restaurant. There are also many local snacks such as baked cakes steeped in mutton or beef soup.

■ **Others** *Lintong's specialties are pomegranates and persimmons. Handicrafts are typically replicas of Qin terracotta armies, jade wares and sculptures in the style of Tang Dynasty.*

Opening hour: 8:00 ~ 17:00 (Qin Terracotta Museum); 7:30 ~ 18:30 (Mausoleum)

Inquiry telephones: 029-83911966 ext. 3126 (Qin Terracotta Museum); 029-83914462 (Mausoleum)

Website: www.bmy.com.cn

❀❀❀ Xi'an ❀❀❀

Stone armor

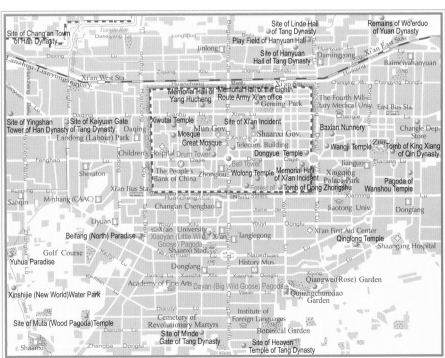

GANSU PROVINCE

General Information

Gansu Province, also called Gan or Long in short, has its capital in Lanzhou City. With an area of more than 390,000 sq km, it has under its administrative jurisdiction 11 prefecture-level cities, 1 prefecture, 2 autonomous prefectures, 4 county-level cities, 59 counties, and 7 autonomous counties. The province has a population of 25.68 million and ethnic groups including Han, Hui, Dongxiang, Zang (Tibetan), Tu, Man and Mongol.

Environment

Located in the northwest of China, it borders with Mongolia by the northwest corner. The entire province straddles three major highlands of Qinghai Plateau, the Inner Mongolia Plateau and the Loess Plateau. The landscapes are mainly plateaus and mountains, most of which are more than 1,000 m above sea level. It has diversified climates, namely the northern subtropical climate, warm temperate climate and middle temperate climate. The average temperature from northwest to southeast is -10 ~ 2°C in January and about 23°C in July, with an average annual rainfall between 40 ~ 800 mm.

Places of Interest

Gansu has a long-standing history with a treasure of numerous cultural relics. Fuxi, the ancestor of the Chinese nation, taught fishing here, and Marco Polo made a stopover here during his journey to central China. The Mogao Caves in Dunhuang are the invaluable treasures left over by the ancients. The Jiayuguan Pass of the Great Wall earned its fame all over the world for its magnificent posture. Thousands of human and cultural scenic and historical spots are scattered along the Silk Road in Han and Tang dynasties. Maijishan Grottoes, Bingling Temple Grottoes, Wenshushan Grottoes and the meeting place of the Red Army in Huining are key sites of cultural relics under state protection. Mogao Caves is included in the World Heritage List. Wuwei, Zhangye, Dunhuang and Tianshui have become famous cultural and historical cities of China.

Gansu has a vast area with a scenic landscape of natural beauty. The boundless Gobi desert, the vast grassland, the crystal glacier, Kongtong Mountain, Mingsha (Echoing Sand) Mountain and the Crescent Moon Spring are reminiscent, as written in the verses of the old days:"In the great desert one straight plume of smoke, By the long river

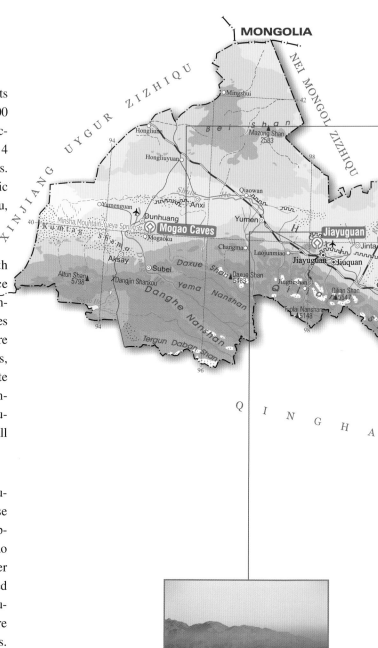

at sunset a ball of flame".

Local Specialties

Lanzhou melons, Lanzhou Dongguo Pears, lily, black melon seeds, Jiuquan luminous jade cup, and Tianshui carved lacquer ware.

SCALE 1 : 6 000 000

① The Great Wall

0   60   120   180   240km

Height(m)

5000
4000
3000
2000
1500
1000
500

NEI MONGOL ZIZHIQU

104

102

angyc
Shandan
Minle
Yongchang
Jinchang
Hexipu
Minqin
Wuwei
Gulang
Dajing
Jingtai
Lenglong Ling
▲4843
Maomao Shan
▲4070
Tianzhu
Yongdeng
Baiyin
Honghui
Honggu
Jingyuan
Gaolan
Lanzhou
Yuzhong
Yongjing
Huining
Linxia
Dongxiang
Dingxi
Lintao
Hezheng
Gaoyuan
Weiyuan
Tongwei
Zhuanglang
Xiahe
Longzhong
Niaoshu Shan
▲2600
Qin'an
Hezuo
Longxi
Joné
Wushan
Gangu
Tianshui
Luqu
Min Xian
Li Xian
Mt. Maiji
Maqu
Tewo
Dangchang
Cheng Xian
Hui Xian
Anyê Maqên Shan
Zhugu
Wudu
Kang Xian
SICHUAN
Wên Xian

38

38

102

36

36

102

34

34

102

104

106

NINGXIA HUIZU ZIZHIQU

Shancheng
Huan Xian
Huachi
Maojing
Qingcheng
Zhenyuan
Qingyang
Ziwu Ling
1687
Pingliang
Mt. Kongtong
Jingchuan
Ning Xian

108

108

36

SHAANXI

Jing He

Huan Jiang

Ziwu Ling

Vajra

Mogao Caves

☐ **Name:**
Mogao Caves
☐ **Geographical coordinates:**
40° 02' N, 94° 48' E
☐ **Date of inscription:**
December 11, 1987
☐ **Criteria for inclusion:**
I, II, III, IV, V, VI of cultural properties

Sutra Cave

⊙ Overview

Mogao Caves are located on the cliffs of Mingsha Mountain 25 km southwest of Dunhuang City, facing Daquan River in the front and Sanwei Mountain in the east. The climate is dry, with little rainfall and large daily temperature range, the highest temperature being 40.6°C and the lowest -31°C. The annual average rainfall is 23 mm, and annual evaporation is 3,479 mm, 150 times higher than that of rainfall. The extremely dry natural environment has made it possible for the Mogao Caves to survive intact. The caves are situated at the key position of the ancient Silk Road, where there was a transit spot for the trade between the East and the West, and religions, cultures and knowledge converged. Mogao Caves have preserved more than 700 grottoes that were built between 4th-14th Century, of which 492 were renowned in the world for their exquisite sculptures and murals. The grottoes are lauded as the world's biggest, richest, oldest and most well-preserved Buddhist art treasure house, which reflect the ancient way of life in many respects, and provide valuable visual materials for the study of ancient China and Central Asia in terms of politics, economy, science and technology, military affairs, religion, archi-tecture, transportation, garments, music and dances as well as folk customs.

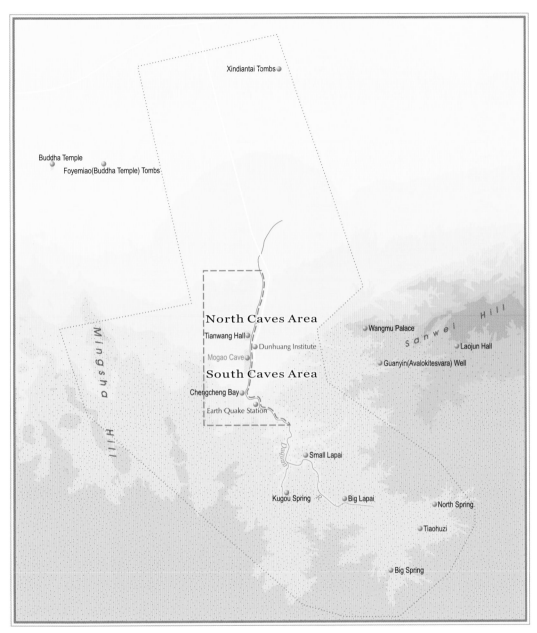

Mogao Caves

⊙ Description

Construction of the Mogao Caves started in the 2nd year of Jianyuan in Early Qin Dynasty (366) and continued until the Yuan Dynasty (1271-1368). For about 1,000 years, people in Dunhuang continuously made statues, which line up for 1,680 m from south to north. At present, 735 grottoes are in existence, located in four layers on cliffs 10 ~ 45 m above the ground. In 1900, the Sutra Cave was discovered by accident, and more than 50,000 historical relics dating back to 4th-11th Century were unearthed. This constituted a major discovery in China's archaeology at the start of the 20th Century, which shocked the world and gradually developed into a new field of study—"Dunhuangology".

The Mogao Caves are divided into the southern and northern sections. What remain in the southern section are 492 grottoes built in the dynasties of Northern Liang, Northern Wei, Western

Wei, Northern Zhou, Sui, Tang, Five Dynasties, Northern Song, Huihe, Western Xia and Yuan. There are over 2,400 colored statues and more than 45,000 sq m of murals. Of the 248 grottoes in the northern section, only 7 have murals and statues (5 grottoes had been listed among the 492 grottoes of Mogao Caves), while the rest grottoes were built with *kangs* (beds made of bricks and mud), kitchens, flues, habitacles, candle stands and other articles for everyday life and meditation. The southern section is where monks conduct rituals while the northern section is the quarters where monks lived, meditated or were buried. The grottoes in the northern and southern sections make up the complete Temple of Mogao Caves.

The art of the Mogao Caves has concentrated architecture, sculpture and painting all in one entirety. On the basis of inheriting

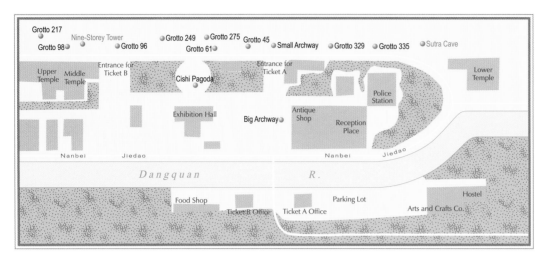

Grotto 217
Nine-Storey Tower
Grotto 98
Grotto 96
Grotto 249
Grotto 275
Grotto 45
Grotto 61
Small Archway
Grotto 329
Grotto 335
Sutra Cave

Upper Temple
Middle Temple
Entrance for Ticket B
Cishi Pagoda
Entrance for Ticket A
Police Station
Lower Temple

Exhibition Hall
Big Archway
Antique Shop
Reception Place

Nanbei   Jiedao
Nanbei   Jiedao

Dangquan   R.

Food Shop
Ticket B Office
Ticket A Office
Parking Lot
Hostel
Arts and Crafts Co.

South Caves Area

China's own fine artistic traditions, it has absorbed themes and presentation of foreign countries, giving rise to a Buddhist art treasure house with unique local style of Dunhuang, which reflects the development and evolution of subjects, presentation methods and styles of Buddhist art through different periods.

In terms of architecture, the Mogao Caves carry different styles for various functions and purposes. There are grottoes of central pagodas, Buddha niches, Buddhist altars, nirvana of Buddha, as well as statue of giant Buddha. The biggest grotto measures over 200 sq m while the smallest one is only less than 1 sq m.

Colored sculptures, which depict Buddha, Bodhisattvas, Disciples, Lokapalas and Vajras, are the main body of the art of Dunhuang. The sculptures are of various styles--some are statues, some are carved on the cliffs while others are mere imprints. Apart from Buddha in Grottoes Nos. 96, 130, 148 and 158, which are mud embodying stone bodies, others are all mud embodying wooden bodies. A Buddha sits usually at the center of a group of colored sculptures and is surrounded by Disciples, Bodhisattvas and others, ranging between 3 to 11 sculptures. The Buddha in a sitting posture in Grotto No.96 is the tallest, with a height of 35.5 m. The smallest Buddha measures only 10 cm. Made with sophisticated skills on various themes, the colored sculptures of Mogao Caves can be justifiably revered as a museum of colored Buddhist sculptures.

Murals of the Mogao Caves are broad and profound, which can be divided into seven categories, including images of Buddha, Buddhist stories, stories from the History of Buddhism, fairies and monsters, decorative patterns, etc. The murals are mainly related to Buddhism but also vividly depict scenes of life, production and social customs as well as international economic and cultural exchanges running through 1,000 years. The murals mainly applied Chinese painting techniques but have also absorbed advantages of painting art from India, Iran and Greece, bringing Buddhist art to a highly sophisticated level.

Dunhuang

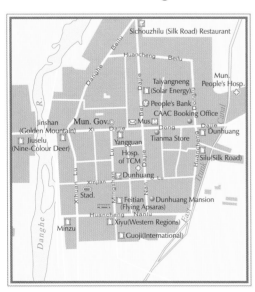

Sichouzhilu (Silk Road) Restaurant
Huancheng   Beilu
Beilu
Mun. People's Hosp.
Taiyangneng (Solar Energy)
People's Bank
CAAC Booking Office
Jinshan (Golden Mountain)
Mun. Gov.
Mus.
Xi   Dalie
Dong   Dalie
Dunhuang
Jiuselu (Nine-Colour Deer)
Yangguan
Tianma Store
Hosp. of TCM
Silu (Silk Road)
Dunhuang   Lu
Xinjian
Xihuan
Stad.
Mingshan
Feitian
Dunhuang Mansion
(Flying Apsaras)
Huancheng   Nanlu
Xiyu (Western Regions)
Minzu
Guoji (International)
Danghe
Danghe

Nine-storey Tower

⊙ Highlights

Nine-Storey Tower The wooden structure outside Grotto No. 96, also known as the Great Buddha Hall, has undergone numerous renovations. It was a four-storey mansion when first built in 695 and was turned into a five-storey mansion by Zhang Huaishen during the late Tang Dynasty (874-879). Two more storeys were added to the building in the 34th year of Guangxu in the

Northern Section, Mogao Caves

Qing Dynasty (1908), when businessmen of Dunhuang pooled the fund for the reconstruction. In 1935, the locals of Dunhuang rebuilt the wooden structure into a nine-storey tower. Except the 9th storey, all the other eight storeys are large 5-room and 6-column structures, each with two peripheral corners turned upward. On top of the octagonal roof of the 9th storey is a 3 m high bottle-like structure. The majestic building, which houses a 35.5 m tall Buddha, is the landmark of the Mogao Caves.

Sutra Cave This is the Grotto No. 17 of Mogao Caves, located on the northern end of the corridor connecting Grotto No. 16. Built in the mid-9th Century, it was used by Hong Bian, a monk in the late Tang Dynasty. The grotto is square-shaped and covered with a dome-like roof. On the northern wall are painted two Bodhi trees, a nun and a waitress. At the beginning of the 11th Century, the monk's statue was moved to other grottoes, and grotto became a secret storehouse of over 50,000 sutras, documents and silk paintings. In 1990, when the antiques were discovered, most of them were lost and are now scattered mainly in Britain, France, Russia and Japan, only a tiny portion remain in China. The grotto now has become a famous historic site for visitors.

Northern Section The cliff in the northern section of Mogao Caves measures about 700 m long, on which there are 248 grottoes. Since only seven of them have murals and colored sculptures, this section has long been neglected. Archaeological exploration in recent years has proved that, apart from the seven grottoes, the other grottoes were used by monks for a wide variety of functions--daily meditation, reading scripture, residing, storing goods, and burying remains and bone ashes of deceased monks. Precious mementos such as books written in Chinese, Western Xia language, Tibetan, Arabic, Mongolian, Syrian, etc, along with some Persian silver coins and Western Xia coins were also uncovered in the grottoes.

⊙ Information

▓ **Transportation** *Airlines reach Dunhuang directly from Beijing, Lanzhou and Xi'an. In peak seasons, there is one flight everyday. Lanzhou-Urumqi, Xi'an-Korla, Lanzhou-Urumqi, Chengdu-Urumqi, Beijing-Urumqi and Shanghai-Urumqi railways all stop at Dunhuang Railway Station, where one can take tourist bus or taxi to reach the city proper of Dunhuang 120 km away.*

▓ **Accommodation** *Good accommodation is available at Taiyang Hotel, Dunhuang Hotel, Dunhuang Grand Hotel and Dunhuang International Hotel.*

▓ **Food** *There are many restaurants of local flavors, which serve noodles and other food with unique local ingredients and preparation styles.*

▓ **Others** *Local specialties include Mingshan dates, Yangguan grapes, Liguang apricots, cups glowing in darkness, sculpted camels, crystal spectacles, carpets, batik, and replicas of artifacts.*

Opening hours: 9:00 ~ 17:30 (January 1-March 31, November 1-December 31); 8:30 ~ 18.00 (April 1-April 30); 8:00 ~ 18:00 (May 1-September 30); 8:30 ~ 17:30 (October 1-October 31)

Inquiry telephone: 0937-8869060

Website: www.dunhuangcaves.org, www.dha.ac.cn

Exterior of Mogao Caves

The Great Wall

Built from the 7th Century BC to the 15th Century AD, the Great Wall is one of the greatest engineering projects in the human history. The Great Wall of the Ming Dynasty (1368-1644) is located in the northern part of China, beginning from Hushan Mountain on the west bank of the Yalu River in the east, to Jiayuguan Pass in the west. It extends across nine provinces, municipalities and autonomous regions of Liaoning, Hebei, Tianjin, Beijing, Shanxi, Nei Mongol, Shaanxi, Ningxia and Gansu, with a total length of about 6,300 km. The Shanhaiguan, Badaling, Mutianyu and Jiayuguan are the important sections on the Great Wall, with numerous beacon towers erected at the most precipitous part of the undulating mountains. The Great Wall is an extraordinary project in the world for its complicated and hard construction work, crucially strategic location, and majestic, solid structure.

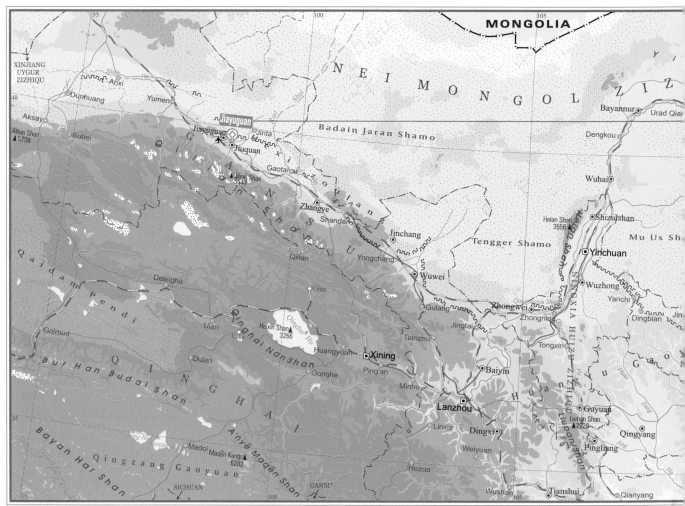

SCALE 1 : 6 700 000   0   67   134   201   268km

Badaling

☐ **Name:**

The Great Wall at Badaling

☐ **Geographical coordinates:**

40° 25' N, 116° 05' E

☐ **Date of inscription:**

December 11, 1987

☐ **Criteria for inclusion:**

I, II, III, IV, VI of cultural properties

⊙ Overview

Badaling, as one of the best parts of this ancient structure, is the most outstanding example of the Ming Dynasty Great Wall. Built with stone slabs and bricks along the mountain, it is 7 m high and about 5 m wide on the top. Terraces, battlements and forts can be seen in the precipitous part. This section of the Great Wall, which has been fairly well-preserved, displays a high level of building technology, and the solid structure demonstrates the superb skills of the craftsmen of the ancient times. It is a key site of cultural relics under state protection.

⊙ Description

Located 60 km northwest of Beijing, the Great Wall at Badaling is winding amid the Jundu Mountain of Yanshan Mountains. To the north of it is Yanqing Basin, and to the south of it is Guangou.

The name of Badaling first appeared in the poems of Liu Ying of the Jin Dynasty (1115-1234). According to *Chang'an Kehua*, from here one could go southward to Beijing, northward to Yanqing, westward to Xuanhua and Zhangjiakou. Badaling got its name as it was a passage that opened out to all directions.

Badaling was the most important fortress that defended the capital, known as the "northern gateway" of Beijing. From here, it overlooks the pass of Juyonguan. Ancient people said the most dangerous part was not at Juyongguan, nor fortress town, but at Badaling.

The existing Great Wall at Badaling was rebuilt in the Ming Dynasty. Emperor Zhu Yuanzhang (1328-1398) accepted the advice of "building high walls" to defend the capital. He sent generals Xu Da and Feng Sheng to rebuild the Great Wall north of Beijing. After 18 times of extensive construction and renovation in 270 years, the Great Wall was completed. It was not merely a tall wall, but also an in-depth and multi-layered defense system. Badaling was an extended line of the Ming Dynasty Great Wall, called "inner frontier". In the 18th year of Hongzhi (1505), a fortress town was built. To bolster defense, the east gate of the fortress town of Badaling was rebuilt in the 18th year of Jiajing (1539). In 1568, general Qi Jiguang reconstructed the Great Wall, especially the section of Badaling. In the 8th year of Wanli (1582), the west gate of the fortress town was rebuilt. After 80 years of construction, Badaling had been built into a defense system linking towers, fortresses and inner towns.

⊙ Highlights

Great Wall Museum of China It is located east of Guntiangou and adjacent to the Great Wall Panorama Cinema. This is a theme museum on the historical development, defensive and offensive tactics, economic exchanges and culture and arts related to the Great Wall. It was built and opened to the public in 1994.

Great Wall Panorama Cinema

It is located east of Guntiangou and adjacent to the Great Wall Museum of China. Adopting the latest technology in the world, the cinema shows the documentary about the landscapes, historical stories (such as the enthroning of the First Emperor of Qin and the legend about Meng Jiangnu) and wars related to the Great Wall on the 360° screen.

Beacon towers They were built on the top of the mountain and used to spread information. Soldiers used fire at night and smoke at daytime to inform each other of the military situation.

Watchtowers The concept was developed by Qi Jiguang, a Ming Dynasty general stationed at Jizhen. The watchtower is composed of three parts--base, middle and top. The middle part was used to store grains and arms, and could also be used for people to live. The top part was used to watch and shoot. As the watchtowers were higher than the wall and close to each other, soldiers from here were able to have a clear view of the situation below.

⊙ Information

Transportation *Shuttle buses link Beijing Capital International Airport with the downtown area. Bus lines go directly to Badaling are No.919 from Deshengmen, Y1 from Qianmen, Y2 from Beijing Railway Station, Y3 from Beitaipingzhuang, Y4 from Beijing Zoo, and Y5 from Beijing West Station.*

Accommodation *The Jinyuanlong Hotel in the area of Badaling has the lodging, meeting and entertainment facilities. Its restaurants offer Chinese food, Western food and local flavors.*

Food *Badaling Restaurant is a large and high-grade restaurant that offers Sichuan dishes, Jiangsu dishes and Guangdong dishes.*

Opening hours: All year round (Open at night during the peak season).

Inquiry telephones: 010-69121383, 69121226

Website: www.badaling.gov.cn

⊱≈⊰ Badaling ⊱≈⊰

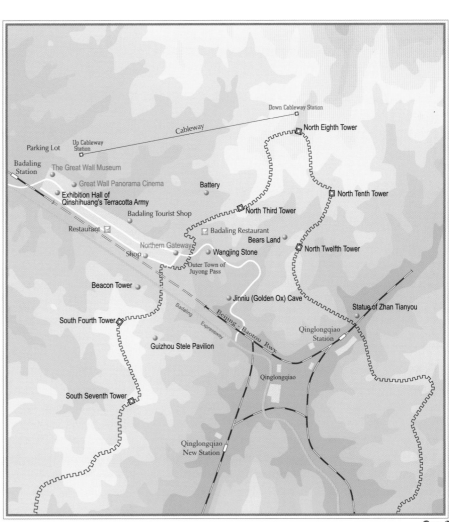

Shanhaiguan Pass

⊙ Description

Shanhaiguan Pass and the Shanhaiguan Great Wall were constructed in the 14th year of Hongwu in the Ming Dynasty (1381). Stretching along the north-south direction, this part of the Great Wall can be divided into nine sections according to its natural run: coastal wall, south-wing wall, pass city, north-wing wall, Jiaoshan wall, Taipingding-Sandaoguan wall, Sandaoguan-Jianshan wall, Jianshan-Tashan wall and Tashan-Jiumenkou wall. Of which, the pass city is the main body, supplemented by six defensive citadels of the south wing, north wing, Dongluo, Xiluo, Ninghai and Weiyuan. The coastal wall is the section where the Great Wall joins the sea, the south wing wall is a section located in the plain area, the north wing Great Wall is a connecting part between the pass city and the mountainous Great Wall from Jiaoshan to Jiumenkou. Along the Great Wall, 10 passes were constructed, including Nanhaikou Pass, Shanhaiguan Pass, Beishuiguan Pass, Jiaoshanguan Pass, Sandaoguan Pass, Lanshui Pass, Si'eryu Pass and Yipianshi Pass. There are more than 20 defensive towers, including the Nanhaikou Pass watchtower, Chenghai tower, the west and north watchtowers of Ninghai citadel, Nanshuiguan Pass watchtower, Jingbian tower, Muying tower, Zhendong tower, Linlu tower, Beishuiguan Pass watchtower, Hanmenguan Pass watchtower, Jiaoshanguan Pass watchtower and Sandaoguan Pass watchtower. These structures, together with 43 watchtowers, 51 platforms, 14 outer beacon towers and 7 base platforms, form a perfect defense system characterized by balanced offense-defense functions.

The Great Wall in the Shanhaiguan Pass Section was constructed against the terrain of the land. In the plain areas, the wall was built on terrains with relatively high elevation, and in the mountains, the wall was constructed on watershed ridges. Most materials used

⊙ Overview

□ Name:
The Great Wall at Shanhaiguan Pass
□ Geographical coordinates:
39° 56' ~ 40° 06' N, 119° 31' ~ 119° 51' E
□ Date of inscription:
December 11, 1987
□ Criteria for inclusion:
I, II, III, IV, VI of cultural properties

⊙ Overview

Shanhaiguan is located in the territory of Qinhuangdao City of Hebei Province. The Ming Dynasty Great Wall began from here, stretching 26 km in the city from Laolongtou (Old Dragon Head) in the south to Jiumenkou in the north. Taking different construction forms, this section of the Great Wall is grand and splendid. It is one of the best sections of the Great Wall, and the only place where the Great Wall joins the sea. Shanhaiguan Pass is regarded as the "First Pass under Heaven". The towering pass is located against the Yanshan Mountains in the north and faces the Bohai Sea in the south, holding a strategic position that connects North China with Northeast China. Famed due to the Great Wall, Shanhaiguan is a historical and cultural pass city and a state-level scenic area, with mountain and sea scenes, unique landscapes, ideal climate and numerous cultural relics and ancient sites.

were local products. Four construction forms were applied: earth with bricks laid as the outer layer; brick-stone wall; block stone wall; and mountain walls consisting of natural cliffs. The 10.3 km section from Laolongtou to Jiaoshan was constructed on the plain area, applying the construction form of earth with bricks laid as the outer layer. The 15.6 km section from Jiaoshan to Yipianshi Pass was constructed on mountain ridges, mainly built with block stones, only a few parts with slab stones or earth with bricks laid as the outer layer.

⊙ Highlights

First Pass under Heaven Also called Zhendong Tower, the east gate of Shanhaiguan pass city is one of the important passes of the Ming Dynasty Great Wall. It was constructed in the 14th year of Hongwu in the Ming Dynasty (1381). The architecture of the pass city tower applied the Xieshan hip-gable double roof, the two ridge ornaments were symmetrical, and it was in the brick-wood structure. The upturned eaves at the four corners were decorated with ridge animals of various descriptions, finely built in vivid shapes. The pass city tower has two storeys. There are 68 arrow windows on the eastern, southern and northern sides. Outside the second storey and inside the first and second storeys, there are three huge wooden horizontal boards inscribed with the Chinese characters "First Pass under Heaven". The characters, written in the form of regular scripts, are big in size, each with a height of 1 m. About 1 km east of the pass city is an outpost citadel--Weiyuan City.

Laolongtou (Old Dragon Head) Laolongtou is located 5 km south of Shanhaiguan Pass. In the early years of the Ming Dynasty, General Xu Da established a pass and stationed troops here. During the reign of Longqing, Qi Jiguang, commander of Jizhen, renovated it and named it Jinglu Watchtower--the first watchtower of the Great Wall at Shanhaiguan Pass. After that, troops stationed here also constructed the Chenghai Tower and the Ninghai City. In the 7th year of Wanli (1579), Qi Jiguang again ordered his subordinate general Wu Weizhong to construct the "Estuary Stone City" at the place where the Great Wall meets the sea. This is the world-famous Laolongtou of the Great Wall. With Chenghai Tower standing above the high platform on the southern wall of the Ninghai City, the structure of Laolongtou looks even more impressive.

Jiaoshan Great Wall It is located 3 km north of Shanhaiguan City on Jiaoshan Mountain, an extension of the Yanshan Mountains. The main peak is 519 m above sea level. High and towering, it looks like the horn of a dragon, thus the name "Jiaoshan". It is the first peak on which the Great Wall stretches. The high and dangerous precipices form a natural defense of

Shanhaiguan Pass, so the mountain is also famed as the "First Mountain of the Great Wall".

Sandaoguan "Upside-down Great Wall" It is located in the steep and high mountains northeast of Shanhaiguan Pass. At the Sandaoguan Pass, the terrain grows more precipitous from bottom to the top, so that "ten thousand people could not overtake it when guarded by only one man". Looking up, the Great Wall seems to be hanging on vertical cliffs. The sight is breathtaking and the place is regarded as one of the most dangerous sections of the Great Wall.

⊙ Information

▇ **Transportation** *Railway: The Shanhaiguan railway station is a large terminal connecting Northeast China with the vast areas south of the Great Wall, all passenger trains, express, through or slow, stop here. Highway: It takes only 2.5 hours to drive from Beijing to Shanhaiguan via Beijing-Shenyang Expressway; and 3 hours from Shenyang to Shanhaiguan. The public bus line from Beidaihe to Qinhuangdao has a stop at Shanhaiguan Pass. From downtown Qinhuangdao City, people can get to Shanhaiguan Pass by taking buses No. 33, 25, 13, 23, 24 and 26, the interval between two buses is 2 ~ 8 minutes. The first shift of the bus starts at 6:20 and the last shift starts at 19:00.*

▇ **Accommodation & food** *Hotels, hostels and restaurants with quality equipment and sufficient accommodation include Haisheng Garden Hotel, Longyuan Hotel, Wangyanglou Restaurant and Muslim Hotpot Restaurant.*

▇ **Others** *Local special products include shrimp, jellyfish, mackerel, sea crab, flatfish, hairtail, yellow croaker, prawn and freshwater crab. Local flavored food includes spicy hotpot, braised dishes, fresh-flower flavored cake and pineapple flavored cake.*
   Website: www.shg.com.cn

❧ Qinhuangdao ❧

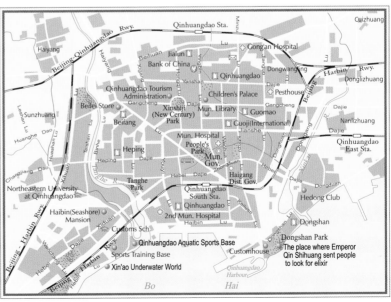

Jiayuguan Pass

☐ **Name:**

The Great Wall at Jiayuguan Pass

☐ **Geographical coordinates:**

39° 37' 58" ~ 39° 50' 29" N,

97° 49' 52" ~ 98° 31' 24" E

☐ **Date of inscription:**

December 11, 1987

☐ **Criteria for inclusion:**

I, II, III, IV, VI of cultural properties

"The Impregnable Pass under Heaven"

⊙ Overview

Located in the northwest of Gansu Province, it was a strategic passage of the ancient Silk Road where confluence of Oriental and Western cultures took place. Lying north of Qilian Mountain and south of Heishan Mountain, Jiayuguan Pass is a typical example of the western Great Wall, and it is also the western end of the Ming Dynasty Great Wall. In the 5th year of Hongwu in the Ming Dynasty (1372), General Feng Sheng of the west expedition army chose the site to construct the pass. The pass city is composed of the outer city, the inner city, the barbican city, the *Luocheng* city, the moat, the north wing wall and the south wing wall. Reputed as the "First Impregnable Pass under Heaven" and the "First Pass in Hexi Corridor", it is an important carrier of the history, geography, military affairs, politics, economy, personage and art and literature of China's western region. In 1961, it was listed as the first key sites of cultural relics under state protection.

⊙ Description

Jiayuguan Pass is the best-preserved and the most magnificent military castle along the Ming Dynasty Great Wall, playing an important military role in the ancient times. To the west of the pass city is the vast Gobi Desert. From the south of the pass city to the Taolai River mound is a distance of 7.5 km, and the terrain is flat, the Great Wall in this area is high above the ground, therefore this section is also called the "exposed wall". From the north of the pass city to the slope of the Heishan Mountain, the Great Wall stretches about 7.5 km, the terrain is undulating, and the Great Wall is indistinctly visible, thus this section is called the "hidden wall". The 15-km-long defense line between the "exposed wall" and the "hidden wall", together with the strategic advantages, strengthened the military importance of the Jiayuguan Pass. East of the pass city is Suzhou, the political, economic and military stronghold in the northwest frontier of the Ming Dynasty, and the supply base for the Jiayuguan Pass.

The region of Jiayuguan Pass has a continental temperate desert climate. The sunshine time

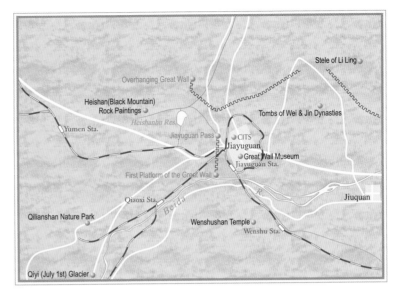

Jiayuguan

is long all year round, the rainfall is low while evaporation is high, windy days are common and daily temperature difference is sharp. The major river in the area is Taolai River, a tributary of Heishui River. The large water surface in the area includes Heishan Lake to west of the pass city and Xinchengcao Lake to the east. The place is rich in natural scenery and places of interests: the vast Gobi Desert, splendid continental glaciers, beautiful lakes, and unique poplar forest. In the area, there are also ancient tombs of the Wei and Jin dynasties (220-420), dubbed "the underground gallery".

Guanghua Tower, Jiayuguan Pass

⊙ Highlights

Jiayuguan Pass It is the western starting point of the Ming Dynasty Great Wall, and also the best-preserved and most magnificent military castle of the Ming Dynasty Great Wall. In the outer city, there are such architectures as the Wenchang Pavilion, the performing stage and the Guandi Temple. In the inner city are the General's Mansion, official well, watchtower, corner turrets and arrow tower. The Guanghua Tower, Rouyuan Tower and Jiayuguan Pass Tower of the inner city are located on an east-west axis. They are all 17-m-high three-storey wooden structures with Xieshan hip-gable of three-eaves roof. The barbican city is the outer protective facility to the gate of the inner city. *Luocheng* city is the frontier defense line of the pass city, on which the Jiayuguan Gate Tower was built.

The First Platform of the Great Wall It was called Taolai River Platform in the ancient times. Constructed in the 18th year of Jiajing in the Ming Dynasty (1539) by Li Han, defense commander of Suzhou, it was the westernmost platform of the Ming Dynasty Great Wall. The Great Wall starts from here and stretches like a huge dragon across the Gobi desert and over the mountains. Standing on the 56-m-high cliff at the bank of Taolai River, about 7.5 km from the pass city, the platform is called the "First Impregnable Platform under Heaven".

Overhanging Great Wall It was constructed in 1539 by Li Han, military defense commander of Suzhou. The terrain of this section of the Great Wall is precipitous and impregnable, hence is nicknamed as "Badaling in the West". The Overhanging Great Wall, an important part of the Jiayuguan Pass, has become a tourist attraction and a major component of the cultural tourism of Jiayuguan Pass. The Great Wall and the Silk Road are the main cultural themes of this scenic area, which consists of Heishan cliff engraving area, Heishan valley Silk Road culture area and Heishan Lake resort area. Here visitors can have a genuine taste of the magnificent western Great Wall, feel the atmosphere of the ancient Silk Road, and enjoy the wild scenery of western China.

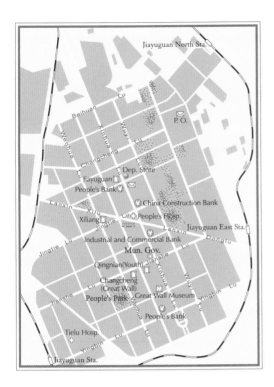

⚛ Jiayuguan City

⊙ Information

■ **Transportation** *Transport to and from Jiayuguan is convenient. Lanzhou-Urumqi railway and national road 312 run through Jiayuguan City; Jiayuguan-Lanzhou-Xi'an-Beijing air route links the city with other parts of the country; road transport in the city and neighboring towns is also convenient.*

■ **Accommodation** *Jiayuguan has good tourist services and accommodations. There are four-star hotels like Great Wall Hotel and Jiayuguan Hotel, and three-star hotels like Jiugang Hotel and Guotai Hotel. They provide full services from accommodation, catering, entertainment to shopping.*

■ **Food** *Minzu (Nationalities) Restaurant serves local food. Local flavor delicacies include barbecued lamb, barbecued mutton cubes and other finely made flour snacks.*

■ **Others** *There are several dozens kinds of tourist souvenirs. The most famous are cups of phosphorescent jade, wind-rain sculptures, Gobi stone, camel-wool pictures and saline cistanche.*

Open hours: 8:30 ~ 18:30, including holidays.

Inquiry telephone: 0937-6396244

Imperial Tombs of the Ming and Qing Dynasties

Scattered in the municipality of Beijing and the provinces of Hebei, Liaoning, Anhui, Jiangsu and Hubei, and built in accordance with strict regulation and highest funerary rites in Chinese feudal history, the Imperial Tombs of the Ming and Qing dynasties are original building complexes planned on a grand scale both above and below the ground.

The Ming and Qing imperial tombs are natural sites modified by human influence, carefully chosen according to the principles of *fengshui* (geomancy) to house numerous building of traditional architectural design and decoration. They illustrate the continuity over five centuries of a world view and concept of power specific to feudal China.

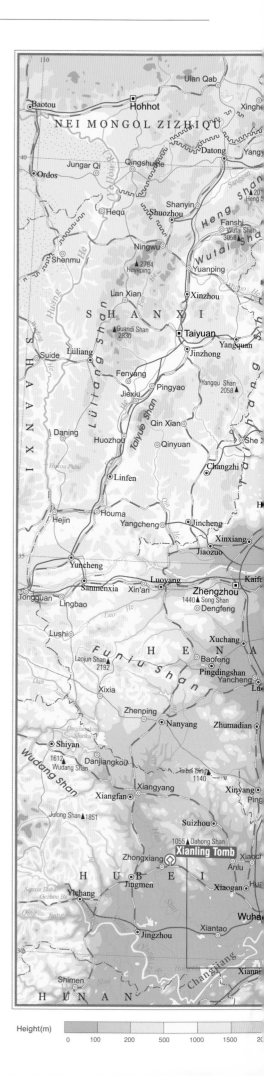

Height(m)

0	100	200	500	1000	1500	20

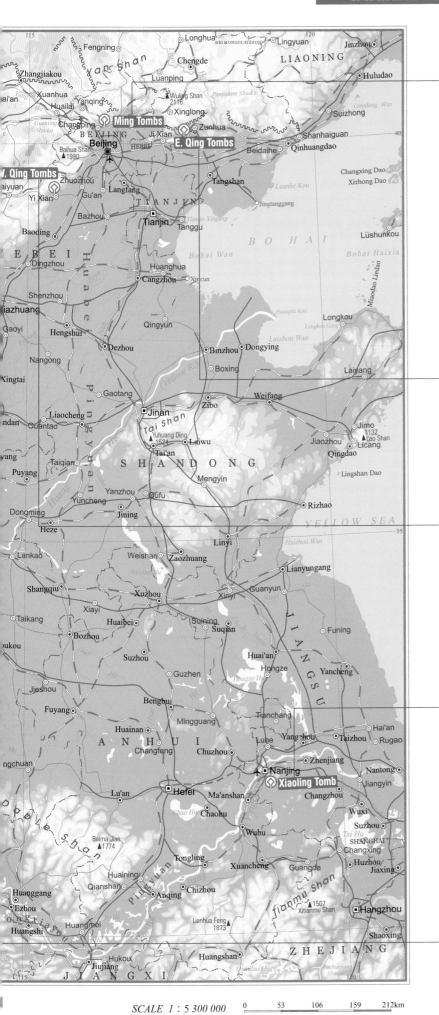

SCALE 1 : 5 300 000

0   53   106   159   212km

Xianling Tomb

☐ **Name:**

Imperial Tombs of the Ming and Qing Dynasties--
XianlingTomb

☐ **Geographical coordinates:**

31° 12' 20" ~ 31° 13' 00" N, 112° 37' 50" ~ 112' 38' 09" E

☐ **Date of inscription:**

November 30, 2000

☐ **Criteria for inclusion:**

I, II, III, IV, VI of cultural properties

Lingxing (Star-worshipping) Gate

⊙ Overview

Located at the Chunde Mountain about 5 km northeast of Zhongxiang City in Hubei Province, it is the tomb where Zhu Youyuan (1476-1519) and his wife Empress Dowager Zhangsheng, the parents of Emperor Shizong (Jiajing) of the Ming Dynasty, were buried together. Construction of this tomb began in the 14th year of Zhengde in the Ming Dynasty (1519) and was completed in the 38th year of Jiajing in the Ming Dynasty (1559), lasting for 40 years. The mausoleum area covers 183.15 ha, and the exterior *Luocheng* (encircling walls) is 3,600 m in circumference. The mausoleum area, consisting of twin cities with over 30 large-scale architectural complexes, is hidden in the mountain and surrounded with water. In January 1988, the State Council listed the tomb as a key site of cultural relics under state protection.

⊙ Description

The architectures of Xianling Tomb are in perfect harmony with the environment. According to the systems for the construction of emperor's tomb in the Ming Dynasty, which stated "tombs should be in harmony with mountains and water", mountains and rivers become the organic components of the tomb. With such a unified planning and layout, tomb architectures are hidden in the mountains and surrounded by water, forming a "natural part of the environment" and therefore becoming a large mountain-backed tomb with spacious surrounding area.

The construction of Xianling Tomb lasted virtually the entire reign of Emperor Shizong. During this period, the Tailing Tomb, Yongling Tomb and Zhaoling Tomb were also under construction, and sacred ways and tablet pavilions were added to the tombs at Tianshou Hill. A certain style was developed due to the similarity of tombs between one and another as the feudal rites required. The Xianling Tomb preserved the styles and formats of imperial tombs. As Emperor Shizong believed in Taoism, Xianling Tomb had its own new features and became the model for the Ming tombs later.

During the construction of Xianling Tomb, some features different from other Ming tombs developed due to political, ideological and aesthetic factors, such as: two tomb chambers at one tomb, inner and exterior memorial ponds, "golden bottle-shaped" *Luocheng*, dragon-shaped sacred way, nine-bend river, and numerous memorial tablet pavilions. All these features are unique among all tombs of the Ming Dynasty.

The construction of Xianling Tomb was an outcome of an important historical event in the early years of Jiajing in the Ming Dynasty - the "ritual dispute". In the 16th year of Zhengde in the Ming Dynasty (1521), Emperor Wuzong died childless. Empress Dowager Cishou and Senior Grand Secretary and Academician Yang Tinghe thus decided to follow the ancestral instruction of "passing the throne down to the brother", and ordered "Prince Xingxian's eldest son Zhu Houcong to succeed the throne". After Zhu Houcong (Emperor Shizong) ascended to the throne, he decided to promote and place his associates and kinsmen to senior posts to form his own small clique, and posthumously endorsed his father Zhu Youyuan as Emperor Gongruixian. His move caused a heated dispute in the imperial court and the society. After a three-year long dispute without a conclusion, Zhu Houcong tyrannically quelled the dispute by relegating, killing or expelling his opponents. Then, Zhu Houcong established his own ritual system, by giving his own family supremacy over that of the deceased emperor. This historical event was called the "ritual dispute", and the construction of the Xianling Tomb served as evidence of this event.

Highlights

One Tomb, Two Burial Chambers   In the 1st year of Jiajing (1522), Emperor Shizong ordered to expand the Tomb of Prince Xingxian, his father, at Songlin Mountain (Chunde Mountain) located in Anlu Prefecture (modern Wuhan), and ordered, in the 3rd year of his reign, to expand and reconstruct the tomb as an emperor's tomb according to the construction rules and systems of the Ming Dynasty imperial tombs. After empress dowager died in the 17th year of Jiajing (1538), Emperor Shizong decided to relocate his father's tomb northwards to Tianshou Hill, so he personally went to Dayu Hill to choose the site for Xianling Tomb, and ordered the ministry of works to give full support to the construction of the tomb, thus a treasure city appeared in the tomb site of Dayu Hill. In the 18th year of Jiajing, Emperor Shizong visited the Xianling Tomb in Hubei and found that Songlin Mountain was good in terms of *fengshui*, so he gave up the idea of relocating the tomb, and decided to transport the coffin of his mother back to the Xianling Tomb in Hubei Province. Because the burial chamber was flooded, Emperor Shizong ordered to construct a new underground palace next to the original chamber. Thus, the tomb of this special emperor got two burial chambers.

Nine-bend River   The Xianling Tomb is different from other Ming tombs in that it has a 1,687 m long river meandering through the mausoleum area. The design of the Nine-bend River was also related to *fengshui*. Because of the artistic design, the river divide the mausoleum area into several zones, bringing the functions of natural factors as mountain, water and trees into full play and making the tomb in perfect harmony with the environment.

Information

■ **Transportation**   *Located in the center of the Jianghan Plain, Zhongxiang City is about 200 km west of Wuhan, capital of Hubei Province, 130 km north of Jingzhou, 160 km east of Yichang, and 120 km south of Xiangfan. The provincial Sisha Highway runs through the city from north to south, and the national roads 107 and 207 go nearby the tomb area on the east and west, connecting with the provincial Zaodang Highway. Wuhan-Jingmen Railway runs through the city. The Hankou-Jingmen expressway is to open soon. There are shuttle buses running between the tomb and Zhongxiang City, and taxi is available and convenient.*

■ **Accommodation**   *There are the three-star Zhongxiang Hotel, two-star Hongyan Grand Hotel, Yangchun Grand Hotel and Xibin Hotel as well as Jinbeihu Holiday Resort in Zhongxiang City. These hotels can accommodate 10,000 visitors. The tourist center of Xianling Tomb will be completed soon.*

■ **Food**   *Local flavor foods include the imperial court coiling dragon dish.*

■ **Others**   *Local special products are wild and green nostoc products, mushroom and fungus.*

Opening hours: All the year round.

Inquiry telephone: 0724-4217387

Xianling Tomb

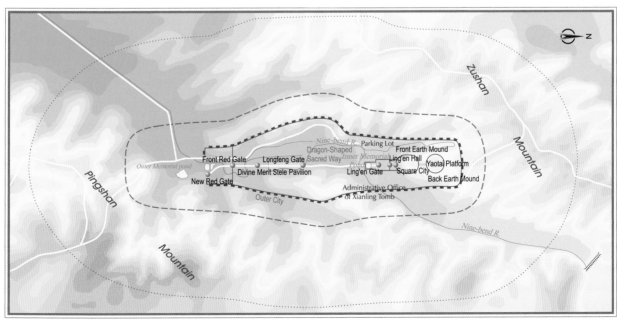

Glazed eaves tile

Xiaoling Tomb

☐ **Name:**
Imperial Tombs of the Ming and Qing Dynasties
(Extension)—Xiaoling Tomb

☐ **Geographical coordinates:**
32° 04' N, 118° 51' E

☐ **Date of inscription:**
July 3, 2003

☐ **Criteria for inclusion:**
I, II, III, IV, VI of cultural properties

Crouching camel sculpture

⊙ Overview

Located in the eastern suburb of Nanjing City, Jiangsu Province, under Wanzhu Peak at the southern foot of Mount Zhongshan, the highest peak in the Ningzhen Mountains south of the lower reaches of the Yangze River, it is the tomb of Zhu Yuanzhang (1328-1398), founder of the Ming Dynasty (1368-1644). It is the first of the imperial tombs built in the Ming Dynasty. In terms of mausoleum system, the Xiaoling Tomb inherited the outstanding elements of the Han, Tang and Song dynasties and made innovations of its own, establishing a system for following in the construction of imperial tombs during the Ming and Qing dynasties. Occupying a milestone position in the establishment of imperial tombs in ancient China, the system and construction mode developed at the Xiaoling Tomb were observed in the construction of all the imperial tombs built in Beijing, Hubei, Liaoning and Hebei during the Ming and Qing dynasties, and were inherited in the construction of the Ming Tombs, Xianling Tomb, the Eastern Qing Tombs and the Western Qing Tombs. It had served as the standard for the overall pattern and feature of more than 20 Ming and Qing imperial tombs built in 500 years, and had exerted profound and far-reaching influences.

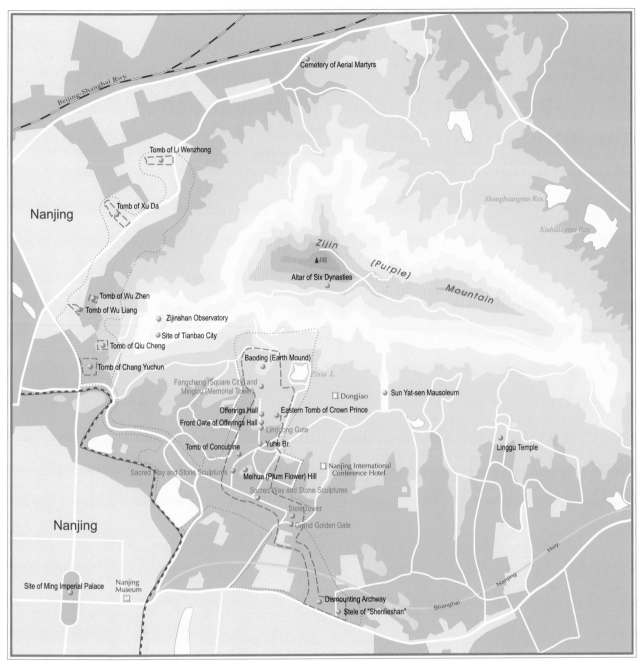

Xiaoling Tomb

⊙ Description

Construction of the Xiaoling Tomb lasted for over 30 years, starting from 1381 and ending around 1413. From the Horse-dismounting Tablet to the Treasure City, where the tomb palace lies, the tomb stretches for about 3,000 m, with more than 30 buildings and stone carvings of different styles, volumes and purposes standing along, forming a massive mausoleum area of cultural relics with rich connotations.

The Xiaoling Tomb was constructed in strict accordance with hierarchy. The surface and underground buildings all have a complete system of their own, well-distributed, massive in size, gorgeous in architecture, and exquisite in craftsmanship. It embodies the top-level burial system in China's feudal society. In spite of wars and natural erosion over the past 600-odd years, the pattern of the tomb has maintained its imposing look and none of the build-

ing sites has suffered any artificial damages or destruction. The underground tomb chambers have been kept in their original state, and no changes have taken place in their environmental features. The major buildings and carvings in the graveyard including the Dismounting Tablet, the Big Golden Gate, the Divine Merit Stele, the stone figures along the Sacred Way, the foundation site of Star-worshipping Gate, the Golden Water Bridge, the Tomb Palace Gate, the foundation site of the front door of the Sacrificial Hall, the Sacrificial Hall and the side halls, the Inner Red Gate, the Square City, the Memorial Shrine, the Treasure City, and the Treasure Dome, all relics of the Ming buildings, have maintained their original architectural authenticity and spatial integrity.

With its massive and orderly layout, winding Sacred Way, mysterious and perfect geomantic environment, harmonious and effective sewage system, and typical architectural style and technical process, the Xiaoling Tomb makes up a masterpiece of imperial tombs. The lofty and delicate stone sculptures standing at the two sides of the Sacred Way represent the level and feature of stone carving in China in the late 14th Century.

The harmony and unity of the humane architecture and the natural environment of Xiaoling Tomb is a typical example of integration between China's traditional culture, architectural art and natural environment. It represents the artistic, cultural and engineering achievements in the construction of imperial architecture in the early Ming Dynasty.

The Xiaoling Tomb has a bearing on several emperors and many important figures of the Ming and the Qing dynasties and has profound connotations of the Oriental culture. It is the product of another peak development of China's feudal era, and a crystallization of the politics, ideology, social culture, aesthetics, architectural technology, and national strength of the early Ming Dynasty.

⊙ Highlights

Distant View of Xiaoling Tomb The Xiaoling Tomb of the Ming Dynasty is situated in a geographical environment of green mountains and clear waters with rich connotations of traditional culture. The tomb palace, built against a background of mountains, is surrounded on all sides by mountains and waters that form a protective ring and create a perfect harmony of humane and natural landscapes. It is a typical example of integration between the traditional culture, architectural art and natural environments.

Autumn Scene of the Sacred Way The Sacred Way is characterized by its perfect combination of artificial buildings and natural environments. Laid out in total conformity with the terrain, the Sacred Way adopted the method of symbolization in planning: following the rules of the heaven and copying the look of the earth to achieve integration of the heaven and the earth and unity of mankind and universe, embodying China's profound traditional ideology and culture and outstanding characteristics of individuality. The stone sculptures along the Sacred Way are varied in style, simple but sturdy in modeling, and massive in overall size and delicate in detail. They represent the highest level of stone carving in China in the early Ming Dynasty.

Memorial Shrine of the Square City It is at the Xiaoling Tomb that a square city and a memorial shrine were first built in front of the covering earth and the treasure city. This pattern added grandeur to the rear palace of the mausoleum. The Big Golden Gate, the gateway, the gate of the tomb palace and other major buildings, all arch-shaped, stand as examples of successful application of big-span brick arches to palace buildings. The model of the plinth and the dragon-shaped ornament on the fastigium first developed at Xiaoling Tomb had been adopted in all official architectures of the Ming and Qing dynasties in Beijing.

Sacred Way

Drooping-ridge
mounted animal ornament

Memorial shrine

Stairway to the memorial shrine

⊙ Information

■ **Transportation** *Access to Nanjing is quite easy by air, road or railway. Once in Nanjing, visitors can take buses to Xiaoling Tomb from Gulou (Drum Tower), Yuhuatai and Hongshan Zoo. Mini-trains and storage battery cars also run between Xiaoling Tomb and the Mausoleum of Dr. Sun Yetsen.*

■ **Accommodation** *Nanjing International Convention Hotel, Dongjiao Hotel, Dongyuan Hotel and Zhongshanling International Youth Hotel are available near the tomb.*

■ **Food** *Snack foods, common dishes and special flavor dishes are served at the Ming Tomb Restaurant.*

■ **Others** *Tourist souvenirs featuring Ming culture (including books on history and culture, picture albums of scenic spots, memorial stamps, postcards, and arts and crafts), Yunjin brocade, and Yuhua pebbles are on sale.*

Opening hours: 7: 00 ~ 18:00

Inquiry telephones: 025-84431991, 84430048

Glazed dripping tile

⊱⊱⊱ Nanjing ⊰⊰⊰

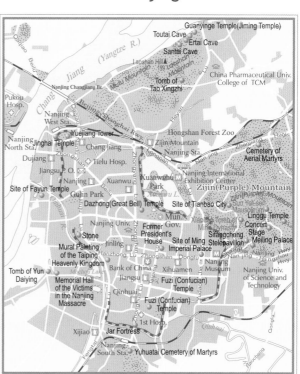

Ming Tombs

☐ **Name:**
Imperial Tombs of the Ming and Qing Dynasties
(Extension)—Ming Tombs

☐ **Geographical coordinates:**
40° 16' N, 116° 15' E

☐ **Date of inscription:**
July 3, 2003

☐ **Criteria for inclusion**
I, II, III, IV, VI of cultural properties

Sacred Way

⊙ Overview

Located at the foot of Tianshou Hill in the north of Changping District, Beijing Municipality, covering a land area of 80 sq km, the Ming Tombs is the collective name of the tombs of 13 emperors after Beijing was established as the capital during the Ming Dynasty. Spanning from 1409 when construction of the Changling Tomb started, to 1644 when Emperor Chongzhen was buried into Siling Tomb, the Ming Tombs serve as a carrier of most of the history of the Ming Dynasty. Careful in selection of the site, unique in design, delicate in con-struction, and selective in the use of materials, the Ming Tombs stand as a typical example of the imperial tombs in China. In terms of their systems, the Ming Tombs inherited that of the imperial tombs built in the preceding dynasties and made innovations of their own to produce profound and far reaching influences on the imperial tombs built in the Qing Dynasty. Apart from the tombs of 13 emperors, 23 empresses and dozens of palace maids buried alive as attendants, standing here are also the tombs of 7 imperial concubines and 1 eunuch, as well as temporary dwelling places of emperors and parks. The historical relics of the tombs provide evidence for the study of the system of imperial mausoleums, the burial ceremonies, the sacrificial rites, the ranking system, the architectural technology and techniques, and the politics, economy, culture and military affairs of the Ming Dynasty.

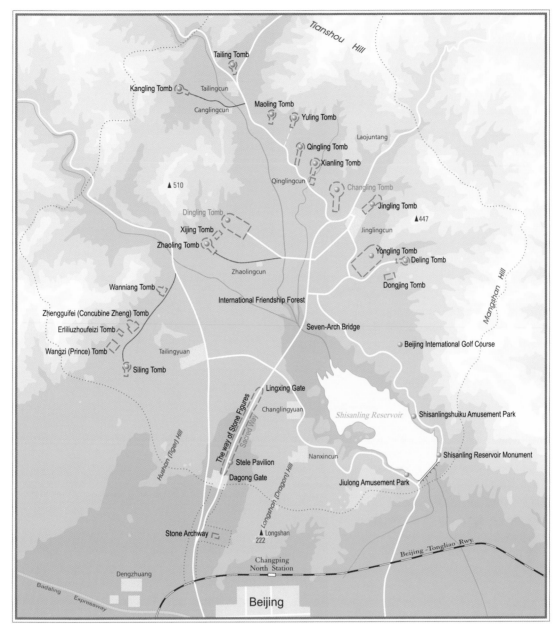

Ming Tombs

⊙ Description

The Ming Tombs are surrounded by hills on all sides: in the north stand the main peak of the Tianshou Hill, the highest peak in the mausoleum area; Mangshan Hill lies in the east; Huyu Hill lies in the west; and Longshan Hill and Hushan Hill lie in the south. Situated among the hills, the site is most auspicious for the tombs of emperors and kings because the hills symbolize, according to China's ancient *fengshui* theory, a perfect location with the Scarlet Bird in the front, the Black Warrior at the rear, the Green Dragon on the left, and the White Tiger on the right.

During the 277 years of the Ming Dynasty (1368-1644), a total of 16 emperors had ruled the country. The founding emperor, Emperor Zhu Yuanzhang, was buried in the Xiaoling Tomb at Zhongshan Mountain in Nanjing because he ruled from there. The second emperor, Emperor Zhu Yunwen (the grandson of Zhu Yuanzhang, with the reign title of Jianwen), became lost in a fire in the palace due to the fight for the throne with his uncle. And as

there was, he was never found. The seventh emperor, Zhu Qiyu, assumed the throne in the Tumu Incident. He was later dethroned during the restoration staged by Emperor Yingzong and buried in the Jingtai Tomb in the Jinshan Hill west of Beijing. The remaining 13 emperors were all buried at the foot of the Tianshan Hill, hence the Thirteen Tombs, another name for the Ming Tombs.

The tombs here are arranged in order according to their time of construction: Changling Tomb, which houses Emperor Zhu Di and his Empress Xu; Xianling Tomb, which houses Emperor Zhu Gaochi and his Empress Zhang; Jingling Tomb, which houses Emperor Zhu Zhanji and his Empress Sun; Yuling Tomb, which houses Emperor Zhu Qizhen and his empresses Qian and Zhou; Maoling Tomb, which houses Emperor Zhu Jianshen and his empresses Wang, Ji and Shao; Tailing Tomb, which houses Emperor Zhu Youcheng and his Empress Zhang; Kangling Tomb, which houses Emperor Zhu Houzhao and his Empress Xia; Yongling

175

Tomb, which houses Emperor Zhu Houcong and his empresses Chen, Fang and Du; Zhaoling Tomb, which houses Emperor Zhu Zaihou and his empresses Li, Chen and Li; Dingling Tomb, which houses Emperor Zhu Yijun and his two empresses Wangs; Qingling Tomb, which houses Emperor Zhu Changluo and his empresses Guo, Wang and Liu; Deling Tomb, which houses Emperor Zhu Youxiao and his Empress Zhang; and Siling Tomb, which houses Emperor Zhu Youjian and his Empress Zhou and concubine Tian. The Ming Tombs is a graveyard where the mausoleum architecture is well conserved and which houses the biggest number of emperors in the world.

The Ming Tombs stand as a typical example of ancient imperial tombs and buildings in China. In terms of layout, the tombs make up an integral whole, with the Sacred Way of the Changling Tomb serving as the "Trunk Sacred Way" of all the other tombs. Closely related with and linked to each other, the stone gateway, the Dismounting Tablet, the Grand Red Gate, the Divine Merit Stele of Changling Tomb, the stone figures, the Star-worshipping Gate, and other buildings bring the tombs together to form an integral whole in which the individual tomb stands in the sequence of its respective rank and seniority. While inheriting the tomb system of Xiaoling Tomb in Nanjing, changes and innovations were made. The stone gateway, for instance, was added in front of the Sacred Way, the Dismounting Tablet was erected in front of the Grand Red Gate, ornamental columns were added in front and at the rear of the Divine Merit Stele, and statues of ministers of merit were included in the stone figures. Stone offerings and star-worshipping gate were added in front of memorial shrine of the square city, a stele of temple name was erected inside the memorial shrine, the walls of the treasure city was thickened, and bridle path and screen wall were added.

⊙ Highlights

The Trunk Sacred Way of the Ming Tombs The Sacred Way of

Trunk Sacred Way

Changling Tomb, 7,000 m long, serves as the Trunk Sacred Way of the Ming Tombs. The buildings along this Sacred Way were first constructed in the 10th year of Xuande (1435) and were expanded in the 19th year of Jiajing (1540). The Stone Gateway, the Grand Red Gate, the Divine Merit Stele of the Changling Tomb, the stone figures, and the Longfeng (Dragon-phoenix) Gate, arranged in order running from south to north, all carry a magnanimous look. The Stone Gateway, standing at the head of the Sacred Way, has five gates divided by six pillars supporting 11 buildings totaling 28.86 m in width and about 12 m in height. Each of the 11 buildings have hip roofs decorated with delicately carved animals, volutes, dripping eaves, and corbel arches. The relief designs on the pillar-supporting stone bases, in particular, are vivid to life and extremely exquisite. This is the oldest stone gateway existent in China.

Changling Tomb Located below the Middle Peak of the Tianshou Hill, the tomb houses Zhu Di (1360-1424), the third emperor of the Ming Dynasty, and his empress. The underground palace of the tomb was built in the 7th year of Yongle (1409), and the archi-

Stone five offerings, Siling Tomb

Grand Red Gate

tecture of the tomb palace was completed in the 2nd year of Xuande (1427). Occupying a land area of 120,000 sq m, it is the biggest among the 13 tombs. The Ling'en Hall of Changling Tomb is the outlet for keeping the memorial tablets, dresses, and daily-used articles of the occupant and the site for implementing sacrificial ceremonies. Totaling 1,938 sq m in space, it is a hall of wooden structure rarely seen in China. The 60 columns made of *nanmu* (Phoebe nanmu) wood supporting the roof of the hall, each over 12 m high and 1 m in diameter at the bottom, are rare and precious timber ever found in the world.

Dingling Tomb Located at the eastern foot of Dayu Hill in the Tianshoushan Mausoleum area, this is the resting place of Emeror Zhu Yijun (1563-1620), the 13th emperor of the Ming Dynasty, and his two empresses, covering 180,000 sq m. Construction of the tomb started in the 12th year of Wanli (1584) and finished in 1590. The underground palace of Dingling Tomb is the only one among the Ming Tombs that has been officially excavated. Excavation started in May, 1956, with approval from the State Council, and was completed in one year. The layout of the under ground palace

Glazed decoration gate, Qingling Tomb

followed the model that characterized the imperial palace, consisting of five halls divided into the front row, the middle row, the back row, the right line and the left line, with solid arches of stone slabs, and seven pairs of stone doors. More than 3,000 pieces of cultural relics have been unearthed from the 1,195 sq m palace. In 1959, the Dingling Museum was established at the same site.

Memorial shrine, Changling Tomb

⊙ Information

■ **Transportation** *There are many buses depart for the Ming Tombs from Beijing everyday. Visitors to Dingling Tomb, Changling Tomb and the Sacred Way can take Tourist Bus 1 or 5 at Qianmmen; Tourist Bus 2 at Xuanwumen, Hangtianqiao or Xiaoying; Tourist Bus 3 at Dongdaqiao; Tourist Bus 4 at Xizhimen and the Zoo; Tourist Bus 5 (feeder service) at Fuchengmen; or Bus 314 at Dongguan of Changping. Visitors to Zhaoling Tomb may simply take Bus 22 at Lishuiqiao.*

■ **Food** *Dingling Restaurant and Changling Restaurant are open all the year round.*

Opening hours: The scenic spots are open to visitors all the year round, whereas the visiting hours change with the season.

Inquiry telephones: Dingling Tomb 010-60761424; Changling Tomb 010-60761888; Sacred Way 010-89749383; Zhaoling Tomb 010-60763104

Website: www.mingtombs.com.cn

Eastern Qing Tombs

☐ **Name:**
   Imperial Tombs of the Ming and Qing Dynasties
   —Eastern Qing Tombs

☐ **Geographical coordinates:**
   40° 11' N, 117° 38' E

☐ **Date of inscription:**
   November 30, 2000

☐ **Criteria for inclusion:**
   I, II, III, IV, VI of cultural properties

Grand Red Gate

⊙ Overview

Located in Malanyu, Zunhua City, Hebei Province, and first built in the 18th year of Shunzhi (1661), it is one of the imperial mausoleums built in the Qing Dynasty, the last feudalist dynasty in China. During the 268-year history of the Qing Dynasty (1616-1911), 5 emperors, 15 empresses, 136 concubines, 3 princes and 2 princesses were buried here. Lying here are five tombs burying emperors, namely, the Xiaoling Tomb of Emperor Shunzhi, Jingling Tomb of Emperor Kangxi, Yuling Tomb of Emperor Qianlong, Dingling Tomb of Emperor Xianfeng, and Huiling Tomb of Emperor Tongzhi; four tombs burying empresses, including the Zhaoxi Tomb of Empress Xiaozhuangwen, Xiaodong Tomb of Empress Xiaohuizhang, Dingdong Tomb of Empress Xiaozhenxian (Ci'an) at Puxiang Valley, and Dingdong Tomb of Empress Xiaoqinxian (Cixi) at Putuo Valley; and five tombs burying imperial concubines, as well as the tomb of Princess Duanminguren, daughter of Emperor Daoguang, lies at the east of the mausoleum area. The Eastern Qing Tombs is the largest and most complete imperial mausoleum existent in China, it not only provides rare materials in kind for the study of the tomb system, burial system, sacrificial rites, architectural art and technique of the Qing Dynasty, but also stands as a typical example for the study of politics, economy, military affairs, culture, science and art of that time.

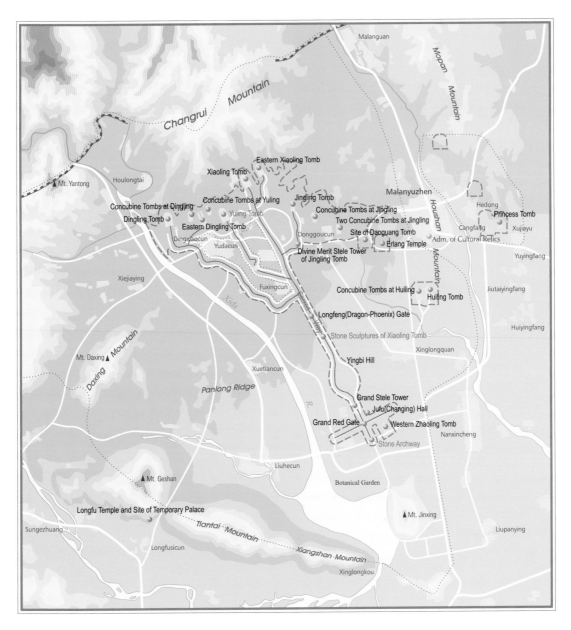

East Qing Tombs

⊙ Description

Based on China's traditional *fengshui* theory, every effort was made to perfect the location of the Eastern Qing Tombs, with full attention to capitalizing on all the scenes of natural beauty and good luck. The Yingfei Daoyang Hill at the east of the mausoleum area looks west like a coiled black dragon protecting the left side of the tomb, while the Huanghua Hill at the west looks east like a white tiger in a squatting posture protecting the right side of the tomb. The Changrui Hill, stretching for over 50 km, serves as the back. And the Jinxing Hill, like a reverted bell, stands in the right south like court officials standing in respect to the emperor. The Yingbi Hill, round and upright in shape, is delicately small to serve as the sacrificial altar, and the Xiangshan Hill and Yandun Hill face each other at east side of the gate of the tomb like two guards on duty. The hills, joined by the waters, form a scene of extraordinary majesty. The Malan River and Xida River flow by the east

and west side of the tomb, full of respect and emotion; and the flat land surrounded by hills on all the four sides, is broad and smooth. In one word, the tomb lies on a treasure land created by nature.

The occupants of the tombs here, from Emperor Shunzhi, the first emperor to rest here in 1663, to the last concubine of Emperor Tongzhi who was buried here in 1935, lasted for a total of 272 years, almost the same length of the history of the Qing Dynasty. In this sense, the Eastern Qing Tombs may be counted as a record of the rise and fall of the Qing Dynasty.

In terms of their architectural layout, the 15 tombs here were distributed according to the traditional ideology of positioning of the senior in the center as a show of respect and clear-cut distinction between the noble and the humble. The Xiaoling Tomb of Emperor Shunzhi, the first emperor to rule inside the Great Wall, stands at the foot of the Changrui Hill in the center of the mauso-

Statue of Avalokitesvara on the stone gate, Yuling Tomb

those leading to the tombs of the emperors they served, and the sacred ways of all the tombs here are linked to the Sacred Way of Xiaoling Tomb sitting over the axial line of the mausoleum area to form a branching network of sacred avenues closely linked to each other. Apparent in indication of seniority and succession, it gives expression to the wish of long life of the imperial family and the imperial court.

⊙ Highlights

The underground palace of Yuling Tomb The underground palace of the tomb of Emperor Qianlong is composed of nine arches and four gates totaling 54 m in length. Starting from the first stone gate, all the walls and arches are carved with Buddhist topics. The carvings, exquisite and smooth, are vivid to life and carefully patterned, winning the palace "treasure house of carvings" and "solemn underground Buddhist hall". The palace provides materials in kind for the study of Buddhism and the art of carving. It is the only of its kind that has been excavated and open to visitors in China.

The three halls of Dingling Tomb at Putuo Valley This is where the mausoleum of Empress Dawager Cixi lies. The Long'en Hall and the side halls at the east and west are all finely built. These three halls, resplendent and magnificent, are unique among all the imperial tombs of the Ming and Qing dynasties. The 64 columns are all twined with gold-plated bronze dragons in bas-relief. The cover walls and eavesdrops, are carved with patterns of auspicious clouds. The stone banisters around the main hall are also covered all over with relief patterns of dragons and phoenixes and seas and rivers. On the red stairway in front of the hall, phoenixes flying in the sky and the flood dragons rising out of water, carved in high relief and transparency, are so vivid to life that the whole work piece presents itself as a rare masterpiece of stone carving.

leum area, a paramount position. The tombs of following emperors stand by each site of the Xiaoling Tomb according to their respective seniority. At the left of the Xiaoling Tomb stands the Jingling Tomb of Emperor Kangxi, and at the right, the Yuling Tomb of Emperor Qianlong. Further left lies the Huiling Tomb of Emperor Tongzhi, and further right, the Dingling Tomb of Emperor Xianfeng. This forms a pattern in which the offspring stands company of their fathers and grandfathers and in respect to their seniors. The tombs of the empresses and the concubines, meanwhile, guard the tomb of the emperor they were dependent on to show the relationship of subordination. In addition, the sacred ways leading to the tombs of the empresses are all linked to

Stone figures of Xiaoling Tomb

Stone sculptures of Xiaoling Tomb Of the eighteen pairs of stone figures, there are three of officials, three of officers, one of standing horses and one of squatting horses, one of standing unicorns and one of squatting unicorns, one of standing elephants and one of squatting elephants, one of standing camels and one of squatting camels, one of legendary beasts of prey standing and one of legendary beasts of prey squatting, and one of standing lions and one of squatting lions. There is also one pair of sacrificial columns. These figures, arranged in excellent symmetry, line up at each side of the Sacred Way for more than 800 m from south to north, forming a force full of power and grandeur. Carved with whole pieces of stone, the figures all look true to life, bold and unconstrained, solid, simplistic, and powerful. They are the biggest in scale and most characteristic among the stone figures of the imperial tombs of the Ming and the Qing dynasties.

Stone gateway at Xiaoling Tomb With a wood-imitated structure, the gateway is five-room wide, divided by six columns and rises 11 floors high. Totaling 31.35 m in width and 12.48 m in height, it is built exclusively with huge stones. At the top of the stones fixing the column are carved unicorns and lions, with the front face featuring relief patterns of dragons and lions playing with balls. Carved into the beams are colored paintings, and the folding columns and boards are decorated with auspicious clouds in relief. Corbel arches, upturned eaves, tile ridges, volutes and carved angle braces are all made of stone, which remain intact after hundreds of years of weathering.

The Sacred Way of Xiaoling Tomb Starting from the stone gateway at the foot of Jinxing Hill and running up to the Treasure City at the foot of Changrui Hill in the north, the sacred way stretching along the mounds of Chaoshan, Anshan and Kaoshan links up the scores of buildings of different systems and in various styles standing in the cemetery to form an imposing, multi-tiered and magnificent axial line. It is the longest and most magnificent and artistic among the sacred ways of the imperial tombs of the Qing Dynasty.

⊙ Information

■ **Transportation** *Located at the triangular belt joining Beijing, Tianjin and Tanggu, the Eastern Qing Tombs is easily accessible. Visitors from Beijing may drive along Beijing-Tongzhou Expressway to the tombs, passing Yanjiao, Sanhe and Jixian; or take Beijing-Shunyi Road, passing Pinggu, Jinhai Lake and Mashen Bridge. One may also drive along Beijing-Shenyang or Tianjin-Jixian expressways. From Tianjin visitors may take Tianjin-Weichang Highway or Tianjin-Jixian Expressway. From Northeast China visitors may drive along Beijing-Shenyang Expressway, branch out at Fengrun, and reach the tomb via Zunhua.*

■ **Accommodation** *There is a three-star hotel 3,500 m east of the mausoleum area that offers catering, accommodation, transportation, tourism, shopping and recreational services. Inside the hotel is a Qing style building with 200 beds in 93 fully equipped guestrooms. Large, medium-sized and small conference rooms are also available in the hotel.*

■ **Food** *There are 20 restaurants in the above hotel capable of serving 600 people.*

■ **Others** *Native products include kiwi fruit, Chinese chestnut, walnut, persimmon, haw, and mushrooms. Handicrafts, glass paintings and iron pictures are also available. Customs and living styles of the Man Nationality are prevalent here.*

Opening hours: All the year round
Inquiry telephones: 0315-6944467, 6944383, 6945475, 6945471
Website: www.qingdongling.com

Stone archway

Western Qing Tombs

A distant view of stele tower, Tailing Tomb

Chongling Tomb

☐ **Name:**

Imperial Tombs of the Ming and Qing Dynasties
—Western Qing Tombs

☐ **Geographical coordinates:**

39° 20' ~ 39° 25' N, 115° 13' ~ 115° 26' E

☐ **Date of inscription:**

November 30, 2000

☐ **Criteria for inclusion:**

I, II, III, IV, VI of cultural properties

⊙ Overview

The Western Qing Tombs, located in Yixian County of Hebei Province, about 120 km southwest of Beijing, was constructed from 1730 to 1915. It includes 14 tombs and two attachments—Yongfu Temple and the temporary dwelling place. The mausoleum area covers 1,842 ha, with a buffer zone of 6,458 ha. Being the last imperial tombs of the Qing Dynasty, it demonstrates the best achievements of ancient architectures in terms of style, technique and architectural thought, and is the best-preserved among all imperial tombs of the Qing Dynasty. These tombs, with abundant materials and historical documents, unveil from different aspects the architectural artistic styles of China's imperial tombs from the 1730s to the early 20th Century, as well as the significant development and changes of the religious belief of the imperial families.

⊙ Description

The Western Qing Tombs is situated at the foot of Yongning Mountain, with Beiyishui River winding through the mausoleum area. Surrounded by mountains and crystal-clear water, dotted with ponds, pines and cypresses, the site is said to be the auspicious place for imperial tombs. Through strenuous efforts for about 200 years, architects of the Qing Dynasty had created a harmony between the architectures and the environment, making the tombs a typical masterpiece in terms of ancient China's *fengshui* theory. The 15,000 ancient pine trees and 200,000 young pines and cypresses form the biggest forest of ancient pines in North China.

In the 8th year of Yongzheng (1730), the Emperor, in pursuit of perfect geomantic location, decided that he should be buried away from his father and ancestors and chose to construct the Tailing Tomb in Yizhou. Hence, the first tomb of the Western Qing Tombs was built. Later, Emperor Qianlong, in order to strike a balance between the Eastern Tombs and the Western Tombs, initiated the "separate burial syste", under which the father and son should be buried in separate places. According to this system, the present burial pattern of the Eastern Qing Tombs and Western Qing Tombs came into being.

The Western Qing Tombs included four emperors' tombs (Tailing Tomb, Changling Tomb, Muling Tomb and Chongling Tomb), three empresses' tombs, three concubines' tombs and four tombs of princes and princesses. Eighty persons, including Emperor Yongzheng,

Ornamental column of stele tower, Tailing Tomb

Western Qing Tombs

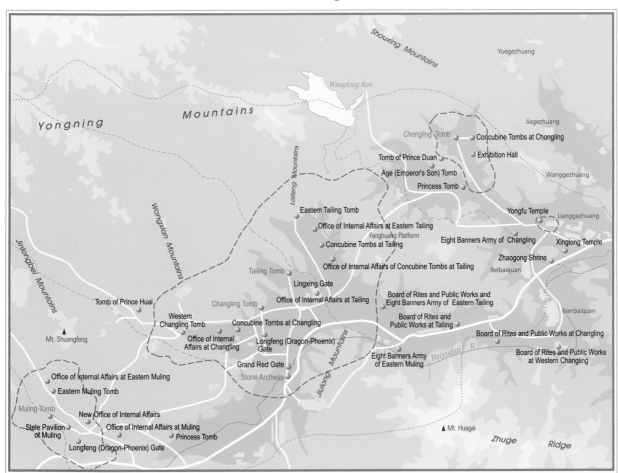

Three-arch bridge with triple lane

Emperor Jiaqing, Emperor Daoguang and Emperor Guangxu (in 1995, the ashes of Aisin-Gioro Puyi, the last emperor of the Qing Dynasty, was also moved and buried in the Hualong mausoleum within the area of the Western Qing Tombs, therefore the site was also called tombs of five emperors) and their concubines and off-spring were buried here.

The four tombs of emperors, with grand and spacious architectures, rational layouts, splendid and magnificent palaces, meticulously-carved stone sculptures, diversified patterns and rich contents, are all best preserved. The tombs of empresses and concubines were constructed in strict compliance with the feudal hierarchy. Most of the tombs of imperial princesses and princes are in good condition. Yongfu Temple, the temporary dwelling place and some of the auxiliary structures as offices and barracks, though having gone through all the vicissitudes, also remain intact. This makes the Western Qing Tombs one of the best-preserved and most complete mausoleums of the Qing Dynasty.

Stone figures of Changling Tomb

The Western Qing Tombs consists of more than 400 structures. Under the principle of strict compliance with feudal rituals and rules, these structures were not restricted to follow the model of other tombs and had their own unique features. The echoing effect of the round-shaped wall and the sacred way to the earth mound of the Changxiling as well as the unique phoenix paintings on the ceiling of Long'en Hall are all special examples of China's ancient mausoleum architecture.

⊙ Highlights

Tailing Tomb Tailing Tomb, constructed from 1730 to 1737, is the tomb of Emperor Yongzheng and the earliest one among the Western Qing Tombs. Covering an area of 8.5 ha, the tomb consists of 74 structures and a 2.5-km long sacred way. It is the largest among all the Western Qing Tombs.

The stone archways of Tailing Tomb The three archways in front

of the Grand Red Gate are the most unique architectures of the Western Qing Tombs. They are located in the square in front of the Grand Red Gate, with one of them facing the south and the rest two located at the east and west separately. These archways, together with the Grand Red Gate in the north, form a spacious courtyard. 12.75 m high and 31.85 m wide, each of them has five rooms and six pillars. Although they are made of greenish white marbles, no ironware was used; instead they were connected with mortises and tenons. This is the only imperial tomb in China where three stone archways were constructed.

Carved nanmu dragons of Muling Tomb The Muling Tomb, built between 1832-1836, is the second tomb of Emperor Daoguang (the first one was constructed at the Eastern Qing Tombs but dismantled due to water leakage). The tomb is famous for its *nanmu* (Phoebe nanmu) wood dragons which, superbly carved, are considered wooden carving masterpieces.

Stone archway

Changling Tomb

Information

Transportation *Visitors may take trains to Baoding, Beijing or Gaobeidian and then take buses to Yixian where the tombs are located. Within the mausoleum area, electromobile service is available. Driving to the tombs is also convenient. National road 112 runs through the mausoleum area, and joins Beijing-Shijiazhuang Expressway and Beijing-Guangzhou railway about 45 km east of the tombs.*

Accommodation *The temporary dwelling place of the Western Qing Tombs was constructed during the reign of Emperor Qianlong, and served as the place where the emperors and empresses lived on their journeys to pay tributes to the Western Qing Tombs, and now it serves as a hotel. In the area, there are Longhu Holiday Resort, Yanxiang Hotel, Baiyicheng Hotel and Taipingyang Hotel. In the villages of the Manchu nationality in the scenic area, visitors may choose to stay in local people's house and taste Manchu dishes.*

Food *There are many special dishes in the place, the most famous include imperial court-style pig leg and imperial court-style buns.*

Others *Special local products include millstone-shaped persimmon, wild jujube, walnut and hawthorn; handicrafts include Yishui inkstone, Yizhou colored pottery and artificial landscape stones.*

Opening hours: Summer 8:30 ~ 17:30; Winter 8:30 ~ 17:00
Inquiry telephones: 0312-4710012, 4710016, 4710038
Website: www.qingxiling.com

Stone archway of Yongfu Temple

About the World Heritage

UNESCO

On November 16, 1945, 37 countries signed the Constitution of the United Nations Educational, Scientific and Cultural Organization, which was ratified later in 1946 by 20 states. They became the first founders of UNESCO. The Organization is now comprised of 190 Member States and six Associate Members. The permanent Headquarters of the Organization is situated in Paris.

The purpose of the Organization is to contribute to peace and security by promoting collaboration among the nations through education, science and culture in order to further universal respect for justice, for the rule of law and for the human rights and fundamental freedoms which are affirmed for the peoples of the world, without distinction of race, sex, language or religion, by the Charter of the United Nations.

World Heritage Convention

The Convention Concerning the Protection of the World Cultural and Natural Heritage was adopted by the General Conference of UNESCO in Paris, on November 16, 1972, in response to the growing concern about the state of our world's cultural and natural heritage, which is under constant threat by the growing pressures of natural and human-made dangers. To date, a total of 177 countries have adhered to the Convention, making it one of the most universal international legal instruments for the protection of the cultural and natural heritage.

The World Heritage Convention is a unique international treaty by which countries recognize that the sites located on their national territory, and which have been inscribed on the World Heritage List, without prejudice to national sovereignty or ownership, constitute a world heritage "for whose protection it is the duty of the international community as a whole to co-operate".

The World Heritage List consists of cultural properties, natural properties, and mixed (cultural and natural) properties. As of December 2003, 754 cultural and natural sites of outstanding universal value are inscribed on the World Heritage List.

World Heritage Committee

The World Heritage Committee is an intergovernmental organization established under the terms of the Convention Concerning the Protection of the World Cultural and Natural Heritage adopted by UNESCO in 1972. The Committee consists of twenty-one States Parties. They are elected for a period of six years at the General Assembly of the state parties held every two years. Each General Assembly replaces one-third of them.

The sessions of the World Heritage Committee are held once a year and hosted by one of its member states on its own land in turn. A total of 27 sessions have been held since 1972. The major tasks of the sessions are: approving sites nominated for inscription in the World Heritage List; examine and evaluating the state of protection of World Heritage properties in various countries; assisting the state parties in their protection of the properties through supply of technical assistance and professional training; providing emergency assistance to the properties exposed to sudden threats; rendering support to the state parties in their public activities organized for the purpose of protection of the properties; encouraging the people in areas housing World Heritage properties to take part in the protection of the properties, etc.

World Heritage Center

The World Heritage Center is the secretariat of the World Heritage Committee and a functional sector of UNESCO for handling matters relating to World Heritage properties. The Center takes specific charge of and co-host the sessions of the World Heritage Committee with the host state member, provides consulting services to the state parties in the nomination of the properties, raises emergency funds, manages the World Heritage Fund, organizes seminars, carries out publicity on the protection of the properties, and keeps contact with international organizations concerned in the protection of the properties.

Definition of Cultural Heritage

According to the Convention, the following shall be considered as "cultural heritage":

Monuments: architectural works, works of monumental sculpture and painting, elements or structures of an archaeological nature, inscriptions, cave dwellings and combinations of features, which are of outstanding universal value from the point of view of history, art or science;

Groups of buildings: groups of separate or connected buildings which, because of their architecture, their homogeneity or their place in the landscape, are of outstanding universal value from the point of view of history, art or science;

Sites: works of man or the combined works of nature and man, and areas including archaeological sites which are of outstanding universal value from the historical, aesthetic, ethnological or anthropological point of view.

Criteria for the inclusion of cultural properties

According to the Convention, each property nominated should meet one or more of the following criteria:

(i) represent a masterpiece of human creative genius; or

(ii) exhibit an important interchange of human values, over a span of time or within a cultural area of the world, on developments in architecture or technology, monumental arts, town-planning or landscape design; or

(iii) bear a unique or at least exceptional testimony to a cultural tradition or to a civilization which is living or which has disappeared; or

(iv) be an outstanding example of a type of building or architectural or technological ensemble or landscape which illustrates (a) significant stage(s) in human history; or

(v) be an outstanding example of a traditional human settlement or land-use which is representative of a culture (or cultures), especially when it has become vulnerable under the impact of irreversible change; or

(vi) be directly or tangibly associated with events or living traditions, with ideas, or with beliefs, with artistic and literary works of outstanding universal significance (the Committee considers that this criterion should justify inclusion in the List only in exceptional circumstances and in conjunction with other criteria cultural or natural)

Definition of Natural Heritage

According to the Convention, the following shall considered as "natural heritage":

Natural features consisting of physical and biological formations or groups of such formations, which are of outstanding universal value from the aesthetic or scientific point of view;

Geological and physiographical formations and precisely delineated areas which constitute the habitat of threatened species of animals and plants of outstanding universal value from the point of view of science or conservation;

Natural sites or precisely delineated natural areas of outstanding universal value from the point of view of science, conservation or natural beauty.

Criteria for the inclusion of natural properties

(i) be outstanding examples representing major stages of earth's history, including the record of life, significant on-going geological processes in the development of land forms, or significant geomorphic or physiographic features; or

(ii) be outstanding examples representing significant on-going ecological and biological processes in the evolution and development of terrestrial, fresh water, coastal and marine ecosystems and communities of plants and animals; or

(iii) contain superlative natural phenomena or areas of excep-

tional natural beauty and aesthetic importance; or

(iv) contain the most important and significant natural habitats for in-situ conservation of biological diversity, including those containing threatened species of outstanding universal value from the point of view of science or conservation

Cultural Landscape

Cultural landscapes represent the "combined works of nature and of man" designated in the Convention. They should be selected on the basis both of their outstanding universal value and of their representativity in terms of a clearly defined geo-cultural region and also for their capacity to illustrate the essential and distinct cultural elements of such regions. The term "cultural landscape" embraces a diversity of manifestations of the interaction between humankind and its natural environment. The protection of traditional cultural landscapes is helpful in maintaining biological diversity.

World Heritage Emblem

The Emblem symbolizes the interdependence of cultural and natural properties: the central square is a form created by man and the circle represents nature, the two being intimately linked. The Emblem is round, like the world, but at the same time it is a symbol of protection. Around the circle are written "World Heritage" in English, French and Spanish.

Tentative List (part) of Properties for Nominations in China

- [ ] Red River Hani Terrace
- [ ] Karst in China
  The cone-shape karst, Guizhou
  Furong River in Wulong County, Chongqing
  Karst in Guilin
  The Sky Hole and Grand Crevice in Fengjie, Chongqing
- [ ] Yin Xu Site
- [ ] Mount Maijishan Scenic and Historic Interest Area
- [ ] Reserve for Giant Panda in Sichuan
- [ ] Kanasi Scenic Interest Area in Xinjiang Uygur Autonomous Region
- [ ] The Historic Monuments of Macao
- [ ] Kaiping Diaolou
- [ ] Traditional Buildings in Fujian Province
- [ ] Mount Wutai